Beyond the
Disappointment
of Sex

This book is dedicated to my parents,
Freddie and Elsie Stafford, who had the
happiest of marriages

Beyond the Disappointment of Sex

Understanding the Roots of Partnership Conflict

Margaret Christie-Brown

sussex
ACADEMIC
PRESS

BRIGHTON • PORTLAND

2 4 6 8 10 9 7 5 3 1

First published 2004 in Great Britain by
SUSSEX ACADEMIC PRESS
PO Box 2950
Brighton BN2 5SP

and in the United States of America by
SUSSEX ACADEMIC PRESS
920 NE 58th Ave   Suite 300
Portland, Oregon 97213-3786

British Library Cataloguing in Publication Data
A CIP catalogue record for this book is available from the British Library.

Library of Congress Cataloging-in-Publication Data
Christie-Brown, Margaret.
   Beyond the disappointment of sex : understanding the roots
of partnership conflict / Margaret Christie-Brown.
   p. cm.
Includes bibliographical references and index.
ISBN 1-84519-036-X (pbk. : alk. paper)
   1. Marital conflict.   2. Marriage—Psychological aspects.
3. Married people—Psychology. 4. Sex in marriage. 5. Man–
woman relationships.   I. Title.
HQ728.C482   2004
306.872—dc22
                                                                2004010992
                                                                CIP

Typeset and designed by G&G Editorial, Brighton
Printed MPG Books, Bodmin, Cornwall
This book is printed on acid-free paper.

Contents

Outline

and omnipotence. It summarises the physical and emotional changes of puberty.

Part III   Love and the Family

7   *Drawn to Love* looks at how we learn to love. It explains why the experiences of boys and girls are different.

8   *Familial Situations* discusses how factors such as the quality of the parental relationship, the number of siblings and the positioning of a child within the family can affect the child's psychological development. The chapter also briefly addresses the difficult issues of abuse and incest.

Part IV   The Gender Dialectic

9   *Gender Roles* examines gender stereotypes and their effect on self-esteem. It shows how these they affect boys and young men differently from girls and young women. It considers how gender difference can be used positively within a heterosexual relationship.

10   *Gender Conflict* describes the ways in which gender roles can cause conflict, both within individuals and between men and women. The chapter looks at strategies used by men and women to deal with this internal and external conflict in society in general and within personal relationships. It considers some of the issues faced by homosexual people.

Part V   Fertility and Infertility

11   *The Quest for Fertility* covers the effects of fertility on sexual relationships. It talks about why people choose to try for a child and introduces the issue of infertility.

12   *The Impact of Infertility* looks at infertility in detail. The chapter explores the different effects of infertility on women, on men and on the relationship between them. It introduces the psychological causes of infertility.

Part VI **Enduring Love**

13 *The Power To Change* argues that sexual experience can be improved by following a tried and tested programme of action. This programme builds on the discussion in the previous twelve chapters. The programme is explained in detail. Advice is given and possible outcomes considered.

Acknowledgements

My greatest thanks go to my husband Jeremy who endlessly supported and helped me through the several years this book took to come to fruition. Also thanks to my daughter Sarah who, on many occasions, polished my prose and my sons Dominic and Jonathan who nobly read it and gave good advice.

Professor Neville Brown and Dr. Earl Hopper have my gratitude for their support, suggestions and encouragement which gave me the confidence to carry through the enterprise.

Finally I pay homage to the hundreds of patients who have taught me so much.

INTRODUCTION

Sex affects us in a myriad of ways. It can give wonderful pleasure and it can be horribly disappointing. It can enhance a relationship and it can destroy a relationship. It created us and it can persecute us all our lives because it seems everyone else is having better sex.

A major problem is that sex means such different things to different people at different times in their lives and so all our demands are different. The two sexes, the many races, religions and social groups, all have different agendas and this can lead to confused expectations.

On top of these, often opposing, issues we have the media who would persuade us that everyone is having a lot of sex and that it is natural and easy. Yet the truth is that most people have difficulty with sex at some time in their lives, many always find it troublesome and, with many, after the first year of commitment, it does not happen all that often. Because it is quite possible to survive and to enjoy life without having sex, some people transfer their attention to something else the moment there is any difficulty with it. Indeed, it may seem infinitely preferable to ignore the problem rather than to discuss feelings of sexual failure, particularly if one thinks that nothing can be done about it.

Sadly, some people have never enjoyed sex, but those who have know that they can feel wonderfully good after love-making. They can feel physically good and they can feel emotionally good The sense of a unique intimacy, of well-being and of life having a purpose produced by this unifying and healing act, can last for days. Despite this, many people find themselves too busy to make it a top priority. Why is this? One obvious reason is that sex is not good every time. For those who expect it should be, the fear of satisfaction waning is enough to cause them to avoid the situation and then for sex to become a bit of a threat. There are many other reasons which are more specific to each individual, and these will be explored later. Sexual problems are mostly about misunderstandings and misinterpretations. People can be mystified by their feelings; there are those who think they want sex yet in the

1

event try to avoid it; some used to enjoy it but now they don't; others cannot understand why it seems tremendously important to some but not to themselves; they have to listen to stories of amazing orgasms which they themselves have never experienced.

There is a great myth that because sexual intercourse is natural, it should be easy, Remove our social brain and this would probably be so, but human sexuality is not just based on instinct, it is very complex. Like all animals, we have a reproductive drive without which our species would not survive. But this instinctual sex drive has to combine with our personal experience of life to create our unique attitude to sex. If we find difficulty with sex it means that the effects of our upbringing, our early encounters with the opposite sex, and our attitude to society and religion have somewhere come into conflict. Our ability to express emotion, to reveal our feelings to another, to be able to be intimate and to tolerate imperfections depends on internal balance and harmony between these factors. Of course, no-one feels entirely peaceful within a relationship, indeed it would be rather boring if there were no dispute but too much and we become anxious and unhappy. The more we understand our internal conflicts the more we can shift those attitudes which block good feelings within our relationship.

And what about love? The song says 'All you need is love'. It sounds good and makes us feel better for a moment. But when the music stops we start to wonder. What exactly is love, have we got it, do we give it, how do we keep it? When we have a partner these questions can become quite threatening. In fact, the more committed our relationship the more worried we may be by the questions.

We use the word love indiscriminately to describe feelings about issues which range from food to friends, cars to children and pets to partners. Put another way it means 'that which gives a good feeling'. Obviously some good feelings are more important than others and can infuse a sense of general well-being. These are good feelings about each other. If we are getting on well with our partner, parent, friend, or colleague, we feel content and life feels good.

'Falling in' love is special and clearly one of the most powerful feelings. Parents have deserted their children for it. The single long for it and the married are afraid of it. As a society we think this powerful emotion is romantic and like to read about it. It is the one time that we don't feel ambivalent, when everything is clear. Because it gives such extra good feelings it is greatly sought after. It doesn't last for long in this pure state because in real life our nearest and dearest disappoint us. Then we have bad feelings which can be so powerful that they can cast a shadow over everything and even threaten to kill our love.

Not everyone 'falls' in love yet most people can love someone and everybody knows disappointment. If we can find a way to reduce the effect of this by understanding and tolerance, the good feelings will still flourish and we can stop being defensive.

Another threat to partnerships is the fact that we develop, as we pass along, a set of priorities which will affect our choices. These may cripple us. For example, in our teens, if our priority has always been to please a parent and our parents have certain plans for us, we may fail to discover our own unique plan through feeling obliged to follow theirs. We may resent this but feel helpless. This can later intrude into the relationship when it may be difficult to put the partner's needs before continuing parental demands, thus causing problems between partners. Recognising our set of priorities, questioning them and understanding where they have come from is one important way of finding the answer to the quest for love. If the maintenance of mutual good feelings in the partnership can be made top priority instead of a tidy house or sticking to some earlier principle, most problems fall into place.

Understanding our own attitudes also helps us to be more perceptive about the rest of the world and, of course, our partner. It involves sorting out the ways in which we are similar and the ways in which we are different from one another and learning to value the differences. Obviously this is important in terms of gender but also in a more general way. Most importantly, everybody wants to be loved yet everyone has different ideas about what love is and how to get it.

Insight comes from looking at our lives from a different angle to the one we have become used to. To do this we have to take a step-by-step approach which starts with examining our life as a child and leading to where we are in the present. The reader will almost certainly find that nothing is quite as they thought and that the origins of any problem are different from what they imagined. This means that those who leap to those chapters that seem the most relevant to them, jump over the heart of the matter and miss the vital points. In particular, turning to the last chapter – "Enduring Love" – in the mistaken belief that following the apparently simple instructions will be enough, without the trouble of reading the book, will inevitably fail. In the long run only a change of attitude can fortify the programme. But, worked through systemati- cally, *Beyond the Disppointment of Sex* can increase awareness of internal conflicts, attitudes to sex and their origin, and the interdependent way sex depends on good feelings and good feelings depend on sex. While this is not easy, the insights gleaned can have a cumulative effect which is exciting and lead to the point where we can adapt our behaviour and so increase mutual enjoyment. Nevertheless, some of the ideas may produce emotional turmoil and be resisted. Previously unrecognised anger may upset the equilibrium that has been developed over the years. The risk then is that avoidance by shutting the book means the loss of a chance to understand the meaning of such a strong effect. This resistance should be anticipated and seen as part of a process of regeneration because real change requires a willingness to face the problem.

Case studies help to bring ideas alive. All the cases described here are true in their psychological essentials, but have been altered to remove anything that could identify the people involved. Names, places and the like have been changed.

Expect to be challenged – expect to be annoyed – expect to want to reject but most importantly, aspire to understand.

PART I

The Sexual Dialectic

1

The Role of Preconception

If we are to explore the important issues in partnership problems, we first need to understand how we come to have the attitudes and prejudices which play such a large part in these problems. Our attitudes are fundamental influences on the kind of lifestyle we pursue, the type of partner we choose and whether or not we stay with that partner. However, we are often unaware of the way in which our attitudes influence us.

Attitudes

Our attitudes are fixed ways of thinking which are set up in the past, retained, and coloured by our feelings. They become entrenched and so give us quick ways of reacting without having to bother to think.

They are formed by our experiences. Each experience has associated feelings which are recorded in memory. For example, if someone called Emily was very kind to you when you were small you may forget Emily herself but retain her name in your unconscious linked to a good feeling. You may call your child Emily in later life and not know why. If you were evacuated to a part of the country where they were unkind to you, it is likely that you will never choose to go on holiday to wherever that was, however much the guidebooks plead. These memories form part of the system we use to make decisions. If we look back and see how we behaved in a previous situation, we can predict that if similar circumstances prevail we are likely to behave in the same way again.

Having had a pleasant feeling leads us to assume, not necessarily correctly, that similar situations will produce similarly pleasant feelings. This means that we are encouraged by good experiences to explore further along paths that seem likely to be rewarding, constantly increasing our experience and therefore our knowledge. Likewise, an unpleasant feeling leads us to assume that a similar situation will produce similarly unpleasant feelings. The avoidance which follows this means that we tend to curtail our experiences and draw in our boundaries because our brain receives a message about the link between the feeling and the activity. The strength of that link makes it feel like an automatic danger signal which leads to a tendency to avoid the activity at its next occurrence. If we have too many unpleasant experiences in childhood, we may remain rather naïve as adults because we will be reluctant to take the risks needed to learn about life.

How Attitudes Develop

The foundations of many of our attitudes are laid down in childhood and are principally influenced, in one way or another, by our parents.

Personal Attitudes

Attitudes begin to be formed at birth when the baby perceives that food and comfort come from its mother. It assumes that mother is all-powerful and knows what is good and what is bad, and its own judgment system will naturally develop from that of its mother. If, for example, the mother dislikes pink, pink will remain an issue in some way. It may be that part of a later rebellion will mean that pink becomes the apparently favoured colour. Later we will see that numerous exceptions to this creep in as life gets more complicated but, for a long time, our appraisal of what happens in our world is filtered through that of our mother. This can persist right through adulthood, as happened to Jeremy:

> Jeremy, aged 27, refused all invitations to go out in the evening after he had washed his hair – his mother had told him he would catch a cold if he did this. It follows that he was locked out of many other more important activities through remaining too closely involved in his mother's attitudes. In particular he had deep sexual anxieties about cleanliness and a morbid fear of sexually transmitted diseases.

The rigidity of our attitudes tends to be in proportion to the amount of emotion shown by our mother over any issue. If she shows anger or distaste to her child when caught masturbating, this can produce a sense of fear and isolation from her love which is very distressing and may lead to the anxious avoidance of masturbation and other sexual interest in the future.

During a child's first years other members of the family increasingly have influence, and then the child leaves for the wider experience of school. Here other powerful figures like teachers, bullies and 'knowing' friends, introduce new ways of thinking. The secure child will face the conflict which begins to arise as opinions different from those of its parents are introduced. The less secure child will start to wear blinkers in order to conform to its mother or father.

> Luke had an older sister who seemed good at everything she did. He tried to be as satisfactory as he could but despite this his sister stayed at home with their mother while he was sent to an all boys' boarding school when he was only eight years old. Here he was very keen to please other authority figures as he had always tried to please his rather unresponsive mother. As an adult he had no desire to see his mother but became very attached to his mother-in-law who showed that she valued him.
>
> At school Luke was a great academic and sporting success. He was rather priggish but was tolerated by his peers because of his athletic prowess. Nevertheless he managed to avoid hearing any 'dirty' jokes or talk about masturbation until he was 17 when he was shocked to have his first wet dream. At the age of 30 he, together with his wife, sought help because he still had a problem with accepting the sexual side of his nature and had very little interest in sex.

Cultural/Social Attitudes

As we develop, other influences of the culture we belong to and the society we live in become increasingly important. The fact of sex in these wider arenas can be interpreted in many different ways. Depending on the individual's culture, it may be seen as being under the jurisdiction of religion or divorced from religion; it can be harnessed to love or it can be totally promiscuous; it can be greatly valued or completely rejected. Because of the variable attitudes in our multi-cultural society, some people are brought up to have powerful beliefs in the absolute rights and wrongs of sex, and they have to live alongside others who have very different views and standards. At school the child of parents with fundamental views and belief in arranged marriage may sit next to a child whose parents believe in 'free love'. To make matters more complicated, within ourselves we have parts conditioned by our parents, siblings and perhaps our religion, living alongside parts conditioned by our friends and the media, so that we may feel one thing yet believe another.

In Victorian times, for all the faults of the prevailing morality, at least everyone knew where they stood as far as sex was concerned. Sex outside marriage was held to be wrong, and if you did wrong you just had to hide the fact and put up with the fear and guilt. Today, what is right for some is wrong for others, producing a sort of civil war in which the changing standards in society collide with individual attitudes.

Societies, like individuals, are divided in their attitude towards sex and the potential pleasure involved. Most societies value the harnessing of sex for the care and protection of its children. The nuclear family has been the basis of this in Britain for many centuries. The advent of effective and available contraception has separated the reproductive and pleasurable aspects of sex.

Contraceptive clinics for unmarried women, which effectively sanctioned extramarital sex, were set up in Britain in the 1960s. Some people feel that the clinics were set up in response to an existing increase in extramarital sex, others that their existence caused such an increase. A change in attitudes towards sex certainly followed the advent of these clinics, to the point we have reached today where unmarried couples living together is now seen by most sections of the community as quite normal.

Also, advances in medical technology mean that young people are now living through a period of more rapid change than ever before, and this will have a profound effect on attitudes. In the field of conception, an infertile couple can no longer come to accept their loss and disappointment, allowing them to invest in life in a different way. Because of the possibilities offered by medical technology, there so often seems to be yet another small chance of their achieving what they long for. It is obviously very unsettling to be weighing up the financial and physical risks of surgery as in IVF, not just once but sometimes ten or fifteen times, with as many hopes and disappointments to be borne along the way. Similarly, tests for abnormalities in the developing foetus seem a wonderful advance, except there is some risk to the foetus in having the tests. In particular, for those in the older age group who may have waited years to conceive, taking this risk can cause immense anxiety.

> Janet had been trying to conceive for the last five years. She had been married for ten years but had a demanding career which until she was 36 had been very satisfying. Things began to go wrong at work and she looked at her life and realised she had only a few fertile years left. She expected to get pregnant as soon as she wanted but this did not happen for a long time. At 40 she was delighted to become pregnant but was told she should have an amniocentesis as the risk of a Down's syndrome baby were high. She was dismayed to be told of the risk to the pregnancy of this procedure and after many family discussions and arguments, she refused the amniocentesis. She was lucky.

Many, faced with a recommended termination of pregnancy following a positive test result, have not thought the issue through properly with their doctor and cannot go ahead with it anyway on moral grounds.

So, a change in social circumstances will affect people's attitudes which in turn will affect the values in society.

Anyone who has painstakingly achieved some internal stability is surrounded by a world where the ground shifts and new choices are being offered all the time. We are constantly having to balance our internal expectations and attitudes against the changing opportunities and risks presented by the society in which we live.

Prejudice

Where the assumptions associated with attitudes are very powerful, they become prejudices. The basis of a prejudice, therefore, is a powerful assumption that similar circumstances always produce similar feelings. Our apparently rational lives and stable personalities are actually built on the unstable foundations of prejudices, which themselves derive from all sorts of experiences in both childhood and adulthood. If as a child you loved and admired a teacher who had curly auburn hair, you are likely to be drawn to people with curly auburn hair and to consider them trustworthy long after you have reached adulthood. Likewise, if you had an unkind fair-haired teacher, this could lead to a lifelong avoidance of perfectly kind fair-haired people. This is a very simple example: it's obvious that both of these are unsound predictions – prejudices, in fact – which lead to disappointment or missed opportunities. Yet much of our behaviour is conditioned by just such prejudices, which are lifelong, as Glenys's story shows:

> Glenys felt antagonism to another mother at her child's school. As she had never spoken to this woman she found it difficult to understand her reaction. One day, after many months of mixed feelings of fascination and hostility, she was dismayed to come across a photograph of her mother as a young woman, and realised that she greatly resembled the woman in question. This evidence of her hidden hostility to her mother was unwelcome but had far-reaching beneficial effects. It eventually helped her to achieve freedom from lifelong neurotic symptoms caused by her need to hide this fact from herself.

How Prejudice Develops

Prejudice can spread by association. To take a simple example, my mother loved opera, sang well, and in particular would sing highlights from *Madam Butterfly*. She took me as a very excited eight year old to see this opera. There was an extra large soprano singing the heroine and I was not prepared for the very long bits in between the highlights. I have rarely felt so bored and trapped, and did not go near an opera house until aged 30. I still get rather fidgety. This example is fairly trivial, but the principle that bad experience causes us to reduce our choices is important. It is made even more important by the fact that this avoidance might not be restricted to opera, but might extend to all theatre by association.

Children are as intelligent as adults but lack their experience. The sense they make of things is essentially logical but the premises are limited by lack of knowledge. When a child has an experience, as we have seen, its intelligence leads it to predict that a similar event will produce a similar feeling. A lot of experience is needed to achieve the realisation that this is oversimplified and leaves out one important factor: that since every experience is made up of several components, a change in one component affects the whole experience.

A return to our opera example illustrates this point. If the unwilling child is dragged off to another opera, which turns out to have more accessible music and an interesting plot, the child's opinion of opera may become favourable as a result. Conversely, the first time a child is left on its own at a party can be a traumatic experience. If the child has enjoyed parties before, in the company of a familiar adult, it may expect to have a good time. However feelings of abandonment and fear can prevent enjoyment and turn the party into an ordeal, which will then mean that the next party is feared and avoided. Joan, aged seven was invited to a birthday party of the small girl next door. She did not know anybody as her parents recently moved house. Entering the party room, she brushed against a bowl of crocuses on a small table, knocking them all over the floor. The mother of the house barely suppressed her annoyance. Feeling very lonely and afraid, Joan did not enjoy the party and became resistant to going to any parties after that. She did not at first tell her mother what had happened because she felt ashamed. A few weeks later she started her new school. The memory of feeling abandoned and fearful affected her attitude to being left at school. Her mother was surprised because she had always been happy at school before. The association with being alone in the company of unfamiliar people produced the expectation of unpleasant feelings even though she did not yet know whether she would like the school or not. She was sure she would not.

While prejudice can be induced by an unpleasant experience leading to an association, it can also be overcome by breaking that association.

This occurs frequently during childhood. To extend our previous example, the new schoolchild may have a great aversion to school to begin with, but as it is the law that every child in this country must attend school, there is no opportunity for avoidance. Most of us will remember our own experience of starting school, and those of us who have had children of our own at school will remember their experiences even more clearly. Some children take to school very readily, but for those who don't, no matter how much they detest it at first, there is no choice – and as school-hating children return to school, day after day, get to know their teacher and begin to make friends, they come to realise that it's not such a frightening place.

When we are older, however, and have more power to control our own lives, having a bad experience is more likely to lead us to avoid a possible repeat of it. As we now know, the more we avoid something, the stronger becomes our prejudice against it. This is because each avoidance confirms to the mind that there is something dangerous in the situation to be avoided, so it becomes increasingly automatic to continue to avoid it. The original fears can become buried in the unconscious mind so that we may have no awareness of the origins of the prejudice. Some prejudices don't have a noticeable effect on our lives, but if the situation that comes to be avoided is important, it can be disastrous. It means that often without good reason, part of life's experience is denied to the individual.

Norah was three years old when her brother was born. Her mother was in hospital for two weeks and when she came home, instead of welcoming her little daughter with open arms, she put out a restraining hand in case Norah touched the baby. This left Norah feeling rejected and displaced; as a result, she became very clingy and was always trying to please her mother. Her jealousy of her brother became hidden. She was fearful at school, and later at work, and always avoided taking risks. She made girl friends but always felt excluded from an inner circle when they became interested in boys.

Norah was attractive and had many admirers but she could not get close to a man, even though she longed to be married and have children, because her hidden hostility to her brother prevented her from relating to men. The main feature of her life as an adult was her need to feel important and significant, but her avoidance of risks meant that she felt inferior to her friends who had better careers or who had married. Psychotherapy made her aware of the roots of her problems and so at the age of 40 she became able to understand her intense feelings of resentment which would regularly be aroused. For example, she recommended her doctor to her best friend, but when she heard that her best friend made an appointment to see the doctor, she felt a blow to her stomach similar to the one she had felt when her mother put out the restraining hand and seemed to choose her brother. Her unconscious felt that her best friend was about to be chosen by the doctor and that once again she would be rejected and displaced.

Avoidance diminishes conscious anxiety while increasing unconscious anxiety. This can be dangerous. It can lead to avoidance of important specific things like visiting the doctor or dentist. It can also lead to the avoidance of broader and more subtle issues such as leaving home at an appropriate time, changing career or having a baby. Many women who say that the reason they don't want children is financial, or that it is because of their career, or that it is selfish to have children as there are already too many people in the world, are in fact rationalising their prejudices about childbirth or responsibility. Usually a previous experience has caused them to make negative assumptions about what happens in childbirth or, more often, how they would cope as a mother.

> Rachel was very indecisive. She found it difficult to decide to marry her boyfriend of ten years. Once married she found it very difficult to decide to have a baby. She was an intelligent and well qualified woman, yet, typically for her, she had no definite career.
>
> Rachel used to produce reasons for her hesitation that were excuses rather than the truth although she, herself, believed them. She would say she worried about having a child as there were already too many children in the world, and she felt strongly that this was the real reason for her hesitation.
>
> The origins of Rachel's deep indecisiveness were complicated. One important fact was that she was the youngest of a large family and came along seven years after her nearest sibling. She always felt that everyone else knew everything and, even as an adult, always expected to be told what to do. She then felt angry and rebellious and often avoided doing what was suggested, although she rarely showed these feelings.
>
> Rachel retained into her thirties a sense that she was the child and could not be ready to marry and have children. She slowly gained confidence with every risky step she took, and now has four children.

Many eldest girls develop prejudices about having children because their first experience of a baby in the family is a bad one. The associated feelings are of rejection, jealous feelings towards the baby and angry feelings of unrequited love towards the mother, as well as anxiety about having those feelings of jealousy and anger. Frequently these girls grow up not liking babies, avoid their friends' babies and have grave doubts about a baby of their own. Early experience has prejudiced them to such an extent that any natural wish for a child has been overwhelmed. However, if women's anxieties can be overcome, the experience of childbirth and motherhood can turn out to be quite different from what they have expected. The same sort of problems can apply to men as well, as Alex's story shows:

Alex's wife Lulu had started to avoid having sex with him. She had agreed when they first married that they would not have children as Alex was adamant that he did not want a child. She now felt resentful and was certain that her loss of libido was because he was denying her a child. Although her background revealed many insecurities, she was unwilling to explore what might lie behind this rationalisation.

Alex agreed to come and talk about their problem because it seemed reasonable to suppose he might have an irrational worry. When he was 12 years old his sister of 18 became pregnant and their mother agreed that she should return home with the baby. Alex had to give up his room and his mother took over much of the care of the baby. The baby cried a great deal and Alex stopped being able to sleep at night. He had no conscious memory of disliking the baby or hostility towards his sister, but he did remember his insomnia and being taken to the doctor because of this. We talked about this complete disruption of his life and his helplessness in that situation, and how it related to his reluctance to have a baby. He would say things like 'supposing the baby liked rugby or pop music?' as he was very antagonistic towards these activities.

Eventually Alex saw that although a new baby would disrupt his life, as an adult he was not helpless, that it would be his child and he would have a power he did not have before. After this insight Alex and Lulu had a son, of whom he was very proud, and who was a great compensation for the fact that Lulu continued to avoid sex!

So far we have seen that prejudices can affect many aspects of our daily lives, from the trivial to the important. They diminish our capacity to profit from experience, whether by simple enjoyment or by acquiring knowledge. Of course, we do not only acquire prejudice through direct experience, but also by adopting or reacting to the prejudices of others.

Our parents' prejudices are particularly influential, as Harold's story shows:

Harold had a very dominant mother and a passive father. His mother would 'train' her children the hard way, both by being angry and by smacking if they failed to behave perfectly. At 30 he had had no sexual encounter of any kind since the age of 6 when he remembers being in bed with his younger sister. That was the closest he had got to anyone.

Harold enunciated very clearly, his conversation sounded pedantic, and he was moralistic and prudish, yet he longed to 'join the rest of the world' and have a close relationship. However, he had so internalised his mother's perfectionism that everyone failed to be good enough.

At a social level prejudice, which causes us to react without thinking, can cause great difficulty. Encounters with people from different backgrounds with different conditioning can feel like a threat when the differences seem to question the attitudes and assumptions of our lifetime. While racial differences immediately come to mind, the most commonplace example of this is encountered in gender differences. Men and women have very different aims and ideals with very different influences in their backgrounds and often feel quite alien to each other. Despite this, in heterosexual relationships, they have to learn to make a life together and fulfil one another sexually. In such relationships two sets of gender-related prejudices may come into conflict leading to a very complex situation. It requires all our understanding and intelligence to cope with the anxiety, disappointment and resentment that can follow.

A common example, because of his own experience, is that a man may assume that a 'normal' woman feels a drive to sex in the same way that he does. He therefore believes that if the woman does not respond in the same way that he would, she is not interested in him. The fact is that women have a different sexual response to men and so this type of logic is based on the wrong premise. Women are often more interested in someone's personality than in sex.

Conversely, a woman may have been brought up to believe that men are only interested in sex for its own sake, and so cannot see that for some men it is an expression of love. It is, of course, true that a man may be only interested in a woman for sex, and it is important for women to realise that this possibility exists. Problems arise when a woman assumes that this is always so, rejects sexually the man who loves her and can only believe in his love if he makes no sexual demands.

When we apply these insights to sexual problems it becomes clear that it is an area which is particularly vulnerable to prejudice. The potential result of such prejudice is a serious disruption of the personality if, by early conditioning, we are put off sex.

To summarise so far, prejudice is an inevitable part of development and yet is a dangerous phenomenon for a number of reasons. Prejudice is attitude charged with powerful feelings. The reasons underlying these feelings may lie hidden from our conscious awareness. Prejudice can cause us to avoid what might be good for us and to seek what might be bad for us. We make assumptions about other people and situations without bothering to find out the truth. We become unable to discuss politics, religion or sex because our attitudes are set in anxiety and we become angry if we have to justify them. What is more, we often don't realise that it is our attitudes we are justifying. We are inclined to consider our anger to be a just reaction to a set of particular facts.

The Power of Unconscious Prejudice

We have already encountered the idea that much prejudice operates outside our conscious awareness and understanding. It is useful at this point to expand on the concept of 'the unconscious' and how it works. The unconscious can be defined as 'the deepest level of the mind, usually inaccessible, which holds suppressed memories of feelings that affect behaviour'.

While many people think of the unconscious mind as something completely unknown and unknowable, it is important to realise that it is only dislocated from our consciousness in the immediate present. We have all already been face to face with all its contents at some time because the unconscious contains records of all the experiences we have had throughout our lives. Those records include both the facts of those experiences and the feelings they evoked in us. It also contains records of our dreams, our thoughts, and the feelings produced by those dreams and thoughts. Some things seem impossible to remember because they happened before we were old enough to talk about them, and now we are so reliant on language that it is hard to describe a period when it didn't exist for us. Some experiences seem beyond recall because they were not important enough to make a strong imprint, and conversely, some were so unpleasant that we resist remembering them because we want to avoid the associated discomfort.

The origins of our attitudes and prejudices are often unconscious, so that we think that we have reasoned something out and that our attitude is rational, whilst it is in fact influenced by an unconscious emotional weighting. The more we fail to recognise the emotional element, the less satisfactory will be our position. In any given situation, to come to the best decision we have to take our whole system into account and include powerful emotion as well as rational analysis. Those who can understand this dual and often opposing influence in themselves are more able to see and therefore override any destructive prejudice.

There are a number of reasons for the dominant power of the unconscious. It has a wider brief than the conscious mind. It has the responsibility for keeping the person safe while the conscious mind is concerned with other issues. It manages the day-to-day biological functioning of the body. It protects from many potential disasters and has antennae out even during sleep. Many drivers have experienced at some time having driven for miles, without having been aware of the process of driving, and while thinking of something else entirely; this is possible because the unconscious is in control.

In order to maintain this control, the unconscious has access to much more information than the conscious mind. There are two sources for this extra information. First there is the external stimuli which the conscious largely ignores while it thinks about something, and second is the wealth of experience which has been forgotten by the conscious. One of the most important functions of the unconscious is as an archive system which leaves our minds uncluttered by too much ready information. However, the unconscious is dominated by the past experience it stores, and the emotions attached to that experience. It is powerful but fallible, like the most autocratic of rulers who think they know what is best for their country but who are out of touch with contemporary changes of attitude.

Because the extent of the influence of the unconscious is largely unrecognised, it can work in a subversive way, allowing a person to think they are making a conscious choice when in fact unconscious factors are controlling the decision. For example, a man who has suppressed anger with his wife may decide on the way home that the reason he does not intend to make love with her is because he has had a hard day at work. He believes he wants to make love but is just too tired. He may feel impotent but reduces anxiety over this by reassuring himself that his problem is fatigue. However, he is preventing himself from recognising that he does not feel good about his partner and really does not want to make love; even further, that he wants to punish her for hurting him. I have seen many middle-aged men complaining of loss of interest in sex who have dominating wives with whom they feel angry. It usually takes time to expose the anger and eventually for them to recognise that they have found a way to upset and control their wife by making her feel unwanted.

Nicholas was referred with his wife Gail because he had lost interest in sex. Gail refused to come to the sessions.

Nicholas was a quiet passive man who had been the youngest in a family of five. His oldest sister had been very important when he was a child. She had bossed him about but also looked after him. He spoke of how articulate she was and how envious he had been of her ability to talk with their father at mealtimes, whereas Nicholas was very nervous if spoken to.

Gail was an ambitious career woman whom Nicholas admired but found intimidating. They were both devoted to their daughter but as the marriage progressed he found Gail's wish for confrontation, and the lengths to which she would go in order to win an argument, harder and harder to take. He became upset.

Nicholas was not aware, when I first saw him, that he was very angry with Gail. He thought he was simply hurt that she was prepared to speak to him as she did. He gradually stopped being able to have sex with her because he would lose his erection. This loss of function caused a conscious anxiety, on top of the unconscious anxiety about his hidden anger with her, which made him look for excuses so that he did not even have to try. He started working late and coming home too tired for anything other than television. He was not able to talk to Gail in a frank way about his feelings, and as she refused to see that the problem was anything to do with her, there could be no satisfactory outcome.

Nicholas was able to explore the parallels between his relationship with his sister and his wife, but was not able to change his way of relating to his wife, and he was unable to break from her because of fear of losing his daughter.

The main cause of the power of the unconscious is that reason is no match for emotion, and emotion is under unconscious domination. In a tug of war between reason and emotion, a forgotten memory, with its emotionally-charged prejudice to avoid pain and seek satisfaction, provides a powerful pull which the careful reasoning of the conscious mind cannot counteract.

As well as guarding us from external danger, as when we are preoccupied while driving a car, the unconscious also tries to guard us from the internal threat of emotional instability. It tries to prevent us from becoming too angry, upset, tired, stressed or frightened, and it does this by influencing the conscious mind to decide, apparently on rational grounds, what would be the safest action. Unfortunately the safest action is not always the best action. This can be seen most clearly in people with severe phobias such as agoraphobia where the sufferer can be too frightened ever to step outside the front door of their house. Clearly the power of their unconscious to stop them becoming too frightened is working so well that it limits their life choices to an extreme extent.

This unconscious protective system often breaks down, bringing a tug of war between conscious and unconscious out into the open, when a change in an individual's life challenges their unconscious defence mechanisms. If powerful unconscious forces are challenged by circumstances and the problem cannot be resolved, it may eventually cause a physical breakdown or an emotional breakdown, or a combination of the two. Barry's story shows how this can happen.

Barry always rationalised the fact that he never went abroad for his holidays as due to lack of finance or there being 'nothing abroad as good as England', although in fact he was unconsciously afraid to travel beyond the familiar boundaries of his native land. When his job required him to leave England he became very anxious as his defence was on the verge of breaking down. He became ill, which naturally meant that he didn't have to go. It is clear that the 'best' action for Barry would have been to go abroad, find out the reality and therefore allay his fears, but his unconscious felt that it was safest to get him out of the difficulty by causing an illness so that he didn't have to become too frightened.

Barry experienced a physical breakdown following an emotional upset in which his unconscious could not control the external circumstances and failed to cope with his internal conflict.

Reducing Prejudice

Insightful parents and educators will help children to retain their freedom of choice by minimising prejudice. They will try to reduce the production of unpleasant feelings by careful judgment of what the child can do without too much anxiety, and by identifying with the child's feelings rather than concentrating on its behaviour. If the child has a nasty experience, it is important for parents to be aware that their natural reaction of overprotection may not be the best way to help, because it can reinforce an anxious child's tendency to avoid similar experiences. Although I emphasise the importance of childhood experience in this context, the same mechanisms operate in adult life, as Amy's story shows:

> Amy and Karen were both 18 when they went to work abroad together. A month after arriving, they were both raped. They not only had to cope with the after-effects of the rape but also with a court case which, in a foreign country, was more than usually traumatic.
>
> Amy came to see me several months later. Karen had gone back to her job in Europe but Amy was afraid to work at all, even in her own country. She told me that her parents hadn't wanted her to go abroad in the first place, and now they and her doctors were encouraging her to stay at home, rest and recover. The result of this was that she was becoming more depressed, anxious and phobic about the outside world in general, while Karen who was 'biting the bullet' was doing well.

So, just as prejudice is spread and strengthened by association and avoidance, it is obvious that where good feelings can be maintained there is a comparable expanding process. Each new experience has peripheral new associations which can then be recognised as similar to those already made. For example, a child may be taken to the local cinema for the first time, enjoy it and look forward to a return visit. The next time parents may decide to visit the cinema in London. If this is again pleasurable and without anxiety, then not only is the cinema enjoyed but it is associated with London. The child now has a new pathway to experience: going to places away from home is associated with an expectation of pleasure.

Priorities

We are beginning to see that the formation of our personality is a step-by-step process, with the reaction to each experience depending on previous ones. If we take a snapshot of ourselves today, it would mark the end result so far of all the thousands of experiences that have formed our character up to this point. Tomorrow we may be different depending on our experiences today. In each experience we try to avoid pain and pursue contentment in an attempt to find fulfilment. Setting apart such impossible questions as 'what is the meaning of life', we can observe that, in the widest sense of the word, what people seek to fulfil is their potential.

We have not one but many different potentials, all of which have to try to fit in with each other. Like the external society in which we live, we have an internal society living inside us. This internal society has a number of factions such as sex, love, career, spirituality, relaxation and fun. Each faction requires recognition and fulfilment, but each has to relinquish some power in order to allow another aspect to have expression. This leads to more tugs of war. For example, someone's spiritual aspect may be in conflict with their ambitious aspect, and their wish to conform and please may be in conflict with their wish to pursue forbidden activities.

In the course of living our lives we form a set of priorities, and in order to find fulfilment it is important that this is a good set. However, choosing the right set of priorities is a difficult task, and one we need to re-think continually because without so doing we tend to revert to our parents' set. Our unique set of priorities will be greatly influenced by our parents' unique set of priorities, although this does not necessarily mean that they will be the same. Where parents have extreme attitudes, their child is likely either to share their view or rebel against it and adopt an opposing and equally extreme view.

In relation to sexual potential, many people have formed an attitude to sex which makes them feel the need to suppress it to a greater or lesser degree. This is for the sake of the other 'factions' which have been presented by the family or friends as more valuable. For example, some people who have been brought up to value only the spiritual aspects of life feel that sex is not only unnecessary but actually undesirable. Others, who have been conditioned by their families to feel a need for success, may invest heavily in a career and so siphon off time and energy into achieving a public recognition which seems more valuable than private satisfactions. Any attempt to change our priorities depends on understanding our own sequence of parental influence and how our personal experience has led to the attitudes and prejudices we now hold.

Can we Change?

This is the big question. Is it possible to change? More specifically, is it possible to change if we are so full of unconscious attitudes and prejudices which influence our every decision? And if it is possible, how can we do it?

To address these questions, we have first to be aware of what can be changed and what cannot. We cannot change our own genes, or our past, or (to any great extent) our environment. This means that we have much less free will than we like to think.

As we have seen, our past has a major effect on us. Our store of past experiences contains memories of events and their associated feelings, and those memories and feelings have created our attitudes. Our attitudes mould our personalities and predict how we are likely to react in any given situation. Our conditioning, therefore, means that choices and decisions are automatically made on the basis of past experience, and the fact that we are largely unaware of this reduces our free will even further.

It is possible to change this situation but only if we can first realise just how much we are controlled by our past. Only this knowledge will allow us to make the great efforts necessary to fight our conditioning and change our automatic responses.

It is difficult to grasp that we are basically living robots unless we actively take control. The idea is not pleasant and the temptation is to reject it. People commonly react by denying that events from their past influence their present actions, but by now we can recognise that the denial is a defence mechanism we use to protect us from a frightening thought. And it is frightening, particularly when we realise that to take control actively we must be willing to take a big risk: the risk of going against our natural inclination to react in the usual way. This is frightening because we know from past experience what is likely to happen when we react as we usually do, and we have no idea what will happen if we react differently. Nevertheless, taking this risk is the only way to find out that it is safe to change. Otherwise, as we have seen, we set up patterns of behaviour which are repeated without thought, and we make the same mistakes over and over again. And in this way we may be regularly prevented from fulfilling our potential.

So, the ability to take control of our destiny depends first on being able to recognise how little control we have at present. This frees us from the assumption that we automatically have a free choice when we make our decisions, and allows us to consider what we have to do to increase our freedom of choice. If we want to counteract the effects of our conditioning, we have to be prepared to use a great deal of effort to go against the instinctive reaction of the programmed biological computer which is our brain. People may argue that those members of society who rebel must have done this and broken away from their conditioning. Certainly many have broken free and done their own thing, but rebellion often means swinging right around into an automatic position of opposition to authority, and is as unthinking a reaction as that of people who habitually conform to authority.

We are usually encouraged during our upbringing and education to be decisive and to hold firm opinions. These are certainly valuable qualities in some situations, but, particularly in today's rapidly changing society, we also need the flexibility to change with our circumstances – and this applies to internal as well as external changes.

Sanjida's story provides a very straightforward example of this system of internal change:

> Sanjida was the only girl in a family of five, and was dominated as a child by her brothers and her rather rigid parents. As a result of this early experience, she developed an automatic reaction which led to an intense resistance to doing anything anyone else wanted her to do. An example of this was that when she was driving in heavy traffic, she would never allow anyone to come out of a side road in front of her.
>
> I suggested to Sanjida that this reaction represented her vulnerability and showed that she did not feel 'rich' enough to be generous. The insight she gained from our discussion allowed her to experiment with taking different action in this situation. She discovered a pleasant feeling of power from acting generously, and this provided a model for changing her reaction in other situations.

This story illustrates that a small change of behaviour can lead to wider changes, and demonstrates that counselling can facilitate such changes. This is so with all sorts of personal problems, including sexual ones.

Key Points

- Our attitudes are fixed ways of thinking which are set up in the past
- The changing standards in society collide with individual attitudes
- A change in social circumstances will affect people's attitudes which in turn will affect the values in society

- We constantly have to balance our internal expectations and attitudes against the changing opportunities and risks presented by the society in which we live

- The more we avoid something, the stronger becomes our prejudice against it

- Avoidance diminishes conscious anxiety while increasing unconscious anxiety

- Prejudices diminish our capacity to profit from experience

- The unconscious can be defined as 'the deepest level of the mind, usually inaccessible, which holds suppressed memories of feelings that affect behaviour'

- Our unconscious contains records of all the experiences we have had throughout our lives

- The unconscious mind is much more powerful than the conscious, and in most conflicts between them the unconscious will win, unless the conscious mind can become aware of the conflict and the reasons behind it

- The main cause of the power of our unconscious is that reason is no match for emotion, and emotion is under unconscious domination

- In the course of living our lives we form a unique set of priorities

- Any attempt to change our priorities depends on understanding our own sequence of parental influence and how our personal experience has led to the attitudes and prejudices we now hold

- If our defences are successfully maintained, nothing can change because the truth behind the defence cannot be seen.

2

Defensive Withdrawal

As we have seen, one of the ways in which we protect ourselves from anxiety is by avoidance. We now need to explore the other ways in which we may protect ourselves from painful feelings such as anxiety, anger, guilt and love. These methods are generally known as defence mechanisms. Some defence mechanisms work very well and produce immediate relief. It is natural to repeat defence mechanisms if they relieve anxiety, so it is inevitable that people will reproduce a defence mechanism which seems to work. Therefore, much of our recognisable personality is determined by the way we tackle problems and the defence mechanisms we use. The early success of a defence mechanism is such a powerful influence that it explains why we tend to continue to use it even when it doesn't work any more, and so repeat mistakes instead of learning from them as we would otherwise expect to do.

Conscious Defence Mechanisms

There are a number of conscious defence mechanisms. These are a deliberate attempt to control our situation and avoid things that upset us but are also about what we intend others to see about us. For example, many people initially show dislike to a member of the opposite sex to conceal the interest which is what they really feel. This may be a dangerous game but, being conscious, the individual at least knows that a game is being played and thus has the choice to stop.

A common problem arises if a person says that they don't want to make love because they have a headache. There are three possibilities here. First, they may have an unpleasant headache of organic origin which genuinely leaves them feeling unwell and disinclined to make love. Secondly, there may be no headache present at all, and the individual may be consciously lying to their partner for reasons of their own.

Thirdly, the headache may be painful and unpleasant but of unconscious emotional origin. Here the individual is completely unaware that hidden resistance to making love has caused, either by tension or in more complicated ways, an excuse for them to avoid it. This allows the one with the headache and also the partner to believe that if it was not for the headache, pleasurable love-making would have occurred. In other words this protects the relationship as much as the individual concerned. This latter is an example of the unconscious defence mechanisms which we are about to look at.

Unconscious Defence Mechanisms

An important feature of the unconscious mind is to protect us from unpleasant memories and emotions. This process can be beneficial or detrimental. These protective processes are our defence mechanisms, and we are usually unaware that they are operating. The negative side to this is that where a defence mechanism has become a long-term solution to anxiety, it means that there has been a dangerous distortion of feelings. It leaves the individual unaware of which are their true feelings and which belong to the defence mechanism. This happens particularly in the defence of denial.

Denial

Denial is a defence brought into play by the unconscious to protect the conscious mind from too much distress. Let us begin to explore this by examining the case of Sally, who was labelled as 'frigid' because she was completely sexually unresponsive:

> Sally was upset and angry that all her friends seemed to be having exciting relationships at university while she was not. She was very attractive and had many admirers whose company she enjoyed. In fact she was a great flirt until the first sign of sexual interest from a man, at which point she would freeze. Sally concealed this as much as she could, but even kissing caused her distress, and no relationship prospered.
>
> Sally was an only child and had no one she felt she could talk to about this. In her sessions with me it emerged that she had been a very relaxed outgoing child until, at the age of six, she had a playmate to stay. This little girl had brothers and sisters who had introduced her to masturbation and she duly showed Sally. The two were enjoying this new excitement together in the shower when they were seen by Sally's mother. A great upset followed as the playmate was sent home, a complaint made to her mother and Sally was beaten with a hairbrush. Sally did not ever masturbate again and learnt to take no interest in sexual matters

in order to maintain her sense of security. A long struggle followed. Sally was desperate to change things, but at the same time she found it difficult even to read any book on the subject. She would often avoid her session with me if she felt I had pushed her too hard the time before, but gradually she allowed the safe blanket of coldness to be lifted to reveal the real person beneath. Even so she remained half fearful of her desires and unsure of whether she enjoyed the loss of control in orgasm.

This is an example of the defence mechanism known as denial. We can see from Sally's story that the frigid individual is not born frigid with no hope for revival, but that there are possibilities for change. Nevertheless it is hard to retrieve an interest which has been completely denied for years. This is partly because it can be difficult to convince someone that they have any interest in sex to retrieve when they have denied it to themselves for so long; and partly because the original unconscious anxiety remains, making them afraid to take an interest. In such cases the mind has failed to recognise that the situation has changed and that it is now not only safe, but necessary, to have the interest.

Parental attitudes played an important part in the development of frigidity in Sally's case. Parents themselves are at the mercy of their own upbringing and the moral codes of the time, and are often unsure of what is the best attitude to take to their offspring's natural but intense interest in bodily functions. Because of their own conditioning they often react vehemently against their children's masturbation, even if they have consciously resolved to be more benevolent than their own parents. They may unconsciously feel that the safest way is to forbid and deny sexual interest even if they consciously think it is permissible.

Fortunately, however, most children retain their interest in sexual matters and tolerate feelings of anxiety about the possible revelation of this interest. Despite some open anxiety about sex, this is a healthier solution than that of the child who manages to control their anxiety through the successful denial of the interest. With this denial sexual interest is lost, sometimes for ever.

Many frigid people are not simply uninterested in sex but feel very strongly repelled by it, which shows that the suppression of sex does not always reduce its passion. The feeling of repulsion is equal in intensity to the original feeling of sexual interest. We have already seen this at work in Sally's case.

Unconscious emotion is usually stronger than reason. The defence mechanism of denial makes it difficult to know whether you truly want something (conscious emotion) or just think you need it (reason). It also makes it hard to know whether something you think you don't want (reason) might be something which in fact you do want but more strongly fear (unconscious emotion). For example, if a child who loses a parent deals with this terrible loss by pretending that it doesn't matter because they didn't like the parent much anyway, the pain may be relieved and the child may seem not to feel the loss greatly. This gross distortion suppresses the truth of an important relationship. What is more, it can lead to a tendency to distort the truth of future relationships, by making it difficult for the child (and later the adult) to allow important people to matter too much in case they should be lost.

When a lot of denial is present in someone's personality, it can become impossible for them to satisfy their emotional needs, as they continually avoid what they want and seek what they do not want. Taken to the limit, if a defence mechanism is complete, it is ultimately unsatisfactory even though it might feel good. We need to experience some of the pain of the situation we are responding to or we will lose touch with an important part of reality.

Denial of this kind can be clearly seen at work in Dolores' story:

> When Dolores was 30 she came to my clinic complaining of loss of libido and depression. She had been engaged to Tony for ten years, and when I asked her why she was still only engaged to be married she said she was 'too busy' to get married.
>
> The major trauma of Dolores' life was that her father had left home when she was aged 11. Her parents divorced and shortly after this her father died. It seemed to me that she had convinced herself at this time that her father was unimportant and that her mother was all important, because she became very angry when I questioned her about these events and suggested that they must have been very upsetting. She denied that the loss of her father was of any importance; indeed her anger was such that she justified not wanting help from me at all because my questions were obviously ridiculous.
>
> It was clear to me that Dolores was very tied to her mother and reluctant to leave home, and that she did not want to face this fact. This meant that she was very defensive and found it impossible to explore her real feelings. It was impossible to help her because she could not believe that she could cope with her real feelings and preferred to defend her 'safer' feeling, which was that only her mother mattered.

Joan's story also illustrates extreme denial, but with a happier outcome:

> Joan came with similar complaints to those of Dolores. Joan's parents divorced when she was five, and she also became resistant when I introduced the idea that the loss of her father might have upset her at the time. She denied this because she had managed to convince herself that since she was very close to her mother she did not really need a father. Nevertheless her relationship with her mother was more complex than she first implied. Joan had left home at the

age of 16 to live in considerable poverty in London, because she thought her mother tended to be more generous to her brother than to her and she felt less loved than he. As a young adult, therefore, she had effectively cut herself off from both her parents. Joan's was less strongly entrenched than Dolores and could tolerate a breach of her defences, probably because she felt she had nothing to lose. She stuck with counselling, was able to gain insight and finally to regain her father who she had rejected for some 15 years.

Another example of denial I have often seen is where a child, enraged by a brother or sister, has hit them where it hurt most. Guilt and anxiety over the injury, reinforced by parental disapproval, may make that child more than usually afraid of its aggressive feelings. It may decide never to become angry again and try to do this by denying feelings of anger, as shown in Guy's story below. This means that future anger is allowed no conscious recognition or expression but, because it still exists in the unconscious, it will find other means of expression. For instance, an inexplicable tendency to be late for appointments is often a characteristic of apparently non-aggressive people, but is frequently found to be an expression of unconscious anger.

The use of denial separates a person from their real but unsafe feelings by helping them to convince themself that they have safe feelings, but these safe feelings are not real or true. Life becomes difficult for the denying person because they are so unaware of their own motivation and often behave in a way that even they do not understand. Guy's story shows how this can work:

Guy was a professional man of 26 who refused to drive a car and would only ride a bicycle. This was because he saw a car as a potentially dangerous weapon, and although he was more likely to be hurt on a bicycle, it was more important to him that he was unlikely to hurt anyone else. His profession often required his immediate availability and this problem was, therefore, crippling to his work. He was a particularly passive man who showed his tendency to denial by managing, during his therapy, not to notice my pregnancy until I pointed it out the week before I was due to give birth.

Guy had been a normal, naughty little boy until the age of seven when he had become angry with his sister and had hurt her quite badly. The whole family had rejected him for a time and he had felt so bad that he took the strong measure of 'deciding' never to be angry again. This, of course, changed his personality as he now suppressed any anger, which led eventually to a number of problems as his normal aggressive drive sought other forms of expression. For example, he tended to dream about the violent death of his mother, not necessarily by his hand but enough to foster his fear of being a dangerous person. This ultimately led to his fear of driving a car lest he should cause an accident and hurt someone.

Projection

Projection is another defence mechanism which is important for sexual problems. Projection occurs when someone denies a failing of their own while attributing that failing to someone else. This distorts the individual's perception of themselves by maintaining their belief that they have no such failing. It also distorts the perception they have of the person to whom they attribute the failing because that person will be blamed for the problem. Projection is a frequent cause of relationship breakdown because constant scapegoating of a partner in this way causes so much mutual anger. Projection within a relationship allows the individual to feel good about themselves which reduces their anxiety, and it allows them to feel justified in discharging their anger towards their partner without guilt. This distortion leaves the partner feeling helpless and angry on their own account. Jonathan and Alice's story shows the effect of projection:

> Jonathan was very angry with his wife Alice. In particular he blamed her for their lack of friends and claimed that she was unsociable. He would occasionally admit that he had always had difficulty in making friends, but would quickly revert to blaming Alice for their poor social life. This mechanism freed him from responsibility for something he found difficult, but also acted as a conduit for the deep anger he felt towards women in general and Alice in particular.

Jonathan tried to deny his own tendency to be unsociable, although he clearly was, and perceived Alice as unsociable, although she clearly wasn't. The particularly damaging result of this kind of projection is that the blame is placed on one partner for the deficiency of the other which increases resentment on both sides.

Reaction Formation

Another defence mechanism which we see operating in sexual problems is that of reaction formation, which we touched on in the discussion of frigidity earlier. This is where there is a strong distaste for sex which is equal and opposite in power to the feeling it is hiding. This is a very powerful defence, and is often used by children for extra safety when their parents strongly disapprove of their interest in bodily matters. They feel revolted by sexual matters in a way which they assume their parents share, and thereby feel safe and united with their parents because they have so totally disguised their forbidden interest.

This defence is particularly pertinent in cases of child abuse. There are many different sorts of child abuse, and some simply leave the child hurt and frightened. However, for many the abuse is by a loved family member or friend, in which case their feelings can be very mixed. Despite its undoubtedly being abuse, it may also have been gentle and arousing. There may, therefore, amidst the fear and anxiety, be exciting sexual feelings which produce intense guilt in the child. One way of dealing with this guilt is to react to the feelings of arousal by forming feelings of utter distaste. This then protects the child from the anxiety of the forbidden sexual feelings which have accompanied the sexual abuse. The memory of the reaction being formed sinks into the archives of the unconscious, so that the adult may only be aware of the distaste, and will be angry and defensive at any other suggestion. This results in the difficult situation for the abused person that whenever they feel sexual arousal it seems to them that they are feeling distaste. It is obvious that there is likely to be great resistance to undoing this reversal of feelings.

Sue's story gives a clear example of reaction formation:

Sue was referred to me for counselling because of her distaste for sex following years of abuse by her stepfather. He had been sent to prison for this offence.

The important factor to emerge in Sue's case was that she had accepted his abuse of her for years, and enjoyed it. She convinced herself that she was protecting her mother and the family by this relationship with him, until she found out that he was also interested in her young sister, at which point she reported him.

When Sue began to talk more freely she revealed that her stepfather was only 12 years older than her, and that she was very fond of him. She was an open-minded young woman and was prepared to work with the idea that it was jealousy of her sister and a sense of betrayal that caused her to 'shop' her step-father. Unconsciously her guilt and anger were turned into a rejection of sex and allowed her to feel the victim, which of course, she was.

Facing the truth about her part in the betrayal of both her mother and her stepfather eventually freed Sue to get on with her life. She allowed herself to enjoy sex with her boyfriend again.

In a way this whole book is about the importance of defence mechanisms in our lives and in particular in our relationships. At this stage, you may find this chapter difficult to relate to because, by definition, any defences that you have are there to prevent you thinking about things that worry you. If you find the explorations difficult now, once you have finished the book you should be able to look back at what you have read with more understanding and be able to repeat the explorations more freely.

Key Points

- An important feature of the unconscious is to protect us from unpleasant memories and emotions through defence mechanisms
- Where a defence mechanism has become a long-term solution to anxiety, it means that there has been a dangerous distortion of feelings
- Unconscious emotion is usually stronger than reason
- We need to experience some of the pain of the situation we are responding to or we lose touch with reality
- Our attitudes are fixed ways of thinking which are set up in the past
- The changing standards in society collide with individual attitudes
- A change in social circumstances will affect people's attitudes which in turn will affect the values in society
- We constantly have to balance our internal expectations and attitudes against the changing opportunities and risks presented by the society in which we live
- The more we avoid something, the stronger becomes our prejudice against it
- Avoidance diminishes conscious anxiety while increasing unconscious anxiety
- Prejudices diminish our capacity to profit from experience
- The unconscious can be defined as 'the deepest level of the mind, usually inaccessible, which holds suppressed memories of feelings that affect behaviour'
- Our unconscious contains records of all the experiences we have had throughout our lives.

3

Basic Emotions

Importance of Insight

It is important to recognise is that our feelings dictate our behaviour. Actions flow along in the wake of emotions unless a powerful effort is made to stop them. Many times we are unaware of the way this happens, but sometimes – having wondered for years why we feel a certain way in a given situation – we may suddenly come to understand the reasons for our feelings and therefore our behaviour. This insight allows us to perceive the real significance of an idea or feeling for the first time.

Acquiring insight into how our feelings work can enable us to use a change in feelings to produce a change in behaviour. A change in behaviour can then result in good feedback from increased positive feelings. Carol's story illustrates this:

Carol's partner Simon told her that her body was abnormal, particularly in the genital area. He repeatedly insulted her about this with the result that she became more and more inhibited and avoided sex. Her anxiety persisted despite reassurance from gynaecologists that her body was perfectly normal.

Carol stayed with Simon for a number of reasons. First, she was dependent on him financially. Secondly, she thought she was too old at 50 to find another partner. Thirdly, her mother's relationship with her father had conditioned her to believe that women were subordinate to men. This led Carol to fear that Simon might be right and that, despite having had three children, there might be something wrong with her.

In counselling with Carol I introduced the idea that Simon's vulnerability and fear of his own impotence made him protect himself by accusing her. This new idea allowed her to begin to doubt his judgment which increased her confidence. She started to feel more powerful, applied for and got a flat of her own, and was determined not to continue to rely on Simon. The result was that he immediately valued her differently and begged her to stay. When she refused he became helpful in a way he had never been before, e.g. in decorating her flat, and the result was that, valuing each other more, sex improved for both.

There are many conflicts in relationships which can be overcome without too much insight being necessary. For lasting satisfaction, though, there is usually more to understand than people think.

Range of Sexual Problems

Sexual behaviour in our society ranges from those who have never have sexual intercourse in their lives to those who have multiple sexual partners. We all fit in somewhere between the two poles. Not everyone wants or has a committed relationship. But for those who do, if one partner has a problem then it also becomes a problem for the other. Strangely, it is common for a person to camouflage a problem of their own by choosing a partner with an even more obvious problem. David's story is a good example of this.

> David's first wife left him for another man. He was very hurt by this and wanted to make sure it never happened again. His second wife, Jenny, wasn't interested in sex, which made him feel safe because he thought that, unlike his first wife, she would never leave him. David thought he could make Jenny respond to him sexually, but her problem was deeply rooted so this wasn't possible. David experienced this as a second rejection which made him very angry. He 'sent' Jenny for counselling and only reluctantly came with her later to 'help with her problem'. After several sessions he found the courage to reveal his anxieties and share the responsibility for their situation.

We have to distinguish between problems in casual sex and those within a committed relationship. Casual sex is outside the scope of this book because there is no time to tackle any problems before new more satisfactory prospects are sought. Even in a committed relationship we have to distinguish between sex in the beginning with its new exciting freshness and sex in the long term with the very different pleasures of the well-known comfortable old dressing gown and the, often difficult, hangover of the daily life together. Commitment alters sexual responses, often dampening them down to some extent. For example a knowledge that sex can be had at any time lessens the excitement and uncertainty of finding suitable opportunities. This and other effects of commitment will be looked at in detail in Chapter 6.

We also have to note the different emphasis of the problems found in the two sexes. This is due to the effects of difference of physical power, type of sexual performance and emotional priority. These important issues will be fully discussed in Part IV. The differences between the sexes can add to the excitement and charge of the sexual experience, but can also lead to tension and conflict. Since a woman's arousal is largely hidden and need only be revealed if she wishes and she can simulate an orgasm if she chooses, her worries are very different from those of a man. The emphasis for her is on the quality of her feelings, since performance is within her control. Men, on the other hand, predominantly worry about their performance, because it is not under their conscious control. They cannot feign arousal and inability to achieve an erection is experienced as failure. Men's self-esteem is closely bound to their sexual performance. These issues apply within heterosexual and homosexual relationships.

The table below offers a simple classification of the most common sexual problems.

Men	Women
Impotence with no interest	Failure or difficulty in arousal
Impotence with interest	Pain on intercourse
Premature ejaculation	No orgasm
Difficulty in ejaculation	Difficulty in reaching orgasm
Lack of interest in sex	Lack of interest in sex
Reduced interest in sex	Reduced interest in sex
Medical problems	Medical problems

Before dealing with the differences between men and women, it will be useful to look at the issues which are the same for both sexes. To begin with we need to consider the important question of how emotional upset can disrupt sexual response. The common ingredient in all sexual problems is anxiety. This is an unpleasant feeling which we wish to avoid. So the effect it has is to make us withhold sexually in varying degrees from our partner.

Anxiety

Anxiety is a general response to threat which, when the threat is real, has a value in promoting the survival of the organism. There is no obvious threat in having sex when it takes place between consenting adults. However, anything which causes us to fear for ourselves in any way can be felt as a threat, and people have many fears to do with sex.

35

Some of these are easily understood fears with external causes such as the fear of becoming pregnant or contracting AIDS. Others are more obscure and have internal causes. Examples are fear of parental disapproval or difficult feelings like anger, disappointment, guilt or helplessness. Some people still fear the loss of a parent's love or fear that their own 'bad' feelings could destroy their present relationship. All these emotions can have a profound effect on sex.

Anxiety causes a response by focusing attention on the perceived danger and works through the hormonal and nervous systems to place the body on alert for fight or flight. This response, in the wrong context, can have a damaging effect on sex and other bodily functions. If a woman is worrying about whether she should be having sex, her attention will not be on her experience of sex with her partner. Similarly, if a man is worrying about whether he will be able to maintain his erection, he will not be paying attention to his partner. This self-consciousness, caused by anxiety, reduces the likelihood of a mutually satisfying sexual encounter.

Almost all sexual difficulties are caused by anxiety. This anxiety is often unconscious, but can still be strong enough to make someone hold back from sexual intercourse. Direct results of such anxiety include loss of desire, impotence, frigidity, premature ejaculation and lack of orgasm. These are ways in which underlying anxiety expresses itself and results in the inability to experience sexual satisfaction. Of course, in a few cases such physical problems are caused by a disease such as diabetes or certain types of medication.

Anxiety may be produced by a situation in the present. Also it may be conjured up by thoughts or memories from the past. For example, memories of failure on holiday in Italy may have become built-in and always lurking. Anxiety may, therefore, be anything from a brief reaction to an ever present millstone. Some sexual anxiety arises directly from the fact that much of our sexual response is controlled by unconscious forces. Any process which is controlled by unconscious forces is, by definition, outside our conscious control. This in itself can create anxiety, particularly for people who place great importance on being able to stay in control of their lives. Faced with the process of sexual intercourse, where arousal is not under conscious control and where loss of control is required if orgasm or ejaculation is to be experienced, such people will inevitably feel great anxiety which will affect their performance. Thus anyone may be humbled by sexual failure – intelligence, status, social class, clothes or money confer no immunity. Indeed, I have frequently found that the more someone demands success or perfection in their sexual performance, and the harder they try to achieve it, the more elusive that success becomes.

> Sean had left his wife of 20 years with whom he had had a satisfactory, if not exciting, sex life. They had been childhood sweethearts and married at 18 which had been necessary in the small community from which they came. Sean lost his job and came to London where he fell in love with a sophisticated woman who returned his affections. Sean was desperate to meet, what he imagined were, her sexual demands with the result that he became completely impotent. Each failure increased the anxiety and made failure more likely. In fact, although his partner was concerned about his sexual performance she was far more interested in his love and companionship and when he became convinced of this his anxiety diminished and his performance improved.

So, the most obvious example of this anxiety is male impotence. The ability to achieve an erection is largely under unconscious control. Erections come when they are not wanted, particularly in the young, and often refuse to come when they are wanted, particularly in the mature. This makes a man very vulnerable and plays a large part in the formation of his character. It means that one cause of anxiety is a sense of helplessness and shows that conscious control, otherwise known as will-power, is not enough to solve this problem.

A particularly common result of anxiety in women is pain on penetration. A woman's anxiety can prevent arousal, leave the vagina dry and cause tightening of the muscles surrounding the entrance to the vagina. This means that the man has to force his way in, which puts him off, and so establishes a means for her to escape sexual intercourse. It is difficult for women to accept that the severe physical pain they feel which is preventing them from experiencing sexual intercourse is caused by unconscious anxiety, when consciously they may think that sexual intercourse is something they really want. The problem will not go away until the cause of the unconscious anxiety has been discovered and understood. There is usually a coherent reason why the individual concerned wants to avoid sexual intercourse, but to find that reason, she will first have to accept the principle that at some level she is avoiding it. Most people are resistant to such ideas, and Hattie was one such:

> Hattie was referred to me by a gynaecologist, following an operation to enlarge her vagina. She had been married four years but was, despite the operation, quite unable to have sexual intercourse. I was surprised to find when taking her history that she had, in fact, had perfectly satisfactory intercourse for three years of her marriage which seemed to make the operation redundant. It was done out of desperation because no one could see anything else to do.
>
> We explored Hattie's relationship with her husband Jake and it emerged that she had been increasingly resentful that he spent each weekend on the golf

course and she felt that he preferred playing golf with his friends to being with her.

Hattie had to accept that in her disappointment she had withdrawn from Jake emotionally and that for her, this also meant withdrawing sexually. While on the one hand she was distressed that pain stopped her having intercourse, on the other hand her 'tight' feeling about Jake caused her to be 'tight' with him and this caused pain. Talking about her emotional pain and eliciting a compromise over the golf allowed her to relax and re-introduce love-making into her life.

Anxiety causes major problems because it is a very unpleasant feeling and people try to avoid it as far as possible. What may start out as one upsetting episode can gradually build up into a phobia if it leads to avoidance of an activity, whether that activity be flying in an aeroplane, riding a horse or having sexual intercourse. A phobia is a specific anxiety caused by something that most people do not fear, and is so powerful that it interferes with what we would wish to do. It tends to occur if we regularly avoid doing something that makes us feel anxious. This is because our brain establishes a link between the anxiety and the activity and a danger signal then registers whenever the activity presents itself, which prompts us to avoid it. This avoidance then becomes self-perpetuating. It is for this reason that a riding instructor will try to persuade a pupil who has fallen from a horse to get straight back on again. If they don't, they are unlikely to come to the class again.

Another consequence of avoidance is that gaps develop between instances in which a confrontation of the anxiety-provoking activity has to occur. During each gap anxiety puts down roots and becomes stronger. The bigger the gap between incidences of facing the frightening thing, the greater the anxiety when it finally has to be faced. This means that problems that are not tackled tend not only to stay for ever, but usually to get worse. A common example I have encountered many times in sexual counselling is that those women who, despite some reluctance, regularly have sex from the beginning of their marriage and do not try to avoid it are likely to have a long and satisfactory sex life. Those who avoid it or manage greatly to restrict its frequency may never overcome their underlying resistance.

If sex causes anxiety, for whatever reason, there will be a tendency to avoid it. This resistance causes many different types of dysfunction in the smooth running of a sexual relationship. These are all greater or lesser expressions of a wish to withhold, either from sex itself or from the partner. This not only creates the obvious conflict with the partner but also creates conflict within the individual.

Conflict

Such feelings of internal conflict are closely linked with anxiety in the field of sexual problems. The natural tendency is to avoid anything causing anxiety. In sex it is complicated because there is also likely to be a strong wish for sex to take place. This is for three reasons:

1. Our biological sex drive is manifest in the wish for sensual arousal and relief
2. People recognise that it is 'normal' to want sex and we all want to be 'normal'
3. We wish to please our partner

This third reason introduces a state of conflict when someone's anxiety is related to feelings of anger with their partner, so that the wish to punish the partner conflicts with the wish to please them. In this state of conflict it is not possible to avoid all anxiety. This is because getting involved in sexual activity carries the risk of failing to punish the partner, while withholding sexual activity carries the risk of failing to please them.

It is sometimes possible to resolve conflict by replacing anxiety with a different response. For example, Mary wants to masturbate. There is conflict because she believes her parents would object and she fears losing their approval. If she decides that avoidance of trouble is the more important thing, she will not masturbate and will thereby feel safer. She will find another way to deal with her frustration and thereby feel more comfortable. However, this can cause problems if the situation is repeated so that Mary learns to lose interest in her sexual feelings. The need to feel comfortable may become a way of life and produce a 'good' child. The adult who was a 'good' child often says 'sex is not all that important' when coming for counselling. In order to rediscover the importance of sex as an adult, she would have to re-experience her original anxiety (which led her to decide that sex had less importance in the first place), and remember its cause. It is only possible to relieve anxiety by coming to understand the reasons behind it.

We have seen that anxiety is the primary emotion which interferes with sexual expression, partly by directly affecting physical response and partly by causing avoidance. It is closely associated with internal conflict. Anxiety alone, or in combination with conflict, can cause sex to be withheld for various reasons, many of which initially seem to be physical.

Laura was to be married in three months but had never used Tampax and never been able to allow penetration although she had had several boyfriends and was 32 years old. She experienced great pain when she tried to have intercourse . Her gynaecologist, however, had examined her and declared that there was no physical problem. With counselling her problems with sex were revealed to be connected with her ambivalent relationship with her father who had left home when she was three years old. While achievement of pleasure would take longer counselling, she was able to to overcome her physical resistance to penetration in time for her wedding. This was achieved by first recognising that this problem was not due to some physical abnormality, by recognising that something the size of a baby could use this passage and finally by being encouraged to use Tampax. This last was helped by a holiday in the Bahamas when her wish to go swimming when she had a period overcame her resistance to touching this part of her body.

There are four main areas of emotional difficulty which can lie behind sexual anxiety and conflict:

1. Disappointment
2. Anger
3. Fear of losing control
4. Fear of punishment

Disappointment

Most single adults naturally seek a partner, but actually having a partner is very difficult to cope with. This is a fact that people are reluctant to face. Romantic stories and films usually end with the making of the union, but the real test comes after that. Most of us are unprepared for this, having hoped or even assumed that with the right partner we would live happily ever after without trying. The first few years together in a committed relationship are sometimes fraught with anxiety as couples come to terms with feelings of loss of illusion, frustration and helpless entrapment. This can lead to power struggles between the partners and the loss of good feelings.

One of the most profound causes of anxiety is having negative feelings about a person we love. This anxiety is particularly acute when we are young and have not yet matured enough to recognise the fact that there are mixed feelings in every relationship and that hostility does not mean the end of love. Hostile feelings cause anxiety because, on top of the difficulty of experiencing the feelings themselves, they can seem to be a sign that the wrong partner has been chosen. This can create great fear early in marriage when it may seem to imply that either a divorce, or a lifetime 'trapped' with the wrong partner, is inevitable. Such fear can cause a loss of closeness, and withholding from sex can be used consciously or unconsciously, both to express this feeling and to punish the partner.

The way a person deals with their hostility makes all the difference to the outcome. Arguing or sulking are part of most people's repertoire and, although not ideal, are at least forms of expression. Problems are likely to arise if a person tries to ignore or deny their hostile feelings. These strategies will cause internal conflict, which will lead to the hostility being expressed in a less direct way, such as through the avoidance of sexual contact. Denial of hostile feelings can be so complete as to leave the person unaware that they are resisting sexual intercourse itself. It can lead them to believe that they need to avoid it because of a physical problem. In women this is usually an ailment, and in men fatigue due to work problems, or in either sex it can be a physical sexual difficulty.

This concentration on physical problems is a protection, which may be conscious or unconscious, against the worries about the relationship itself. It is an attempt to divert attention from, and protect the partnership from, hostile feelings. In this way sex can become a scapegoat so that, apart from the fact that sex is being avoided, the partners may be getting on well. Sometimes this manoeuvre ensures a mild and useful separation from the ultimate closeness which, after a short time, restores good feelings. More often it can become a way of life and set up a situation in which sex avoidance is commonplace.

Understanding the reality of relationships in a true and unromantic way can, paradoxically, improve the sexual situation dramatically. There is nothing more dangerous to a relationship than unrealistic expectations about romance. This means thinking about what our expectations of our partner are and tracking down the origins of these expectations, whether from literature, the media or our parents. Above all, it means facing the fact that our partner will also have expectations and will also be suffering from disappointment.

Anger

Anger may be minor and temporary, such as the partner not ringing to say they will be late or bringing home duck for supper when chicken had been agreed. It may be a more serious issue such as being unpleasantly drunk or worse, perceived to have been unfaithful. Whatever, the most common reaction to feelings of anger is simply a conscious wish to withhold the giving of the self until the issue at stake is resolved. It is therefore difficult to combine anger and sex, because satisfactory sex requires that both partners are willing to be exposed and vulnerable, and anger in this situation can cause deep anxiety. The angry person may be anxious that their suppressed anger could break through during intercourse and lead to violence, or the non-angry person may sense and fear the other's anger. It can therefore feel safer to withhold, either partly or totally, from sexual intercourse.

Anger can also be completely unconscious. This usually applies to passive and non-violent people. Men of this type make unconscious attempts to cope with their angry feelings which will take the form of turning them upside-down into feelings of powerlessness or physical impotence. This reassures men that they have no dangerous feelings to deal with, but it makes their partners feel rejected and angry, which increases the tension between the couple. Jim and Molly's story illustrates this effect:

> Jim and Molly came for help because, after finding each other through a shared interest rather late in life, they were having difficulties due to Jim's impotence. He had always had a problem with maintaining an erection for long enough to penetrate, and although Molly knew of this, she felt angry and rejected when she couldn't change it. In their partnership there was a continual cycle of anger over impotence, producing more anger and consequently increasing the impotence.
>
> At first they were drawn to each other because Molly was very dominant and Jim was very passive. However, his passivity became more controlling and frustrating as she became more demanding and her anger fuelled his need to avoid her. This pattern of behaviour originated with Jim's mother who was also dominating. She had had a very close relationship with him as a child, but they lived abroad, and she suddenly banished him to boarding school in England. This produced conflicting feelings of angry rejection and devoted love, which Jim had never quite been able to grow out of, and which seemed to be reflected in all his relationships with women. His unconscious wish to punish women he loved for his mother's rejection had to be neutralised. This made him hold back and feel safe with his impotence but also gave him the satisfaction of punishing his partners by frustrating them.

In Jim's case, the factors were largely unconscious. Sometimes, however, there is a perfectly conscious decision to punish the partner for whatever has caused the anger by showing no interest. This is a normal, if childish, reaction which is unlikely to cause too much trouble in the long run. It is when the anger is unrecognised, and the need to protect and punish unknown and denied, that more serious difficulties arise.

Fear of Losing Control

Society is fascinated with the failure of human beings to maintain control, as seen in the popular media reporting of rape, murder, adultery and revenge. At the same time as being excited by it, we fear the power of sex to make us so excited that we lose control. A drive, whether sexual or aggressive, is inherently propulsive and needs to be controlled. However, because the sex drive is instinctive, it is not easily manipulated by that part of our brain which expects to control our body. This potential lack or loss of control creates anxiety in itself.

Men are strongly muscled and have a high level of testosterone, the hormone which gives strength to the sexual drive. Women have weaker muscles and a lower level of testosterone, resulting in a comparatively controllable sexual drive. Each gender has some reason to fear the other. Men fear women because of women's capacity to arouse excitement in them which they must then control. Women fear their own power to arouse men and the demands on them that will follow. So the woman may wear tights for protection and carry a nailfile in her purse just in case she needs a weapon. Young girls unsure of their sexuality may dress provocatively and then feel indignant at the effect.

A man may frequently be afraid of his impulses, particularly when he is angry, and a woman may also be afraid of a man's impulses even when he is not angry. Many men complain of the woman's power to goad and drive them to violence. It may well be that women have developed verbal skills to supplement their weaker musle power only to fear the possibility of a thumping if they succeed in riling their partner.

Fear of Punishment

A different question is how our personal and sexual development from childhood can interact with adult problems to create anxiety, conflict and sexual difficulties. In some cases this may seem obvious but in others, particularly where the sexual failure comes after a period of successful sexual activity, the importance of the past may be missed.

Every society has evolved a network of taboos, customs and laws which regulate the expression of sexual excitement. Parents are especially important in this process. For the young child, it is parents who represent this process of control, and because their influence is early, its effects tend to be profound and long-lasting. However, just as it can be difficult to control sexual excitement, it can also be difficult to control its regulation; finding the middle road between too much excitement and too much suppression is very difficult.

Sexual excitement is provided by biology, while social influences supply its suppression. Childrens' sexuality can tolerate some suppression of excitement and still function, but if the suppression in childhood is too great, it may be difficult for an adult to maintain a sexual response. For example, Toby was constantly reprimanded for taking an interest in his own genitals and learnt to suppress his interest so thoroughly that it completely disappeared. He did not overcome this and marry until he was 50 years old. Tom showed the extreme effect of too much suppression that sexual excitation was stored up until it broke through in an uncontrolled way. Brought up in a middle-class family he had had a girl friend for years who he had only kissed. However, when a young girl who he hardly knew came to stay with his parents he went to her bedroom and would have raped her had she not called for help. During the day he had shown no interest in this girl and had been reprimanded for being rude to her. This is most likely to happen where extreme strategies, such as total denial of interest, are in place. These leave the individual unprepared if the strategy breaks down, because no other resources have been developed, so the individual is totally vulnerable to their newly revealed passion, as shown in Colin's story:

> Colin was the only child of older parents and had a strict religious upbringing. He met his girlfriend Annie at their strict and puritanical church. They married but sex was unsatisfactory. When they had been married for about six months, Colin began to have abdominal pains which eventually led to an operation and a spell in hospital. Here he was tended by nubile young nurses and a very obvious change in personality followed. Annie noticed this change while he was still in hospital when he openly made suggestive remarks to all his nurses. His former Christianity was forgotten and his behaviour became extremely permissive and promiscuous. A year later they were divorced.

The other biological drive which causes similar problems for parents is the aggressive drive. We will see in Chapter 6 how the two instinctive biological drives of sex and aggression can interact such that each increases the difficulty in controlling the other. The aggressive drive equips us to fight, if necessary, for our survival, but it can obviously be dangerous if uncontrolled. Once again it is the responsibility of parents to control their young child. Parents who are unsure of their ability to control their own sex or aggressive drives are likely to be anxious about the same drives in their children. In turn, those children are likely to become anxious parents, unless they can gain some insight into their problems. People are understandably reluctant to blame loved parents for their problems. Bringing up children is probably the most difficult job in the world and it is not possible to do it perfectly. Parents can be very loving, act with the best of intentions, yet still unwittingly cause problems for their children which persist into adulthood.

It often happens that people refuse to explore their difficulties out of loyalty to their parents. This loyalty sometimes hides fear: fear of disillusionment, fear of finding hidden hostility, or fear of punishment for failing to follow parental rules. Understanding the source of our anxiety depends upon our ideas about life and people, and understanding the position of our parents is part of that process. Parents have needs, as well as children, and there is not always an ideal balance such that both parents and children get their needs met in full.

Too often those with sexual problems undervalue their own adult judgment because they hold on to a childish illusion that parents know best and that failure to follow parental advice could prove disastrous. The right perspective is to see parents as ordinary human beings, just like ourselves, with no magical powers. This allows us to consider parental dictates from an adult point of view and to accept or reject them on their merits, rather than to accept them unconditionally which prevents us forming our own moral code.

Sex, therefore, is a complicated interaction between instinctive, emotional, intellectual and social drives, some of which are conscious and some unconscious. Achieving a satisfactory balance between these factors is crucial to our success as human beings; imbalance leads to anxiety and internal conflict. Disappointment, anger, fear of loss of control and fear of punishment may lie behind such anxiety. The manifestation of these problems is different in men and women.

Key Points

♦ The most effective approach to solving sexual problems addresses both the emotional and physical sides of sex

♦ Within a committed relationship the physical expression of sex depends upon its emotional foundation

♦ For lasting satisfaction there is usually more to understand about unconscious emotional influences than people think

♦ Almost all sexual difficulties are caused by unconscious anxiety

♦ It is only possible to remove unconscious anxiety by learning to understand the reasons behind it

♦ Parents can be very loving, act with the best of intentions, yet still unwittingly cause problems for their children which persist into adulthood.

4

War Without End

Most people are well aware of a conflict or 'tug of war' inside themselves over many issues. With any decision we weigh the pros and cons, and the outcome of this internal debate is that one side wins. This seems to be done at a conscious level; although, without realising it, we may be driven by unconscious factors. We want, but should we have, another drink or even another potato? It seems like a clear choice, but we may be unconsciously influenced by our mother's voice in our conscience saying 'you have had quite enough' and the rebellious child inside us, still feeling it must assert itself, saying 'I want it'.

In particular the tug of war is a useful metaphor to show the fluctuating state of our feelings about sex. It shows that at any one point during adult life we have a fundamental state of equilibrium in our attitude to sex, which may be pro-sex or anti-sex. This equilibrium may be shifted at any time by changing external factors, which can be as simple as a squabble with our partner or as complex as becoming a parent. We often try to make things better by changing the external factors, and this can have some effect. A new job which reduces money worries or resolving a dispute with our partner can all have a temporary beneficial effect on our relationship, and therefore on our sex life. However, if the basic attitude to sex has become negative for some reason, a more fundamental shift will be required for a permanent improvement.

The number of complex issues surrounding love and sex means that we may be very well aware of the tug of war over some issues. For example, in a committed relationship, there is often the temptation to be unfaithful. The tug of war this creates, with the pros pulling one way and the cons the other, is perfectly clear. It is harder to be aware of the unconscious elements of partnership conflict. For example just feeling hostile for no reason or irrationally angry over some minor forgetfulness by the partner can destroy sexual interest. The next eight chapters are devoted to elucidating the hidden power of the unconscious elements which can have a destructive effect on sex and love. This insight allows some control over previously helpless feelings.

The diagram below represents the personal world of a human being as the field on which a sexual tug of war is being held. It names the two teams, Pro-Sex and Anti-Sex. Each team has an anchor with a fundamental role: in the Pro-Sex team, the anchor is called Sex Drive (SD), and in the Anti-Sex Team, the name of the anchor is Basic Insecurity (BI). The individual competitors in each team are also named, as you can see in the diagram.

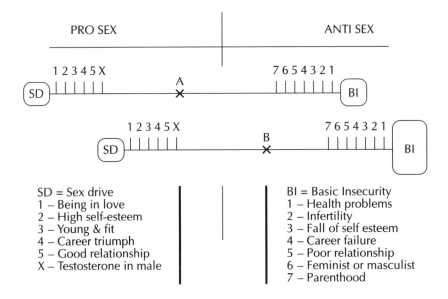

SD = Sex drive
1 – Being in love
2 – High self-esteem
3 – Young & fit
4 – Career triumph
5 – Good relationship
X – Testosterone in male

BI = Basic Insecurity
1 – Health problems
2 – Infertility
3 – Fall of self esteem
4 – Career failure
5 – Poor relationship
6 – Feminist or masculist
7 – Parenthood

The Tug of War Model

The Field

The 'field' where any internal tug of war is held is our own personal world. This world has been built up inside us, ever since birth, from our unique experience of life. It is not so much a true representation of the world as the way it seems to us. In our early construction of our personal world, our experience of the environment is limited. This inevitably leads to mistaken assumptions because it is easy for us to misinterpret things. For example, if our mother is cross with us, we may believe that she does not love us. This is a logical interpretation but usually incorrect.

Mistaken assumptions may lead to inappropriate behaviour as we try to put things right. For example, I have seen many male patients whose mothers or grandmothers regularly threatened to cut off their penis if they played with it. Of course they didn't mean it, but these children mistakenly assumed that castration was a real possibility. This resulted in deep anxiety about what was acceptable to women and often played a large part in subsequent sexual impotence.

When we have a sexual problem, it is therefore important for us to see if we are being influenced by mistaken assumptions. Adult knowledge together with insight gives us a chance to free ourselves from the deep-seated anxieties of childhood.

The outside world, and its reflection in an individual's personal world, are both full of contradictions. This makes it difficult for us to decide how to behave. At first our instinctive biological needs pull us in one direction and the influence of our family pulls us the other way. These are the fundamental pulls. Other pulls result from our own intellectual evaluations and interpretations which develop as a result of wider social demands. As the intellect increasingly comes into play there is an attempt to make logically perfect decisions which are free from the less controllable pulls of emotion and instinct. The individual, therefore, has to find a way to satisfy instinctive, emotional and intellectual needs and decide what behaviour produces the best feelings. As we have seen, sexual activity involves all three types of need, and if the balance between them is not correct for the individual, a problem will result.

The Anchors

The sexual tug of war in an individual represents the ebb and flow of their available sexuality. Some people will fluctuate more than others, but there is a basic stability in the opposing forces which determines whether the individual's Pro-Sex or Anti-Sex team is likely to win. This is because, as in the traditional tug of war team, there is a competitor on each side who is more important than the others: the extra-strong anchor. In our analogy the anchors represent the central issues which have been with us since childhood and which have become part of our personality. It is the anchors who control the game.

Pro-Sex Anchor: Sex Drive   In the Pro-Sex team the anchor is the Sex Drive. A drive is a built-in biological pressure with the aim of securing the survival of the individual or the species. The Sex Drive is primarily for the survival of the species, while the aggressive drive is primarily for the survival of the individual.

The Sex Drive is active from early childhood. As we have already seen, the pressure of the Sex Drive is what worries many parents: remembering their own fears of loss of control, they are anxious about the behaviour of their child. One reason for this is that from birth onwards the child becomes a representative of its parents. They feel responsible for their child's behaviour which seems to reflect both their ability as parents and their value as people. The child to some extent personifies the parents' own unconscious fear of doing something socially unacceptable. In other words, the parents are anxious to control in the child those drives which they fear in themselves.

Anti-Sex Anchor: Basic Insecurity   This fear in the parent produces in the child the Basic Insecurity which is the anchor of the Anti-Sex team. Basic Insecurity is a cluster of anxieties which arise during early development and are essentially a response to parental concern about behaviour. Basic Insecurity can be seen as a defence, induced by parental and social control, against the inherent Sex Drive of the child.

Several issues can influence Basic Insecurity. These include a wish to please parents, resentment over sibling displacement or anger about gender favouritism. All these issues will be fully discussed in later chapters.

The Other Competitors

The other competitors in our internal tug of war game are issues which arise in adult life and have a positive or negative influence on our sex life. They are emotional, physical, social and intellectual matters. We will look at the Pro-Sex competitors first.

Being in love   This is perhaps the most important competitor after the anchors. The state of being in love is very powerful and, in the short term, is capable of overriding much of the Basic Insecurity. However, in the long term it can produce many problems for the unwary. For example, the romantic person does not expect a change to occur once a relationship with their loved one has been successfully secured, nor are they aware that much of their excitement is connected with the uncertainty of not yet having the desired person. The excited state is expected to last forever, but events such as engagement, living together or marriage will cause permanent changes in the relationship, which can result in disappointment and bitterness. This inability to deal with the reality of commitment may be influenced by unrealistic parental ideals which lead to the establishment of unrealistic personal expectations, which are expanded in adolescence on exposure to the myth of romantic love as depicted in films and other media. An immature attitude to relationships is the result. More mature people will expect the changes that occur with commitment and can deal with some of the inevitable disappointment. Those less ready for commitment find it hard: the loss of freedom and the need to consider the partner seem a high price to pay. This disillusionment can tip the tug of war balance in favour of the Anti-Sex team.

Where conquest of the opposite sex is used to allay deep insecurities, in either sex attaining the desired quarry will result in a more rapid and complete loss of interest. However, because men have the assistance of testosterone to keep them sexually excited, the changes that occur in a committed relationship have less effect on them sexually than they do on women, whose sexual desire is more likely to decrease in a committed relationship.

Testosterone in men   This is a very important member of the man's Pro-Sex team. Testosterone is a hormone which has a very powerful physical, mental and emotional effect on men. It supports the efforts of the team's anchor, the Sex Drive. Testosterone causes sex to intrude in a much more physical way on men than it does on women, particularly in puberty but also in adulthood.

High self-esteem   The lucky person with uncritical parents who have created in the child a sense of love and approval even when mistakes are made or marks at school are not the best, will have a sense of self-esteem that can withstand many knocks. This good feeling about themselves will free them from the usual anxieties.

Young and fit   Youthfulness and fitness are states that have an energy of their own. This can create a sense of hope and expectation about the individual's ability to cope with and enjoy what life has in store which can make it a strong Pro-Sex competitor.

Career triumph This competitor has a beneficial but short-term influence on the game. It adds power to the team as a whole, but is not usually persistent enough to be a fundamental influence in a sexual problem. For example, getting a new job can stimulate good feelings for a short time, but the usual pattern will recur within a few weeks. However, the very high achiever seems to get a 'high' from success that results in heightened sexual arousal for as long as the high lasts.

Good relationship In a good relationship where basic anxiety is not a strong player in either partner's tug of war, sex is a source of comfort, restoration and recovery from disappointment. It is a way of making the problems of the outside world seem less important. It is only where conflict and anxiety prevents the use of sex as a healing force that the ups and downs of life make a noticeable difference to the sexual relationship.

The Anti-Sex competitors may be more or less powerful than the Pro-Sex competitors, depending on the shape of the individual's sexual field.

Feminist or masculist Feminist and masculist are simplistic labels for a number of complex issues of gender conflict which will be dealt with fully in Part IV. This is perhaps the most important emotional competitor in the tug of war. This competitor adds its efforts to the Basic Insecurity anchor of the Anti-Sex team. For example, while it can truly be said of men and women that they are equal and opposite, many people who are discontented and envious wish to maintain that they are not only equal but the same. Anyone who is unhappy with their gender and envious of their partner has deep negative feelings to cope with in the relationship, which may well up at any time and spoil activities in which sexual difference is an issue. These feelings may be conscious but are much more often unconscious.

If a woman is unconsciously envious of her partner's position as a man, she will unconsciously wish to undermine him. This will create a destructive barrier of hostility with far-reaching effects on many aspects of their relationship. As the act of sexual intercourse between a man and a woman highlights the physical differences between them, it is a particularly potent provocation of her envy. I have found this to be by far the most powerful competitor in the Anti-Sex teams of women with sexual problems.

If a man is unconsciously envious of the female position he too will

51

unconsciously wish to undermine her. Both sexes tend to undermine by withholding their own arousal from one another, and in the man this can lead, at worst, to impotence. Because sexual intercourse emphasises gender difference it can become the focus of all gender-related problems in a relationship.

Infertility The frustration and disappointment associated with infertility makes it a powerful competitor in the Anti-Sex team. A couple may have achieved a satisfactory sex life, with their Pro-Sex team an easy winner of the tug of war, and then feel it is time for them to have a child. If this does not happen and one partner minds very much, a destructive element can enter the relationship. The responsibility for the failure is usually borne by one of the partners, and the situation becomes fraught with guilt, anger, loss of self-esteem and humiliation, giving the Anti-Sex team the power to win for a time.

Health problems This Anti-Sex competitor can cause major sexual problems all by itself. It is the one competitor which can cause purely physical sexual problems without an emotional component. These include problems resulting from diseases such as diabetes, injuries such as paraplegia, and certain types of medication. The discussion of such physical sexual problems is outside the scope of this book.

A more complicated situation is where a physical health problem arouses unconscious anxiety which then indirectly causes a sexual problem without the link between the two being recognised. It can be difficult for people to grasp that a condition which looks and feels like a straightforward medical problem may have an emotional cause, or that such a condition can in turn be the cause of an emotionally-based sexual problem. I have seen many different conditions which have affected people's sexual responses, and I will outline some of the commoner ones in more detail.

Any malady affecting the reproductive system, from mild thrush to fibroids or cancer, will arouse strong feelings against sex in any individual whose Basic Insecurity is strong. The unconscious anxiety in these individuals is caused by a combination of early conditioning that sex is naughty and the fact that naughty children learn to expect punishment, which leads such people to conclude that sex will be followed by punishment. Claire's story is an example of this:

> Claire came to a family planning clinic for contraceptive advice. Until recently

she had been living at home in the country and having a carefree existence. She now had a job in London and a steady boyfriend.

Living in London changed her in a way she had not expected. While living at home she had been rebellious and difficult. In London she became very responsible, and changed her image from that of a carefree hippie to that of a sharp businesswoman. Six months later she started to experience itching and soreness, and was given treatment for a thrush infection. She was told to avoid sexual intercourse for a week, but found herself unwilling to return to having sex. She denied blaming her boyfriend for the infection, and accepted that thrush could be caught from many sources, but the problem persisted. While talking about herself and her present circumstances she came to recognise the changes that had taken place and became aware that since leaving home she had become anxious and guilty. She felt her mother would not like her to be sleeping with her boyfriend and that the thrush infection was a punishment for doing something wrong. Although she could see, at a conscious level, that she could not blame her boyfriend for something she agreed to, at another level she felt it was because of him that she was experiencing the guilt, anxiety and thrush. It was difficult for her to face that she was frightened at leaving home, particularly because when she was at home she had felt safe enough to rebel against her mother. Suddenly having to be responsible for herself and her actions, with nobody to restrain her, made her feel very anxious – especially when she felt punished by the thrush. Once Claire was able to understand the origins of her anxieties, she began to relax, and was able to return to the sexual relationship she had rejected.

Termination of pregnancy and sexually transmitted diseases present us with obvious moral dilemmas which often result in feelings of guilt. As guilt is a deeply distressing feeling rooted in loss of security and anxiety, people will do a lot to free themselves from it, and many find ways of denying their guilt. This is often done by blaming the partner, labelling them as 'dangerous' and so withdrawing from them for safety. Frances' story is an example of this:

Frances was very much in love with her boyfriend Nick. They had been together for three years, and she would have liked to be married, but he had a deep fear of commitment and was fifteen years older than she was. She had had a Roman Catholic upbringing and was also very attached to her parents and hid from them that she was 'living in sin'. Frances became pregnant through missing two contraceptive pills. Her unconscious may well have prompted this event, but consciously she was appalled. Nick was also appalled and wanted her to have a termination. Frances' need both to please Nick and to avoid causing her parents distress led her to suppress her own wishes and have the operation. After this, however, she was torn by guilt that she had destroyed her baby's life and that Nick had 'made' her do it. Frances continued to see Nick for a while, but she could not bring herself to make love with him, and eventually she left him.

The effect in the tug of war is that guilt strengthens the Anti-Sex team anchor of Basic Insecurity by increasing anxiety. Thus, even in the individual with little initial anxiety, a temporary withdrawal from sex may occur after a termination of pregnancy, while in the individual who already has high anxiety, the withdrawal may be total for many years.

Another health problem which can cause sexual difficulties is a gynaecological condition which necessitates an operation. In particular, the need for a hysterectomy is frequently followed by a sexual problem. Although this may be blamed on the operation itself, it can instead be because unconscious fears lead the woman to feel she cannot have sexual intercourse. Unconsciously she fears that her sexual interest may have played a part in causing her need for the operation. A logical progression of her fear is that further sex may lead to another operation, perhaps next time to cure a more unpleasant illness. Maggie's story is a clear example of this:

> Maggie, who was 48 years old, was referred because she was depressed and felt unable to have sexual intercourse following a hysterectomy. She had not felt worried about the hysterectomy, and had been reassured before the operation that it would only make her better and not affect her sex life at all. She came to see me with her husband Vernon and wept when she said she had not been able to have sexual intercourse since the operation. It was difficult to understand why she 'could not', since this fact distressed her so much, and I felt it was likely to be that she 'would not'. I asked what used to arouse her and she said she had always enjoyed having her breasts touched, so I asked what happened now when her breasts were touched, at which point Vernon interjected with 'I should be so lucky'.
>
> He explained that Maggie no longer allowed him to touch her breasts. It was then obvious that Maggie was resisting being aroused and eventually it became clear that she feared that sexual arousal was dangerous and had diseased her uterus. She was fearful that her breasts might be the next to go. This revealing of her unconscious fears, and linking them to the propaganda against sex which her parents had espoused during her childhood, allowed her to be reassured that this was a child's anxiety which had been resurrected by the need for surgery. This need had frightened her deeply, but she had denied all fear beforehand, and so had not been able to talk through her anxiety. When she could do this, she restored their sex life.

Some people even see an operation as the penance that will finally free them from guilt and actively seek to have one, but this is then followed by the need to avoid further sexual intercourse in order to avoid further guilt. A person may intellectually accept a doctor's reassurance about their physical condition, while continuing to be unconsciously influenced by an earlier and contradictory emotional response which is usually the more powerful. The natural sequel to such fears is to withhold from the activity that is thought to cause retribution. However, as complete withdrawal from sex may be impossible, a partial withdrawal is the frequent result – just enough to cause a problem. Isobel's story is an example of this:

> Isobel came to me at the age of 22, having already seen many doctors. She was complaining of severe breast pain and wanted to have an operation to remove her breasts. Naturally doctors were very concerned about her desire for this operation, and she had been investigated physically in every possible way. Her wish for the operation, which would be the dread of most women, was one clue that this was an emotional rather than a physical problem. Isobel was living with Hamish who was causing her great unhappiness by not making a full commitment to her. His work involved liaising with other young women, and she felt threatened.
>
> At first when the relationship had been going well, she had managed to suppress her feelings of guilt, created by her belief that her parents would not approve of Hamish or of them living together without being married. As her unhappiness grew, she had a conflict to resolve between her guilty feelings, her love for Hamish and her increasing anger towards him which she repressed. This conflict was resolved unconsciously by the production of a symptom which was a manifestation of her anger, which she had repressed in order not to lose Hamish, although in fact she was very angry with him.

Women frequently find sexual intercourse difficult after a thrush infection or a hysterectomy, despite all medical reassurances that sexual intercourse has nothing to do with the problem and that they need fear no after-effects. This unrealistic effect is a good example of how unconscious anxieties come from past experiences but do not take into account changing circumstances. A part of the mind has not recognised that nobody is now in a position to label their sexual activity as 'naughty', and there is no longer an authority who can mete out punishment. That part of the mind unconsciously continues to see the world from the child's viewpoint.

These essentially irrational fears must be distinguished from the fact that we have known since the 1970s that the incidence of cervical cancer is linked with the number of sexual partners a woman has had, and can reasonably be felt to be caused by the woman's sexual desires or by the demands of her partners. Unfortunately, the problem of HIV and AIDS has led individuals with these kinds of unconscious anxieties to feel that it is a 'scourge' which has been 'sent by God' as a punishment, and this has increased their difficulties. Flora's story is an example of this:

> Flora came from a happy home with caring parents who had sheltered her until

she left school, and she was the last in her group of friends to find a boyfriend. It took Winston many months to persuade her to sleep with him, and when she did she took the pill, used a cap and insisted that Winston also used a condom, so certain was she that she would be punished for sex without marriage by becoming pregnant. Despite her anxieties, the relationship was progressing, when information about AIDS hit the headlines and destroyed her shaky peace of mind. Despite the fact that Winston was faithful, she put a stop to their sexual activities and could not be persuaded to return.

Low self-esteem There are many causes for low self-esteem, and these will be explained in later chapters. The person with low self-esteem has no deep sense that they are lovable; they are, therefore, rather depressed and this tends to deflate the sexual drive. The emotional side of the relationship also suffers, because slights are expected and often seen when there are none, and so disagreements within the relationship are hard to heal.

Career failure The effect of a career failure will depend on how complete or how temporary it is. Men are particularly affected since their self-esteem rests so firmly on their ability to provide and compete in the world. Many virile men who are made redundant experience great depression followed by loss of interest in sexual intercourse, and their ability to retrieve the situation will depend on many factors. Fergus' story is an example of this:

> Fergus had been a labourer all his working life. He was persuaded to seek help from me by his partner Bradley because he had lost interest in sexual intercourse. Fergus and Bradley were very interdependent. They had enjoyed a good sex life until Fergus damaged his back at the age of 45. He was off work for three months, and although in some discomfort, he quite enjoyed the break. Bradley was working and they relaxed at weekends by going out in their beloved small boat.
>
> However, it became clear after many medical investigations that Fergus could never do such physically demanding work again. Unfortunately he was not well educated and felt he had no other way of being valuable. He became increasingly impotent as his sense of value diminished, and he felt too ashamed even to go and meet his friends. There was no happy ending for Fergus as he was trapped in his fear of a changed world. He could see no hope for himself and would not let anyone try to help him.

Poor relationship If there is a period when a relationship is poor, which comes out of a recent dispute and can be resolved without too much difficulty, it will not have a strongly negative effect. However, ongoing battles are likely to be persistent enough to have a fundamental influence on a sexual problem.

Parenthood   The issue of pregnancy and childbirth is an interesting one, as it can add power to the Pro-Sex as well as the Anti-Sex team. Some women feel at their best when pregnant and blossom sexually, and some men find pregnant women particularly sexually attractive. Other women and men withdraw from sex because of an overprotective feeling towards the foetus and later, after a long gap and the birth of the baby, may find it difficult to get back to a regular sex life. The story of Denise and Roger is an interesting one:

> Denise was thrilled to be pregnant after trying to conceive for a number of years. She had always wanted a baby, but her husband Roger started to find sexual intercourse difficult, and she had trouble arousing his interest. When she did, he would lose his erection before time. He was reluctant to face the fact that he was unwilling to be a father as he wanted to please Denise and thought she would be angry with him. With discussion Denise came to understand that Roger thought she only wanted a baby and was not really interested in her relationship with him.
>
> With these anxieties out in the open, their sexual relations improved, and she became pregnant. The unexpected then occurred in that she no longer wanted to have sexual intercourse on the pretext that the baby must be protected. More discussions revealed the fact that her interest in sex was less than she realised, because trying so hard to get pregnant had concealed her lack of interest. Roger had been right to fear what a pregnancy could do to the relationship. Denise was able to understand the importance of maintaining the sexual relationship and made a huge effort to explore the reasons for her lack of interest and overcome her resistance.

New parents experience unfamiliar and sometimes overwhelming feelings of fatigue and extra responsibility which collude with any Basic Insecurity to act as an excuse for avoiding sex. The longer the sexual gap, the more likely it is that a phobic reaction towards sex will develop. Difficulty with sexual intercourse after a baby is a very common complaint, and I have chosen Carmela and Pedro's story out of hundreds:

> Carmela and Pedro were thrilled with their baby son. Carmela was breastfeeding, Pedro did his bit with the nappies and they were tired but happy. At six weeks Carmela had her check-up at the hospital and all was well. She returned home to Pedro who had been looking forward to sharing some of the love and affection she was heaping on the baby. To their dismay Carmela found that she did not want to be touched, remained dry and sexual intercourse was painful. They

assumed this was temporary, and perhaps usual, and only started to worry as Carmela became more and more reluctant to have sexual intercourse. She eventually stopped completely and would become angry and tearful if Pedro approached. After six months without sexual intercourse Carmela and Pedro came to me for help. Carmela had to address several issues in herself. She was finding the responsibility of motherhood more daunting than she had expected, and had no family help that she could call on. She felt extremely protective to the baby and felt that her breasts were for him. She felt that she and Pedro were there only for the baby.

Also, Carmela had never really valued sexual intercourse, and saw it mainly as a means to an end, as a result of which she had stopped having sexual intercourse early in her pregnancy. This meant that she became used to a life without Pedro's sexual demands and, when these returned, she found them intrusive and annoying. Three things had to happen for Carmela and Pedro to return to a normal sex life. First, Carmela had to face what she was feeling. Secondly, she had to understand the effect of her feelings on Pedro. Thirdly, she had to be prepared to do something that a large part of her did not want to do, namely to have sexual intercourse.

So, if you are young, fit, successful and in love, your positive feelings will permeate life in general and sex in particular, helping to make things good. The opposite occurs when stresses, financial problems, job insecurity, illness and conflict in your relationship have adverse effects.

The tugs of war of two very different individuals are represented in the diagram on page 47. Person A's Pro-Sex team is winning. This person is usually able to enjoy sexual activity. Life events may cause negative emotional factors to interfere with their satisfaction, but fundamentally A is at peace with their gender and secure in their sexuality. Person B, on the other hand, is not usually able to enjoy sex, and their Anti-Sex team is winning. B has a large amount of Basic Insecurity which dominates and interferes with their ability to gain satisfaction. When B is in love or triumphant for some other reason, the excitement may add enough power to the Pro-Sex team to pull them temporarily into the area of sexual pleasure, but it will not be enough to facilitate the fundamental change required to give B lasting sexual confidence.

Key Points

♦ Changing deep-rooted attitudes is a difficult process which requires courage and determination

♦ The field where any internal tug of war is held is our own personal world

- Our personal world is not so much a true representation of the world as the way it seems to us
- If you are young, fit, successful and in love, your positive feelings will permeate life in general and sex in particular, helping to make things good
- Stresses, financial problems, job insecurity, illness and conflict in your relationship have adverse effects
- Sexual intercourse can be improved if people are open-minded and willing to explore a number of uncomfortable personal issues.

PART II

The Child Within Us

5

Seminal Experiences

The next three chapters will highlight those factors which most affect sexual development. The focus is on understanding the interplay between some of our earliest developmental influences and problems that arise in adult life. We shall first examine the ways in which we may trace and understand the history of our formative years, given that adult sexuality is rooted in childhood experience.

We have seen that as children, we respond to the various influences on us in different ways, some of which work better than others. As adults, tracing our history allows us to see the patterns in our behaviour, and to identify the defence mechanisms we use to deal with difficulties. We may then be able to develop better strategies for dealing with the difficulties we now face, or even dispense with such strategies for self-protection altogether. For example, much anger as a child is due to a sense of being misunderstood, but such expressions of anger as mute sulking become unnecessary and inefficient strategies once the adult is articulate and able to defend themselves verbally. Nevertheless, we all know people who continue to use the old methods of self-protection which they are used to.

Memory and Imagination

In trying to understand our roots we have to develop skills which are not usually recognised as valid in the exploration of truth. These are skills of imagination. Successful understanding of the roots of present problems needs a reconstruction of how we felt in the past, using imagination as one tool. This is, of course, not the same as reconstructing specific events.

Memory, seen by most people as infallible, is in fact an unreliable record. There is a particular obstacle for memories of childhood which is only partly to do with the time scale. This problem is that even for the luckiest of us, childhood is a time of

◆ being frustrated
◆ being separated from what is wanted and needed
◆ fear of loss of control
◆ feelings of helplessness
◆ competition with siblings
◆ failing to gain approval
◆ struggling for attention
◆ a sense of unfairness

All these produce difficult feelings which are coped with using different defence mechanisms according to the character of the individual concerned.

Three common defences used by children are denying, forgetting and pretending. We looked at denial in Chapter 2. Children use denial to avoid the pain of a situation by switching their attention and failing to notice what is obvious to everyone else. For example one day I was walking in the woods with a small cousin aged five called Bruce. Wielding a stick as a sword he accidentally hit my hand on a vein. A very large lump rapidly appeared but when I showed it to him he said very pompously, 'I see nothing'! Forgetting and pretending allow children to deliberately forget what they do not like and selectively remember what they pretend to be true. For example, first children who naturally feel very hostile to a new baby may be expected by their family to kiss, love and look after the baby. To express the jealous anger they feel will result in censure, but to meet their family's expectation will gain the reward of approval and allow the child to feel good. The child has a tug of war between its hostility towards the new baby and its need for approval from its family. Most children cope with this by choosing approval, and therefore remember how 'good' they were with the baby and forget their jealousy and anger. The result of their defence mechanism is remembered in preference to the difficult feelings which they actually had to cope with.

This seems to be a good way out, but it is likely that the unpleasant feelings will cause trouble in some way. As adults these individuals may try to avoid having to deal with a similar situation again, which may lead them to be unhappy about having a child of their own or to find dealing with new members of any group difficult. There may be possessiveness and jealousy in all their relationships yet the cause of that jealousy is long forgotten and camouflaged with love. Thus the original defence mechanism becomes the barrier to our getting to the source of the unpleasant feelings and therefore to the possibility of exorcising their negative effects.

Those who had particularly frustrating and unhappy early years often use the defence of forgetting so that they remember little from before puberty, while others use the defence of pretending to remember their childhoods as they wish they had been. With mature imagination, however, we are able to use our knowledge of the circumstances of our childhood, the experience that we have acquired over the years and the insight of others to build a picture of how things were for us. If we know ourselves and our families now, we can imagine these people in the situation as it was then, and come to understand a great deal of how it must have been. Teresa's story shows this process in operation:

> Teresa was a very possessive young woman who often felt jealous when her friends became parents. She had a younger sister, and at first she could only remember being praised as a child for taking care of her sister. Teresa came to recognise that the jealousy she felt when visiting a friend with a new baby was due to the fact that she no longer had their full attention because of the intrusion of the child. Since this is a very minor displacement compared with suddenly sharing attention for evermore with a new sibling, she could see that she must have felt jealous when her sister was born. Although this sounds rather simple, it was a hard-won insight. Along with many eldest children, Teresa was very resistant to the idea that she had been jealous of a sister she had chosen to see as inferior to herself!

This using of the past to understand the present, and the present to understand the past, gradually builds the whole picture.

As children we were very vulnerable and our parents seemed incredibly strong. Most adults with difficulties have usually failed to recognise that, at an unconscious level, they still feel that they are vulnerable and their parents are strong. What is more, they are reluctant to see it any other way. This is because it is reassuring to believe there is someone stronger who can rescue us if necessary.

True understanding can only be achieved if we can free ourselves from fear enough to be prepared to face unpalatable truths. These unpalatable truths can be, for example:

♦ that our parents were not always kind
♦ that we did not love our parents as much as we felt we should
♦ that we were not always kind to our parents
♦ that our parents found aspects of our behaviour hard to deal with

For others it may be hard to face a realisation that they care deeply for a parent who has upset or hurt them in the past. Many people claim to hate their mothers. They assert that their mothers are the cause of all their unhappiness. These people are often unwilling to be happy and, as in Adam's case, may refuse to become well:

> After a large number of psychotherapy sessions, Adam revealed that he realised he could be better but did not want to 'let his mother off the hook'. He felt that if he was well and happy he would have lost the weapon with which he could punish his mother: his unhappiness. The 'hook' in Adam's case was punishment for his 'betrayal' by his mother who, after seven years in which he was an only child and had her undivided attention, had a second child by whom he felt displaced. His 'illness' was an inability to cope with his rage and wish for vengeance towards the woman he loved, and indeed towards all subsequent women for whom he always felt the same mixture of love and anger.

Blame

It is important to say something about blame at this point. In the exploration of early factors which contribute to adult sexual problems, it may seem as if I wish to place the blame for any difficulty firmly on the parents. This can inhibit progress in two ways. First, people with sexual problems are sometimes particularly protective of their parents, and will therefore resent and reject any implied criticism. Secondly, others, who are only too eager to place the blame on someone else, may use this idea as a weapon with which to attack parents and thus avoid having to take whatever personal responsibility may be necessary.

The aim of self-exploration is always to gain understanding, and true understanding means realising that parents, too, can only be as their experiences have made them. Since the understanding of infant emotional development is relatively recent, most people's parents have had no opportunity even to recognise the danger of their power. Recognition does not necessarily mean that parents will use their power more wisely, but there does seem to be more concern about the feelings of the child when the effects of parental power are understood than when they are not.

It is also important to realise that if we persistently blame parents we put too great a burden on ourselves to, in our turn, be blameless parents. I have found that some cases of infertility seem to come from an unconscious fear of the individual concerned that they would not be a 'good' parent. In reality there is no such thing as an entirely good parent because the job of bringing up a child is too lengthy and complex for anyone to complete without making mistakes. If we can stop feeling that our parents should have been perfect, we can stop needing to be perfect parents ourselves.

In Adam's eyes his mother would have been perfect if she had not had a second child. He is certainly just in his demand that she acknowledge the pain it caused him, but for her to avoid that pain by denying herself a second child would have implied that to be a perfect parent she must protect Adam against all pain and frustration. As we shall see, this would only have weakened him in the long run.

Responsibility

Responsibility comes with understanding. Until we have insight into the effect we have on others and the effect others have on us, our behaviour is controlled unconsciously by hidden parental attitudes which have automatically become ours. We are not in charge, and we do not even know that we are not in charge. Even those who have made a great effort to rebel against their parents are often unaware that they may be as much a slave to rebellion, with effects which are just as crippling, as they would have been a slave to conformity.

Insight brings potential freedom from these states, but it also brings responsibility. We must now think out our decisions in the light of greater awareness. If we then fail to create a better life for ourselves, it is no one's fault but our own, and we can no longer blame our parents, our partners or anyone else.

The trouble is that it takes effort as well as insight to change. We are often willing to have the insight but reluctant to face the effort. Without the willingness to make efforts no one will be able to correct a sexual problem, because we are very resistant to changing programmed behaviour. This is because unconsciously we believe that we have already found the safest way to behave.

No therapy will be effective for people who want effortless change. For example, some people are always late for counselling. Change their regular appointment time and they will still be late. I usually find that this is a general life pattern, and, indeed, most people know someone who is habitually late. They are quite unaware that this behaviour has a purpose and when I first suggest this possibility they find it difficult to believe. For some people, this is because their lateness causes them great distress. Others are calm about their lateness but refuse to see that it has any importance. However, I usually find it is possible to show that lateness is a behaviour pattern with a hidden purpose. This is usually a need to express some unconscious aggression which, because it is unconscious, cannot be expressed directly. It is then necessary for us to work together to find out what original pain made this strategy necessary. When we discover this, and it becomes clear that someone has developed a lifestyle of lateness as a way of dealing with unconscious aggression, they have the chance to decide to change their behaviour and be on time in future. However, as their behaviour pattern has become programmed over many years to leave things to the last moment, it takes great effort to change. There is also a need to find a new outlet for the aggression which was formerly dealt with by lateness.

Security and Insecurity

The first piece of understanding we need about our formative years is to recognise that our early life was dogged by the need to find security. Despite recognising that we are frequently anxious and uncertain as adults, it takes effort to imagine how anxious we must have been as infants. This is for two very different reasons. One is that we convince ourselves that babies cannot really experience anything beyond physical comfort or discomfort. The other is that we have had to try so hard to grow up that recognising how much we may still feel helpless and childlike is very unwelcome. We must make the effort to return, in imagination, to childhood. This will help us to understand

- ♦   What it was like to be a child
- ♦   How helpless we felt
- ♦   How needy and demanding we were
- ♦   How we dealt with the failure to fulfil our needs
- ♦   How we coped with our families

Periods of major change in life are also periods of uncertainty because the future seems less certain as a result. This is so from birth, the first such change we encounter, which becomes the prototype for all subsequent changes.

Babies' brains start to register experience while they are still in the womb. Foetal existence is a sort of nirvana where, for the only time in our life, there are no demands on us which require compliance and we simply have to 'be'. The necessities for life are automatically provided and we are not responsible for our own survival. From the moment of birth this changes. The change in external circumstances produces a change in our internal equilibrium which demands action. We desperately need to breathe as soon as we are born, but our nostrils may be blocked for a short space of time. Suddenly there are bright lights and a change in noise level, together with the loss of the mother's heartbeat which has been our constant companion. For the first time, hunger strikes, and its assuagement seems uncertain. Then when our need for food is met the new feeding method produces pain from wind. This overwhelming change of circumstances beyond our control makes us feel very helpless. This feeling of helplessness becomes the blueprint for the feeling we get whenever our survival seems threatened, which for some adults can happen through the uncertainty of something as apparently innocuous as going on holiday. We can infer, even though we cannot remember it, that we must have felt great anxiety at birth.

The severing of the baby's 'life support system', which is the biggest change it will ever deal with until death, heralds the beginning of a process whereby the baby has to take some control of its destiny or die. Our ability to cope with change produces the pleasant feeling we achieve when we master something difficult. The baby stops crying when it finds the nipple because it is biologically programmed to seek it and is then reassured by its power to get what it needs.

Influence of Mother

The immediate effect of birth on the infant is for it to try to re-establish some sort of security in the face of these changes, and to try to develop some sense that survival is possible and that the separation from the safe environment of its mother's body is not a mortal blow. The baby tries, therefore, to get back to the very close relationship with its mother, whom it recognises as the person who can make it feel better. One's mother smells and sounds familiar, provides food and bodily warmth, and thereby reduces the baby's anxiety and gives it a sense of hope for the future. Keeping close to mother thus equals security, and it follows that a failure to keep close to mother creates a sense of insecurity.

The newborn baby, therefore, develops a perception that the necessities of life come from its mother. The mother, to an infant, is a godlike source of fulfilment of all needs, and is therefore of total importance and omnipotence. The baby recognises that its very survival depends on its mother (or a mother substitute).

There are, of course, many different sorts of mothers. Some mothers have wanted their child while others have not. The child may be the first born to a mother aged 17 (or 40), or the last born to a mother aged 45. The mother may be loving and rich, loving and poor, unloving and rich,

69

or unloving and poor. Apart from these factors every mother has good days and bad days which then means that the baby experiences good days and bad days.

Clearly, then, to understand individual early beginnings in a real way, the individual mother has to be looked at. We cannot talk about a standard mother but there is an important single factor which links all mothers, young or old, and that is their power.

The newborn child has to relate to mother in order to survive. We have now understood that our childhood experiences have a profound effect on our adult life, so we can see that our first relationship will affect all future relationships. Attitudes and expectations will be formed, based on our relationship with our mother, and we will judge later relationships accordingly. For example, if we get on well with our mother, we expect to get on well with other people. Conversely, if we don't get on well with our mother, we will carry negative expectations into other relationships.

Because of her power in forming our basic sense of security in these early stages of development, we remain particularly influenced by our mother's own beliefs and attitudes. This is despite the fact that her beliefs may be wrong and her attitudes inapplicable to us or to our lives. To begin with, because of our mother's godlike quality, anything she says or believes is given particular weight. Even if we rebel later on, the strength of her influence remains.

The effect of our mother's influence may be serious, as when a mother warns her daughter that all men are beasts and only want a girl for sex so she should avoid intimacy at all costs, or the effect may be comparatively trivial, as in the case of Jeremy from Chapter 3 who was unable to go out in the evening after washing his hair as he was convinced by his mother's warning that he would catch cold if he did so.

Our conscience, which can cause us so much anxiety, is formed initially by our mother's rules. The strength of our moral stance tends to be in proportion to the amount of emotion shown by our mother over a given issue. Some issues will be dealt with by our mother in a fairly neutral way, but other issues about which she feels very strongly can have a profound effect. For example, if she shows anger and distaste when she finds her child masturbating, this can produce a sense of fear and isolation from her love which is very distressing and may lead to the anxious avoidance of masturbation in the future, even producing amnesia so that in later years an individual will passionately deny that they have ever masturbated or that they could ever do such a thing.

As we grows towards maturity, we will experience many controversies with our mother which must be worked through. The way we handle these inevitable disputes will depend on the extent to which we have been left with a basic sense of security or insecurity by our earliest experiences. We may be able to establish our independence easily, or still feel at our mother's mercy. Our sense of security may seem synonymous with pleasing mother, and a corollary to this is that many children, who feel it is hopeless to try to please a mother who makes unreasonable demands, turn to behaviour which inevitably displeases her.

The need for a good relationship with our mother remains the foundation stone of a sense of security and the ability to form other relationships. The maintenance of this first relationship is vital to the child. The relationship should develop from the very intimate physical contact with the baby, through the close emotional relationship with the older child, to the point when the relationship is partly internalised by the increasingly independent adolescent who develops their own security. It also becomes partly available in a more appropriate form to be invested in the young adult's chosen life partner, and at this point mother has to relinquish her position as the most important person in her child's life. However, this neat progression may be hard to achieve.

Separation

It is very important for sexual development that the child feels loved and secure enough to be keen to venture forth and cover new ground. This is because, as we shall see, where sex is concerned some rebellion against mother is always necessary, and the insecure child finds it difficult to rebel. Nor is the insecure child, and later the insecure adult, easily able to take part in situations which require decisions to be taken, because of their fear of getting it wrong. It is our biological dilemma that despite the painful 'separation anxiety' induced by separation from mother, and our programming to avoid pain wherever possible, separation is part of a necessary process beginning at birth.

Progressive separation is necessary in order to be able to survive in the adult world and long-term survival plans must take precedence over short-term discomfort. Being able to tolerate some separation without too much anxiety is therefore important. This is best achieved by the child being given time to separate gradually without added stress. It should be like feeling strong and safe enough to let go of the side of the swimming pool. Enough is the operative word here, as we rarely feel entirely strong or safe.

It is an apparent paradox that we need to feel secure enough to tolerate the insecurity of separation. The security we derive from good mothering is something that we carry around with us and incorporate into our own attitudes and outlook. It depends on a mother helping her child to become independent and separate from her, despite her own reluctance to let this happen. We gain a kind of archive of mental strengths and memories to which we can refer. This process is sometimes called the internalisation of a good mother.

As we have seen, the more insecure we have been made to feel early in life, the more security remains our priority in life. We can be said to have internalised a bad mother. We remain unsure of ourselves and feel the need for constant guidance in order to behave correctly. To make a commitment such as marriage, or even a steady relationship, may be very difficult. This is particularly so in the man whose mother is possessive of him and never likes his girlfriends. Such a man may experience an unconscious feeling of insecurity at the thought of "jilting' his mother by making a commitment to a relationship with a girl-friend. He will use various ways to rationalise why he cannot make such a commitment. By using such a strategy he prevents himself from being able to find the appropriate security in an adult relationship, as happened to Tom:

> Tom had a problem with both impotence and a lack of interest in sex. He had been very close to his mother who had always given him a special packed lunch for school while his sisters had ordinary school food. He met his wife Dora when he was 22 and married without telling his family. He pretended he was not married but after two years he owned up and took Dora home to meet them. She had been visiting for two years when I saw them, but Tom was always given his boyhood room with a single bed and she was in a guest room also with a single bed. Tom never dared to ask his mother for one of the double beds that were available in his family home. It was very difficult for him to change this pattern of behaviour, but he came to see that his problems with Dora were due to a deep sense that his mother did not want him to be married.

People with sexual difficulties usually give the need for security too high a priority and are unwilling to experience the necessary discomfort of some anxiety which is always present in progress. This is likely to have been because rebelling against mother was too high a price to pay if she could make life miserable as a consequence.

An appropriate nudge to us to face up to change and progress comes in the well-known injunction in Ecclesiastes 3, where it is said that

> "To every thing there is a season, and a time to every purpose under the heaven,"

poetically emphasising the need for issues to be dealt with at the right time. If they are not, it is difficult to deal with them later on.

At each stage in our development we are coping with different issues to do with surviving as a social animal. As we have seen, the small child is, of necessity, coping with insecurity. If the child has a controlling mother who fails to transfer any of her power to her child, that child will fail to develop a sense of its own capability, and seeking protection is likely to remain the priority issue throughout life. Madge's story shows how this can happen:

> Madge came to me for psychotherapy at the age of 40 because of a succession of illnesses which were thought to be psychosomatic. She looked very young and had the voice of a child. It was some time before she told me she was a virgin, and that she had only had one sexual encounter in her life which was while she was abroad.
>
> Two matters dominated Madge's life: she sought mother figures, and she enjoyed many aspects of illness. She had felt greatly displaced by a younger brother to whom her mother became devoted. She remembered only feeling loved by her mother when she was ill because only then was she paid the attention for which she craved.
>
> Madge had never been able to get close to men of her generation and therefore had no children, which caused her great distress. She was locked into a need to get the attention of mother substitutes, and this completely prevented her from moving on and experiencing the 'rites of passage' at the appropriate time.

Mothers who are very controlling are also likely to be very dependent in their own relationships, although this may not be obvious and they may strongly deny it. They are, though, very reluctant to let go of children and often interfere greatly in any marriage their child makes. Jock's story shows how this can happen:

Jock's mother was very possessive and jealous of his relationships with his father and his sisters. When he was in his teens she had tried to prevent him meeting a girl friend. As an adult he had no close relationship of his own, had never been intimate with anyone and despite many friends, he had no sense that he could ever have a sexual relationship.

> Jock was referred for psychotherapy at the age of 36 at a time of crisis in his life. He had become depressed at the divorce of a couple with whom he had been very involved; he had a close relationship with them both. The wife was very controlling and demanded his loyalty and would not let Jock remain in contact with her husband. She also put up barriers to his seeing any women who had been mutual friends of them all and he allowed himself to be controlled in this way.
>
> Until this point Jock had not faced his isolation because he was a great reader and never felt lonely. He believed everyone else thought he was gay but could not decide whether this was true or not, partly because no one had made an approach to him and partly because he did not allow himself to recognise any sexual feelings towards anyone else.

The wife in the divorcing couple had, in a symbolic way, treated him very much as his mother had done by controlling him and keeping him away from both men and women.

Communicating his thoughts and feelings were difficult for Jock at first because he had intellectualised his feelings, and presented himself the way he thought he should be rather than the way he was. Despite his poor relationship with his mother it became clear that her influence still controlled his attitudes and behaviour. As he perceived this he began to do things she would disapprove of and finally found himself feeling attraction and arousal to someone of his own sex. He had found himself and felt elated and hopeful of a relationship for the first time.

Of course mothers, and fathers too, who realise that their child has become anxious and dependent, can try to override their own wishes and encourage separation.

Need

Need is an important issue. It is related to security and can easily be confused with love, but with dangerous consequences. We shall explore some of the different aspects of love in Chapter 7, but should at this point clarify the potential danger of need.

To do this we must distinguish between reasonable need and neurotic need. Some relationship needs are inevitable and healthy. These are the human needs of companionship, sex, loyalty, help in times of trouble and a sense of personal value through the partner. The individual seeks a relationship in order to fulfil these needs. Some mutual dependency is part of any loving relationship when its aim is to combine the qualities and talents of two individuals such that each can enrich and enhance the other. Each will be prepared, when necessary, to care for the other, but this is not a major part of the relationship. Loss of the partner would be a severe blow and a great sadness but would not be viewed as a mortal blow because survival was not dependent on the other.

Reasonable needs are clear and it is therefore possible to decide whether and, if so, how they can be fulfilled. For example, one partner may earn the money and the other look after the house, or both may earn the money and share looking after the house. One may be good at mechanical things while the other decides on the decorations. These are tasks about living which are to be performed and shared to mutual advantage. (Of course the priority interest of this book is the 'task' of sex performed and shared to mutual advantage.)

Occasionally there may be more difficult, but still reasonable, needs to deal with which upset this balance of mutuality. For example, if on the eve of marriage one partner breaks their back, both will have to decide whether they can share the loss which has occurred and whether they can deal with the new relationship in which one of them needs to take more and the other will therefore have to give more. This problem would make interdependence impossible and thrust much of the main responsibility on to one of the partners.

The distinction between reasonable need and neurotic need lies in the degree to which unconscious needs are in control. Where there is neurotic need, the adult still unconsciously makes the demands of a child, although this is likely to be rationalised and justified. Examples that many people will recognise are those of the 'little woman' who needs to be provided for or the 'weary man' with his important job who must not be bothered with lesser problems. The hidden demand is that the partner shall be a parent as well. This means that one partner takes all the responsibility and the other increasingly feels they can't and don't want to take responsibility. In counselling, it is not unusual to find a couple like Joe and Kath, where one partner does nearly everything:

> Joe was very resentful of his wife Kath. She claimed to have a bad back, and as a result he did a full-time job, went to the shops on the way home, cooked the evening meal and cleared it up. Kath managed, nevertheless, to play tennis. She remained unable or unwilling to understand Joe's resentment. She felt that if Joe loved her, he would want to look after her, but she could not see that the corollary was that if she loved Joe, she would want to help him.

The emotional demand that children make is to have the total attention of their parent. This demand becomes unreasonable in adulthood. Of course in reality a child rarely gets the total attention of their parent and usually learns to accept less while longing for more. The neurotic has not learned to do this and continues to make impossible demands for care and attention as an adult. This unreasonable need for attention is retained in adulthood either because the demand in childhood succeeded too well, usually called being spoilt, or did not succeed at all, leaving a sense of deprivation. In the first case the adult expects the attention because it has always been there. In the second case the adult looks for it because of a hunger which is difficult to assuage; as with some actors, the attention is never great enough. This may cause no problem at the beginning of a relationship, when there may be mutual emotional satisfaction from such role-playing, but problems increasingly arise from it as it becomes an entrenched way of life, as happened with Louise and Derek:

Louise and Derek could not consummate their marriage. They played with each other by pretending to be animals, talking in baby voices and taking it in turns to be baby bunny and big bunny. This would be harmless enough as an occasional game, but in their case it was a fundamental piece of the partnership, which destroyed the possibility of a sexual relationship by becoming an easier substitute for it.

Dependency

The intensity of such a dependent way of relating in any partnership, whether with mother, friend or lover, may seem very loving but in fact hides large amounts of aggression. Once the fantasy of the roles has worn off, the protagonists are left with disappointment and anger. As we saw in Chapter 1, sex is inevitably diminished when this happens.

The aggression comes about in two ways. First, some aggression is inevitable in a situation in which one person feels inadequate and envies the more independent person who seems powerful. Secondly, because the childlike demands to be looked after are so persistent and so unreasonable, they cannot be fulfilled. This failure produces anger and frustration in both partners.

Dependency creates an important power issue. The dependent partner wields an immense amount of passive power by making the other feel guilty and, therefore, that they must try harder to please. There will have been some romantic collusion between them, either with the idea that strength in the man's role means treating women as childlike and in need of protection, or that strength in the woman's role lies in mothering men. Jane's story is an interesting example of this:

> In Jane's first session she told me that she was frigid and made many trivial complaints about her husband Bill. After a while it emerged that in order to feel secure she needed to have Bill with her all the time, allowing him no contact with other women at all. This was obviously impossible and she realised that he had to go to work. She nevertheless felt angry with him that he could not meet her demands, and he in turn felt angry with her for making them.
>
> Without realising it Jane punished Bill for the infidelities she imagined he had by being very resistant to sex, yet by doing this she increased her own sense of insecurity and her fear that he would look for a more desirable partner.

Such demands are often extended to resentments about any interest the partner may have outside their relationship: a baby, golf, gardening or learning Greek. Sarah and Alan's case was an extreme example:

> Sarah came to me complaining of her inability to enjoy sex. Her partner, Alan,

felt that although she had a full-time job, she should be completely responsible for maintaining their house as well. He expected her to shop, cook, iron, clean and decorate. Sarah's problem was that she half thought he was right to make these demands since she had seen her father make the same demands on her mother.

It was difficult to make Alan aware of the unfairness of the situation, because he too had grown up in a household where men were totally supported, and his mother had been a slave to his father and himself. This situation produced resentment in both Sarah and Alan, but once they had gained insight into these feelings, their relationship improved in every way. Sarah then had no further need to punish Alan by withholding sex from him.

It was clearly a problem for Sarah and Alan, as for many other people I have seen, that stereotypes from a previous generation were the models during their childhood and so continued to cause ambivalence in their adult relationships.

Neurotic dependency therefore produces angry feelings which then produce guilty fears of loss of security. Further demands for reassurance will be made and a vicious circle produced. Much effort and insight is needed to break these destructive bonds while trying to maintain constructive ones.

The roots of many sexual problems lie in dependency, particularly when anger causes manipulative games to be played. Fred and Jemima's case was particularly extreme:

Fred was so possessive and demanding that he actually locked Jemima in their flat when he went to work, completely impervious to any needs she might have, and thought it was quite reasonable that her only outings should be with him. He took her to the supermarket in the evening and thought she should feel quite satisfied with her life.

They first came for counselling because of Jemima's lack of libido and inability to achieve orgasm, which doesn't seem surprising in the circumstances. Not so easily understood was the complicated situation of mutual neurotic dependence which the history of the couple revealed. Jemima had known Fred since before his first marriage in which he killed his wife, probably from possessive jealousy, as a result of which he had gone to prison. Despite knowing this, Jemima married him. There was considerable anger and fear in the relationship, yet she felt she had to stay with him.

There was obviously a great deal of neurosis in both Fred and Jemima, which simultaneously seduced them towards and repelled them away from each other. It could be said, therefore, that their case represents extreme interdependence of a neurotic nature.

Helplessnes

Helplessness makes us feel dependent and needy. If our needs can be met we feel relatively strong and open to progress, since we are confident that we shall be able to look after ourselves and acquire what we need. If, however, our needs are not met, we feel weak and angry and have no confidence in our ability to control our environment. We look to others to provide for us. This attitude blocks our progress and keeps us tied to the power source, mother; crumbs from her table may nourish us enough to keep us kneeling there. Later, we may exchange our powerful mother for an adult partner who controls and looks after us, but the relationship will not be well founded and will contain much aggression.

We must recognise that under certain circumstances even the most mature adults can lose command of their lives and find themselves once again experiencing the fear and panic of childhood. Regressing in this way is likely to happen when we are made to feel helpless: by having to go into hospital, by losing a job, or by losing a loved one. It is the helplessness which seems unbearable because it is the ultimate vulnerability of being in someone else's power.

Power

We have seen that young children are naturally insecure as a result of their circumstances. What, then, are the factors in their relationship with their mothers that can increase this level of inevitable insecurity to the point where it interferes with their development and, therefore, with their sexuality?

The main factor is power. As already described, babies are so helpless that a mother has the power to make the child happy, satisfied and as secure as it is possible to be; she also has the power to make it feel depressed, anxious and frightened, just by experiencing a change in her own mood. This power is unasked for, often unwelcome and, for some, an unexpected responsibility which comes with the job of being a mother and can be overwhelming in its magnitude.

There are two major ways in which the state of a child's relationship with its mother can have a destructive effect. The first is where the mother herself has failed to find security, seeks her own security as a priority and is therefore unable to be supportive enough of her child to impart a sense of security. The immature mother is herself fearful of the world. She may retreat to childhood when faced with the added responsibility of motherhood, and is unlikely to impart the hopeful outlook her child needs in order to face the world with equanimity. Thelma's story shows how detrimental the effect of this can be:

> Thelma had a successful career in business when at the age of 39 she began to feel she should have a child before it was too late. She was very undecided because she was the eldest of a large family and this produced two reasons for her uncertainty. First, she saw her mother's domesticity and devotion to her family as something she neither wanted or could aspire to. Secondly, she felt strongly that her brothers were more highly valued and less strictly brought up than the girls, and she was determined to acquire that same value by taking a male role. The result was that although very feminine in one way she was also very unsure and resentful of this side of herself in another.
>
> There was a happy outcome to Thelma's story but it was hard won. She became pregnant but insisted she would be back at work two weeks after the birth, and she employed a full-time nanny beforehand in case the baby was early as she felt so incapable of looking after a baby herself. It was not possible during her pregnancy to discuss the fact that she might want to look after her baby because she always felt that she was being told that this was what she ought to do and she would become angry. After the baby was born she went to work as planned but as the months passed she became unhappy that the nanny had the relationship with the baby while she felt an outsider. Her fear of the responsibility was always intense when the nanny was off-duty but gradually she came to accept the role of mother, to want it and to feel that she was good at it. She began to feel she had missed out on the important first nine months and planned another child. By now she was fully confident of herself as a mother and was lucky enough to have a new baby to plan, this time enjoying the whole process.

Should any mother become physically ill and unable to look after her child herself, several different people may become mother substitutes, all with power and each with different expectations and demands upon the behaviour of the child. This can leave the child not only fearful about the separation and the apparent loss of its mother, but anxious about how to please and therefore maintain its security with the different mother substitutes.

The second, and more pernicious, long-term effect of a mother's power is where the child is made to feel it is failing its mother. In our frailty and vulnerability at the beginning of our lives, we are beggars at the door of mother's approval. The child who has a sense of being adored by their mother, and a sense that even if it does wrong it will be loved, feels strong and able to face the world because it assumes that it will always be forgiven and fears the making of mistakes less than others. The child who feels that it is loved only when it is behaving in a way which is satisfactory to its mother is constantly anxious, to the detriment of its progress. This mother will have very set ideas about correct behaviour and be determined to make a perfect person, free of failings. By making impossible demands, she endlessly makes the child feel a failure. This child feels that safety and happiness would lie in pleasing mother if it were only possible to do so. Even as an adult, there may be no freedom from the sense that if only the way could be found, there would be safety. This fantasy is then a priority, endlessly interfering with and excluding more important achievements. Lucy's story shows just how damaging this can be:

> Lucy's sister Angela was greatly favoured by their mother. Angela did nothing for her mother, rarely visited her and led an independent life with many men friends. Lucy, however, constantly worried about her mother, did her housework and endlessly but hopelessly tried to please her. Her mother spoke rudely to her and compared her unfavourably with Angela, and yet held her in her thrall. Lucy finally found a boyfriend and was to spend a weekend away with him when her mother became 'ill' and she was unable to go.
>
> In Lucy's case no boyfriend was ever 'safe' enough to overcome her deep insecurity, and she was likely to remain at her mother's beck and call.

It is not too dramatic to suggest that insecurity and helplessness potentially introduce a 'brainwashing' situation. This would occur where a mother, without understanding the full outcome, uses the threat of withdrawal of her love to control her child's behaviour. She is so concerned to train her child correctly that she is unable to be interested in its feelings, and is only interested in its behaviour as it affects her own feelings. This then persuades the child to place emphasis on its behaviour and to suppress its feelings. This is not to imply that all emphasis should be on the child's feelings either, but on a balance in which neither the mother's need for good behaviour, nor the child's wish to do only what it wants, holds complete sway.

The power that mothers have to affect our feelings and thus control our behaviour can be hard to grow out of. Adults who retain elements of their response to this tend to react inappropriately to all people who seem to have similar power. Teachers, doctors, bosses, lawyers and politicians all potentially become 'mother' figures with the result that too much dependence is put onto these experts, including the fantasy that they should be infallible. An inability to question our mothers may make it difficult to question other authorities. This can be dangerous: since so many 'experts' disagree, it is clearly important that their expertise must be subject to our own judgment and monitoring of the facts. There may be a danger of the wrong advice being taken because one 'expert' sounds more authoritative and reminds us more of our mother.

Children whose mothers expect them to be perfect are likely, in turn, to expect their mothers to be without fault. The price to pay for continuing submission to mother and, later, 'mother' figures, is that any failing of mother or another authority is met with disillusionment and anger. This is what happened to Lloyd:

> Lloyd was the only boy in a family of four and he was born last. He felt the other children were all cleverer than him and they pushed him about a lot. His mother protected him and they devised small strategies that made him feel important: a letter from his mother to enable him to avoid swimming because he did not like taking his clothes off at school, special packed lunches, the choicest pieces of food at home. He repaid her by being good. He did not listen to dirty jokes and behaved as she would want him to behave. They were good to each other and he expected all grown-ups to be the same.
>
> As an adult he became very dependent on a surgeon he had to go to for a chronic condition and felt that no other surgeon would do. A problem arose when he thought the surgeon had given him bad advice. He could neither question nor complain, but he felt very angry with his idol who had developed feet of clay.
>
> Lloyd was in conflict because he was unable either to stay happily with, or to leave, the surgeon. As a result he developed panic attacks. These attacks occurred in situations which had not previously felt threatening, such as wide open spaces and tunnels. His whole sense of security had become unstable, because of his disillusion with the surgeon and his resulting dilemma, and he only felt safe in his home.

Those who choose to deal with their powerful mothers by rebelling against them have a different problem. All expert advice is automatically rejected; the more authoritative the expert sounds, the more they will be faulted. There is endless difficulty here, because sound advice is not listened to and the advice of other rebels seems more acceptable. In order to function best, it is important to be able to invest some trust in 'experts' but not too much.

The emphasis I have placed on the power of the mother is because in most cases, unless the mother has relinquished her position as carer to the father, his influence as far as power and security is concerned is much less important. It is of a different nature and will be explored in Chapter 7.

Parental power is not the only type of power which causes important yet often unrecognised issues in sexual problems. Power gives the ability to affect and control events, and the greater someone's power the less their vulnerability. We all feel happiest when we feel we are in control of our lives and the people in them, but the problem for partnerships is that if one is in control, the other is not, and is likely to be unhappy.

Before we can find a way to share power it is important to analyse it. Power may be innate and/or acquired. There are several obvious ways in which power can be innate. The greater bodily strength of a man means that physically he is more powerful than a woman or a smaller man. A clever person is more intellectually powerful than a stupid person and a beautiful person is more immediately powerful than an ugly one. Those who have natural power are less likely to need to be constantly concerned with it than those who have not or who feel they have not. A strong handsome man may nevertheless have been weakened by parents and have the need to acquire power by other means. As we have seen, by the nature of their position, parents have power over their child to raise its self-esteem or to make it feel a failure.

There is a fundamental unfairness in innate power that makes those without it feel envious and strive to acquire it.

Power can also be acquired, either by hard work or by association with the power of others. The more our skills meet the needs of others, the more powerful we become. Professionals such as lawyers, doctors or plumbers on whom we are particularly dependent are therefore particularly powerful. An adult can also acquire power by being attached to a strong partner. This used to be the only way a woman could be powerful. It is still the only way some women feel they can survive. Some battered wives return again and again to be hurt, yet feel that they could not survive alone. Not only women acquire power by being attached to men: literature is full of men seeking rich wives or social elevation by marriage. However, the sense of power acquired in this way can be fragile and unstable, as Les's story shows:

> Les, an actor with working-class origins, found himself working with Eleanor, a woman from an upper-class background. He was particularly attracted to the powerful and commanding accent of her voice which proclaimed her class. They married, but when they were with Eleanor's family and friends, Les felt like an outsider. He became acutely aware of the feelings of inferiority which had unconsciously influenced his choice of partner. He had hoped to raise his self-esteem by associating with Eleanor's circle, but he found the opposite happened because his own origins seemed to be highlighted.

The foundations of our sense of power or powerlessness are laid in childhood. Apart from its innate talents a child acquires power in the world in two ways: first, by developing skills which make it a more or less valuable member of society, and secondly, from its parents by being associated with them. However, paradoxically, very powerful parents may inadvertently weaken their child. Any child who either has no need to fight for what it wants, because its parents are powerful enough to give it everything, or else is not allowed to become independent, because its parents exercise controlling power, will not make the efforts necessary to compete with those who are taught self-reliance. Because of its helplessness, though, the child wants the parents to be powerful and protect it against the outside world, so is likely to fight against parents who work to foster its independence. This, then, leads to one of the enduring paradoxes in adult relationships. Everyone wants to do what they want but no one wants their partner to be a doormat!

An added complexity in the development of the child's sense of power is that of feelings of omnipotence. As the child develops, the first world it knows contains itself and its mother. It discovers that crying brings food and gradually recognises that, while mother must be very powerful to have so much food, the child itself is powerful in being able to acquire it. At this point the only world it knows is this one with mother and when it is successful in getting what it needs, it has, for a time, a sense that it controls the world. However, it is clear that if one feels one is in control of the world, any failure to get what is needed feels very threatening indeed. When young, therefore, we have a sense of omnipotence alongside our sense of helplessness which confuses us; retained feelings of early omnipotence also eventually lead to a different sort of anxiety. This will be explored further in relation to guilt.

Apart from the early sense of omnipotence, the child is in fact powerful, but in a passive way. Because the parents love it and want it to survive, it has the power to create immense anxiety, as anyone who has had a sick child will know. The child may be unaware of this power for many years, so concerned is it with the power of the parents. It may even fear that bad behaviour might result in its being sent away. Its own position is, therefore, that it feels very mixed about the power of its parents.

♦ It is also true that the child is powerful because its parents cannot escape their unique responsibility. The parent/child bond is for life whatever happens. For example, many happily adopted children still want to trace their birth mother, and mothers who have their child adopted can never forget. As the child discovers its power there can be a battle of wills which is an important part of development but, as life goes on, roles become reversed and parents may eventually become as dependent as a child. Despite the increasing frailty of her ninety-year-old mother, my friend Joan was nevertheless shocked when one day her mother asked her 'are you my mother?'

From these roots derive the adult sense of power and the way it is used in relationships. We can now see that power comes not only from activity and apparent strength, but also from passivity and apparent weakness. Both types of power can eventually produce resistance and resentment in a partner who is being controlled by whichever means. This is so despite the fact that the active person may choose a passive person who seems to want to be controlled, and the passive person may choose an active one in order to relinquish responsibility. Bruce's story shows how damaging this dynamic can be:

Henry was a homosexual man who had had a very deprived childhood. He had spent his life trying to please his unresponsive mother, and had developed a powerful and caring personality to conceal the hurt child who was longing for someone to look after him. He wanted a committed relationship, but he attracted, and was attracted to, beautiful young passive men who themselves wanted to be looked after.

Henry sought help from me because his potency fluctuated wildly with his emotional state. Trouble would quickly come when a commitment was made and he started living with his partner: he would begin bitterly to resent the fact that the type of person he attracted was not the sort to share the responsibility of the partnership. He was particularly upset if no meal was ever prepared for him when he was out working all day, because originally his mother had failed him in this way. He would then become vulnerable, demanding, unhappy and impotent and finally unattractive to his partner who would then become unfaithful. Henry's tragedy was that he was addicted sexually to the very type of man who would inevitably fail him.

Henry was an insecure man who used power defensively. When this proved ineffective his relationship would end.

When we think of active power, we think of someone actively wishing to invade or take over someone else's territory by greater strength, as in rape, war or making a child eat its greens. It is taking control of someone against their will. It may be done 'for the best' as in greens eating, or it may be done selfishly as in rape. What we may not always realise is that active power may be a strategy we used to protect ourselves against a feeling of potential or actual helplessness.

Active power in relationships is usually brought out by the need and dependency of one of the individuals. This may be reasonable where the dependent person is a child, but for an adult to retain this way of relating can be damaging. For example, if a mother continues to cook and wash for a girl until she leaves home to get married, the girl has not established herself as an independent adult. Many such young women unconsciously expect their husband to take their mother's place. At first he may be pleased with the dual role but as his own work becomes more demanding he will resent feeling he must bear all the responsibility of their life together. Also the image of partner as parent will detract from their sexual relationship.

Sometimes it is not obvious where the power lies. This is important because if someone reacts badly because of feelings of powerlessness, when in reality they hold the power, or if the person is really powerless but acts as if powerful, there will be confusion in the relationship. Often a woman feels less powerful than a man because of her lesser muscle power, and acts aggressively to compensate for this, not realising that the man feels that she has the power because of his sexual need of her.

In all relationships there are issues of power which have to be resolved. Earlier, when discussing dependency, we drew a distinction between reasonable and neurotic need. There are similar aspects to the power issue. The more it is hidden and based on unconscious childhood needs, the more difficult it is to resolve in a relationship. In a marriage where both parties need each other and have different sorts of power, power-sharing, bartering and decision-making must go on with fairness if the relationship is to be successful. Understanding where the power lies and recognising the danger of trying to hang on to it all the time, or of not taking it any of the time, is vital in any partnership. The trouble is that this fairness takes effort and it is easier for us to fall automatically into the games we are used to playing with our partners in order to get what we want.

The more privileged people in society are particularly vulnerable to relationship problems because they find it difficult to accept any power-lessness. Where one partner is very rich or very beautiful they usually expect to get what they want because others value their beauty or money so highly. This means the inevitable difficulties in a committed relation-ship prove too tiresome to tolerate if they can easily find a replacement. Such people are, of course, very vulnerable if they lose their special powers but also they never get the chance to savour the pleasure of being sure they are loved for themselves rather than because they have money, position or beauty. The case of Andrew illustrates these points:

> Andrew was handsome and wealthy. His father left him a large sum of money when he was 23 and he bought a Ferrari. He married Esther but soon lost sexual interest in her and began to have a series of relationships with other women. He had many problems with all his relationships because he was very fussy and as soon as he found any imperfection he looked for another woman. He had no intention of leaving Esther but he had no intention of making love to her either. He sought help over his phobic reaction to sleeping with Esther, but he had turned her into a security figure and expected her to allow him to do what he wanted.

Andrew's behaviour in psychotherapy reflected the problems of his other relationships in that he would go off in his car on holiday and miss his sessions when difficult issues had to be dealt with. It was not, of course, that money caused his problems but that he used it to resolve immediate disquiet rather than working through his anxieties.

To summarize, in this chapter we have started to discuss the emotional life of a child as it relates to the world around it. The relationship issues in this stage of our development affect our feelings and begin to dictate the behavioural patterns we will live with for the rest of our lives unless we make an effort to change. It is in early childhood where love is born and where the first pains of rejections are felt. We often cannot remember but we can imagine how it must have been.

Key Points

- ♦ Adult sexuality is rooted in childhood experience
- ♦ We need to use the past to understand the present, and the present to understand the past
- ♦ True understanding can only be achieved if we can free ourselves from fear enough to be prepared to face unpalatable truths
- ♦ Until we have insight into the effect we have on others and the effect others have on us, our behaviour is controlled unconsciously by hidden parental attitudes which have automatically become ours
- ♦ It is very important for sexual development that the child feels loved and secure enough to be keen to venture forth and cover new ground
- ♦ Under certain circumstances even the most mature adults lose command of their lives and find themselves once again experiencing the fear and panic of childhood
- ♦ Power gives the ability to affect and control events, and the greater someone's power the less their vulnerability
- ♦ Power comes not only from activity and apparent strength, but also from passivity and apparent weakness
- ♦ Understanding where the power lies and recognising the danger of trying to hang on to it all the time, or of not taking it any of the time, is vital in any partnership.

6

Sensuality Emergent

In Chapter 5 we considered how early stages of emotional development including insecurity, helplessness, dependency and power may either be satisfactorily dealt with or leave unresolved neurotic problems which can affect adult relationships. We are now going to look at early stages of physical development, and again examine how what happens to us in childhood can affect our adult life.

Everybody knows that there are areas of our bodies called erogenous zones which carry particularly powerful and pleasurable sensations. These tend to be linked with our body's orifices and can be designated 'exciting'. Their purpose is to ensure reproduction of the species and is, therefore, a serious one. Less specifically, our bodies are sensitive to touch as in massage, which is pleasurable but relaxing rather than exciting. People with sexual problems frequently have a problem with these sensations, and particularly with exciting sensations. Sometimes massage, with its relaxing propensity and association with calming and stroking an upset child, can be accepted and enjoyed, but those with severe anxiety about arousal fear touches of all sorts. Given that bodily sensations resulting from gentle touching are designed to be pleasurable, it is important to understand how this can be interfered with and changed

Feeding

The very earliest sensual development is concerned with those basic functions of the body which are to do with its survival. We have a drive to survive and we get satisfaction and pleasure from the specific functions upon which our survival depends. The first is the pleasure from the mouth in taking in food, with sucking, swallowing and tasting. While this process goes on the baby is very close to its mother; they become as one again, and both get comfort from the experience. This is particularly so with breastfeeding: the mother's milk is always at the familiar temperature of her body, the baby kneads the breast while it suckles and feels her heartbeat, and altogether it seems like old times in the womb. Thus sensual contact gives pleasure and security and the baby is eager for it.

This sensual contact has a sexual element which can perhaps best be understood by watching a cat kneading someone wearing a jumper that reminds it of its mother's coat: it will be semi-conscious with ecstasy. Independent of gender, there is a sensual and sexual contact with mother which, unless the mother is too inhibited, is very pleasurable to both. Mother feels successful if her baby feeds well and her love is increased by this satisfaction. Similarly, the baby's love of its mother is increased by the recognition of the nourishment it gets from her. It is clear, therefore, that feeding fulfils both a physical and an emotional need. It is important to grasp that love in the baby is synonymous with need and this differentiates it from more mature selfless types of love for which there is no separate word.

The important point for understanding later sexual problems is that feeding is a shared pleasure which, if it goes well, greatly pleases both mother and child and relieves anxiety in both. Mothers who reject breastfeeding for reasons other than illness may be rejecting the instinctive sensuality of the process which makes them feel uncomfortable to the point at which they find the idea disgusting. Most mothers are either unconscious of the hidden sensual and sexual element in feeding, or believe that it is a permissible pleasure because it is linked with the child's survival. Similarly, many women enjoy sex only when trying to conceive. Here the serious purpose of reproduction makes pleasure justifiable to those who need to justify their pleasures.

A feeling of sensuality that is welcomed by mother is entirely pleasurable to the baby while, as we shall see, later developing sensualities are not welcomed by mother and are therefore not entirely pleasurable to the child. The approval surrounding feeding lasts and is non-controversial for most. Sharing a meal with people is a permissible sensual experience which is greatly valued in society.

It follows that difficulty over feeding produces much mutual disappointment. Anxiety and insecurity are shared between mother and baby, causing a major deprivation of important good feelings about each other. The bonding between mother and baby is forged through feeding, whether breast or bottle. The new mother needs her baby to feed well so that it will grow well and any refusal makes her feel anxious and inadequate. Anxiety usually makes us feel angry with the source and it is distressing for mothers to feel anger towards their precious and longed-for baby. Equally the baby feels anxiety because it is unsatisfied and it too feels angry. The mother may be able to comfort and reassure the baby but may not be so easily reassured herself. Excessive crying in a baby feels like an accusation and the guilt of feeling angry with a loved one adds an emotional burden to a person already vulnerable as a result of their newfound responsibilities. A baby who cannot be reassured will retain more feelings of insecurity which can have a lasting effect. An older child may use refusal of food or food fads to control and punish parents.

Excretion

Another sensual experience which babies and toddlers share with their mothers is excretion. Again, like feeding, there is a shared potential satisfaction between mother and child. For the child the physical sensations are pleasurable, and for the mother excretion is the proper sequel to the feeding process: a sign that all is well with the child and that, therefore, she is a satisfactory mother. For many mothers, however, this process brings with it the issue of training.

Anxiety can begin when the child first becomes aware of the regular emergence from itself of what it sees as curious and interesting stuff. Excrement is intriguing to the child rather than dirty or unpleasant. If a child is left in a room with a soiled nappy, it will play happily, exploring its environment in the usual way including the nappy and its contents, until its mother rushes in with cries of horrified disgust, at which point the child will naturally begin to assume that faeces are dangerous and not to be touched. Of course it is universally accepted that excrement is dirty and has to be dealt with carefully, but it is easy to make it seem more obnoxious than it really is.

The result of overreacting to this issue is to introduce the idea that the bottom has a different value to other bodily parts. The fact that we cover our bottoms even when revealing all other parts shows that it is universally seen as different and special, as much because of its sexual link as excretion. But it is again a question of degree. How different, in what way special, and how much associated anxiety is produced? Individuals' answers to these questions can tell a psychotherapist whether a real problem has been created.

The issue of control can also have a life-long effect on an individual. This will occur if as a child, their elimination process was experienced as a personal reflection of success or failure by their mother. Many a mother is very concerned with having a 'clean' baby as soon as possible. A well-trained child, rather than simply a well child, allows her to feel proud and have high self-esteem. To please this mother the child is required to control elimination before it is ready to do so. Since failure to achieve control causes at best disappointment, and at worst mother's anger, the whole issue causes anxiety.

A child cannot easily control its excretory function until it is two and a half. It can be forcibly trained by the age of one, but only at the expense of a great deal of tension and anxiety. As urine is produced all day, the child will have to concentrate all day on what is happening in its own body to avoid the anxiety of an accident. Therefore it cannot be free to concentrate on more important issues going on in the world outside. To such a child, the main concern has to be control of excretion, since its mother's love seems to depend on it.

Childpower

During toilet training the child comes to recognise that it has power over, and therefore some control over, its mother. How strongly this new power is used by the child depends on two factors: the child's temperament and the mother's attitude. The power the child discovers is that by withholding elimination, or by eliminating at the wrong moment, it can make its mother anxious and frustrated. If the child is reasonably content with its lot it is more likely to wish to please its mother than to wish to upset her. However, if the mother is very controlling, demanding and insensitive to her child's needs, it may have many hidden scores to settle. This child may find that messing about on the potty causes frustration to its mother and is, therefore, a source of satisfaction. It now recognises that it has the power to please and the power to frustrate and can do a bit of controlling on its own account. The usual way in which a child exercises control is by withholding and refusing to perform, but it is not the only way, as the story of Emily and Henry shows:

> Emily felt very helpless when five-year-old Henry, who had not worn nappies for three years, suddenly started to relieve himself on the carpet when she had friends to tea. He chose the occasion to cause her the greatest distress as a punishment for her apparent rejection of him when she had another child. Extra attention and reassurance finally resolved the rebellion.

This control may be exercised consciously at first, but will eventually become part of the personality. An adult who is very secretive was probably a child who withheld from its mother and got great satisfaction from doing so. As we shall see, sexual problems are much to do with withholding from the partner, and those children who found satisfaction in withholding from their mother to right old wrongs are likely to use the same mechanism when they are adults.

So, we have seen that there are two main issues over toilet training: first, mother's attitude to faeces, and secondly, the power that the child has to please or frustrate its mother. This reflects two of the main struggles in an adult partnership where there is a sexual problem: (1) the attitude to the function of sex may be distorted by feelings of distaste; (2) sex may be used as a weapon or a gift in the power struggles within the relationship.

As these early experiences in our development cannot be remembered, some people dismiss them as fiction. However, not only has much research through analysis shown what happens to us at this time, but we have the evidence in our behaviour as adults which allows us to link with and reconstruct the past for ourselves. It is also true that, if feelings are taken into account rather than just behaviour, there is a logic which we can all recognise.

Genital Discovery

To complicate matters further, at around the same time that the child is trying to cope with parental expectations about excretion, it also has to face the complex issue of which parts of the body it is safe to show interest in. This is a time when the child's attitude to sexuality can be distorted by its family without a single word being spoken. Many people I have seen protest that their parents did not ever speak about sex and therefore could not have put them off it. The opposite is true: because the issue was unspeakable it remains, for many, an unspeakable subject.

The so-called 'genital phase' of development starts from about six months as the child becomes increasingly aware of its own body. The genital area, previously inaccessible because of nappies, becomes an area of particular interest because of the pleasurable sensations aroused when it is touched. As nappies are left off, the child explores its body, just as it explores the world that its body inhabits. At bath time mother's touches are pleasurable so the child will naturally return to play in this area. This becomes a problem if the mother forbids such pleasure. Should the mother herself, influenced by her own upbringing, feel that genital touching is dirty, the child will pick up the tension in her attitude and learn to share it. This is because the child has no other yardstick for judging right and wrong, and cannot differentiate between its mother's judgments and moral judgments.

A less emotionally prejudiced mother, who doesn't feel bad about her child's genital touching, may still forbid it because she thinks it is her duty to teach her child about socially acceptable limits. This will still indicate to the child that its behaviour is unacceptable, and it is still too young to get a balanced perspective on degrees of unacceptability. However, as long as there is no excessive tension in the mother, a reasonable compromise is then reached. An older child of three or four can begin to understand to some extent that there are social rules and regulations and that certain behaviour, while not necessarily bad in itself, is unacceptable in front of other people. This is too complex for a young baby to understand: for a baby things are either good or bad. The result is that most adults feel that sexual pleasure is to some degree 'bad', even if they do not consciously think that it is. This feeling is a bit naughty and exciting for some people, but can provoke extreme anxiety in others, who must then strive to deal with their uncomfortable feelings if they are to enjoy sex fully.

The genital phase of sensual development is therefore a complicated, paradoxical time, full of potential emotional difficulty and conflict with mother. The conflict between the physiological pressures and social demands of excretion and genital pleasure combine to make this a time when the mother feels on trial, with her child's behaviour as her test. The child can also come to feel on trial, and this will affect the development of any behaviour which is an extension or derivation of these issues. As we have seen, one such behaviour is sexual.

Guilt

Guilt is an intensely unpleasant feeling associated with a failure to behave as we believe we should. Originally it is a feeling about the fear of the potential death of the self caused by failure to please outraged parents, and is therefore about insecurity. It begins from the moment demands about our behaviour are made by parents, which are then internalised to become our conscience, and is usually at its height in adolescence when we must co-ordinate innate desires, parental wishes and peer group demands. Some people seem to get off lightly while others are tortured by unreasonable guilty feelings all their lives.

The exploration here is not about what we should or should not feel guilty about, since these issues are debatable and a matter of opinion. It is about what children do feel guilty about. Most young children feel some guilt about sex because they have, to some extent, been made to believe that their parents have no interest in sex and therefore would not like their children to have such interest either. Therefore, in order to develop into sexual creatures, such children must experience the anxiety of rebelling against their parents. This anxiety is in some cases powerful enough for children to decide to avoid it altogether despite the losses involved.

A feeling of guilt, therefore, is a particularly unpleasant sort of anxiety coming from a conflict between the way we want to behave and the way we feel we should behave. For many there is even anxiety about thinking something forbidden, let alone behaving in a forbidden way. There is a tug of war between the safe feeling of following our conscience (which is largely derived from our parents) and the anxious feeling of wanting to grant our own wishes. Guilt, or the expectation of punishment because we believe we have committed a sin, therefore comes about when the desire to do something which is judged by others to be wrong is so strong that it overrides our inclination to stay safe and avoid anxiety.

Guilt also comes about when we feel we have inadvertently done something wrong or have been persuaded to do wrong against our better judgment. We are likely to feel angry with anyone who has caused this to happen. This is why many relationships are destroyed by a decision to terminate a pregnancy. The woman may blame her partner for getting her pregnant in the first place so that she has to bear all the physical responsibility of dealing with an unwanted pregnancy. If he then wants her to have a termination, which for some religious people is made all the worse by being considered a sin, she often cannot forgive him. Many a man feels similar resentment when his partner insists on her right to choose a termination which he feels to be morally wrong. Mary's is a particularly interesting story:

> Mary was a young Catholic woman who came to me because after her marriage she no longer experienced orgasm. She had for some time had an affair with her husband John while he was married to someone else, knowing this to be against her religion but with the comfort of being able to confess her 'sin' each week and be forgiven. During this period she achieved orgasm, but when John divorced his wife and asked Mary to marry him, achieving sexual satisfaction, paradoxically, became more difficult. Marrying John meant that Mary had to choose between him and her church as, according to the Catholic rules, marrying a divorced man was a mortal sin for which she could be excommunicated. She would no longer be allowed to go to confession and receive absolution.

Mary chose marriage, but found that she could no longer experience any pleasure or excitement in sex. She had been able to live easily with her previous situation by using the idea that 'the flesh is weak' and believing that she could be forgiven for this. But she could not live easily without that forgiveness which was now withheld from her. It became clear that she was very frightened by her sense of the loss of God's forgiveness, and was unconsciously punishing both herself for her 'sin' and John for causing her to 'sin'. This punishment seemed to be both a penance with the hope of final redemption and also a superstitious hope that as long as there was no pleasure she could not be blamed.

While our detective work clearly established the cause and effect of Mary's problem and the power of guilt to control her behaviour, the case brought home the fact that the therapist is up against an immovable object in those who have had strongly held religious beliefs inculcated in them from an early age. It was not possible to retrieve Mary's orgasm and I have found that it is rarely possible to help pleasure and enjoyment to be directly linked to sex in those people whose early conditioning about sin, hell and excommunication has led to a sexual problem, because such conditioning is too frightening and powerful for many to contest.

Women are more affected than men because they have little testosterone drive to combat their resistance. They will 'do their duty by their man', particularly if they want to be pregnant, but are often divorced from the pleasure of sex. Many people conditioned in this way deny that their problems can be due to their religion, because they have consciously rejected that religion, and may no longer consider themselves to be religious at all. In fact very early conditioning affects the sexual process so fundamentally that conscious thinking may be quite different from unconsciously controlled responses.

Many women from a Roman Catholic background have come to my clinic with sexual problems following hysterectomy, sterilisation or the menopause. This is because, unconsciously or even consciously, they do not feel justified in pursuing an activity which no longer has reproduction as its pretext.

There are at least three variables which contribute to our levels of guilt: first, the power of the conscience; secondly, the power of desire; and thirdly, the power of anxiety. This last rests on our ability to assess the relative risks in a decision and the amount of anxiety we can tolerate. The maturing self must adjudicate between the demanding self (desire), the internalised parents (conscience) and the ever-changing environment. Psychological freedom from the trap of guilt is achieved when individuals are able to make judgments that they deem appropriate and accept the consequences. Psychological prison exists when it is felt that for the sake of safety, change must always be resisted, however appropriate it might be.

Those brought up under strict regimes with many rules and regulations, either at home or in their church, are particularly controlled by guilt. It is clearly laid down to them that they are in serious trouble either with mother or with God if they do not follow the rules. As life itself seems to depend on mother and God, if they are both frightening, any failure to please will seem very dangerous. If the developing individual can only feel relaxed and safe when following the rules to the letter, great problems will ensue. For example, if someone brought up in a strictly Christian environment reads the writings of St Paul in his First Letter to the Corinthians (chapter 7, verse 8) that it is better not to have to marry, it will be difficult for that person to avoid feeling that even marriage does not really sanction sex and that sex must be less than good. This person will then feel guilt when normal sexual feelings occur. If the guilt is mild, it may affect the feelings unpleasantly, but not enough to spoil the sexual act. More often it affects the feelings just enough to spoil the sexual act by causing some unconscious withholding from the situation, and in some people it prevents any sexual performance at all.

The exploration of a sexual problem may, therefore, require the individual to think and re-think their beliefs before they can see their problem clearly. If they are unable to do this they will be unable to find a satisfactory solution, as Martin's sad story shows:

> Martin was brought up as a strict Roman Catholic. He had been very sexually active but claimed never to have been unfaithful as a husband. His wife developed a pathological jealousy which destroyed their marriage, and he left his country to come to England to work. He felt very guilty about leaving his wife, sent money home regularly and did not divorce. Two years after coming to England Martin met Rachel and fell in love. They got on very well together, but he was impotent with her although he had never been so with his wife. He denied feeling any guilt and could not believe his religious conditioning could have anything to do with the situation.
>
> He was the most desperate impotent man I have ever come across. He was prepared to do anything. While I was working to increase his insight into his unconscious fears and anxieties, he also tried injections of the male hormone testosterone, injections directly into the penis of a drug which gives an erection and finally opted for a prosthesis (a plastic tube inserted permanently into the penis to give an erection).

Martin's desperation was not for himself but from a fear of letting Rachel down. His was a sad problem: his guilt and his need to be a good person for God, his wife and Rachel caused him to be good for no one.

A less 'good' man would have been all right, but Martin had to force a behaviour on himself that his unconscious rejected.

Guilt, then, is felt because of what we have done or because of what we want to do. The anxiety associated with guilt is often at its worst when we are deciding whether or not to do something which has been prohibited by our parents. There is a sort of assessment going on all the time of whether particular pleasures which may be forbidden are worth the risk of being found out. The child even fears that the parents may know by supernatural means that they have done wrong. Infertility patients who have previously had a pregnancy terminated by choice almost invariably have a doomed sense that they are being punished. Indeed in some it may be that they are giving themselves the punishment they feel they deserve. The shock of an emotional upset such as a termination can stop a woman ovulating. The fact that emotional causes are at work in many physical illnesses allows speculation that this may be due to an unconscious rejection of the pain of adulthood and a retreat to the safety of childhood, or it may be that the woman has a sense that she cannot be trusted to carry and raise a child.

It can be surprising, in cases where guilt is powerful, how strong and persistent the expectation of punishment can be. Some people seem to spend their lives expecting some terrible accident or disease as a punishment for the surviving remnant of a childhood misdemeanour or imagined misdemeanour. The most worrying imagined misdemeanour is that of having wished, in anger, that their mother would die. Gillian's story shows the power of such guilt in action:

> Gillian said to me, 'I must get to grips with the problem of my mother, because if she dies before I have sorted out my angry feelings, I will feel that she died because of me and I will feel guilty for the rest of my life.'

The basis of Gillian's anger with her mother was a feeling of lost and unrequited love since the birth of a sibling. This had made her feel guilty on two counts: first, because she had experienced angry feelings of hate which made her feel that she did not love her mother any more and was therefore doomed, and secondly, because in her pain she had punished her mother by behaving badly. This had momentarily relieved her feelings of anger but increased her feelings of guilt and anxiety.

It is not uncommon for people to feel anxious about their parents dying, not only for love of them but because of fear of living for ever with guilty feelings. Gillian recognised that she had invested her mother with the power to make her expect punishment for ever, for having had hostile feelings towards her.

It is often difficult to differentiate between love and guilt because they are frequently combined and both feelings can produce the effect of devotion. Many people remain in their mother's thrall for the whole of their lives under the guise of love. For example:

> Joan wanted to go on holiday, but although Joan's mother of 90 lived in a nursing home, Joan was expected to go to see her every other day. If she did not her mother would become ill. Despite the care her mother was having Joan was unable, for her own peace of mind, to go away because her mother did not want her to. Joan felt that she loved her mother too much to hurt her but really there was very little love in the relationship. The mother was completely selfish and had always been demanding and Joan had dealt with her own anger towards her mother by overcompensating with complete devotion. The more demands her mother made, the more anger Joan felt and the more devotion she showed.

Omnipotence

As well as showing the persistence of the mother's influence and the fear of punishment, Gillian's story also demonstrates the belief of the very young child that it has the power to make its wishes come true. Although children have little experience on which to draw in making judgments, they are very logical, and quickly reach a conclusion that their feelings of omnipotence reduce their comparatively unpleasant feelings of helplessness. Authors writing for children understand this, and they too foster the idea that wishes come true if you wish hard enough.

Similarly much of religious faith is about the ability to move mountains and never to have to face helplessness. While this idea comforts in one way, it burdens the child (and later the adult) with guilt over its responsibility for its wishes. For example, if a mother had upset her child, and the child had reacted by feeling a flash of anger, and shortly afterwards the mother had an accident, the child would fear that it was its anger which caused the accident. Equally, if a mother became ill, her child might fear that it was responsible for causing the illness. This opens the way for the anxiety that thoughts and feelings are as much action as is behaviour. The child comes to feel that it is dangerous and attempts to deal with this by denying its 'bad' thoughts and feelings. Indeed some religions propound the idea that thinking and feeling bad thoughts are as wrong as acting them out.

If there has been a traumatic event in the child's life causing great anxiety and guilt, like divorce or the death of a parent, fearful feelings may become entrenched. Otherwise, ideas of omnipotence usually tend to fade as other possibilities and realities take their place. In all of us, remnants of omnipotent feelings are retained at an unconscious level and can be brought out at times of great stress. The best example is in bereavement, when it is almost universal to feel some guilt that even the most natural death could have been prevented if only different action had been taken. There is much in Western literature to endorse this universal sense of the power of our wishes, from the Bible with its 'ask and it shall be given unto you' to Tinkerbell being saved by the wishes of children everywhere. In a similar way bereaved people often feel they could have prevented the death by being more helpful. Others even fear they caused the death with any angry feelings they may have had towards the loved one.

Adeline's story shows how bizarre omnipotent worries can be retained in the unconscious of an otherwise perfectly normal person.

> Adeline was a highly intelligent woman who suffered greatly from anxiety and unrealistic guilty feelings. She found it necessary to think about any plane in which her husband was travelling, from the moment it left the ground until it landed, with the idea that she kept the plane in the air by her thoughts. In this way she dealt with her fear of herself as a dangerous person whose ambivalent feelings towards her husband could prove fatal.

The corollary of failing to abandon ideas of omnipotence may be a failure to take responsibility for events over which one actually does have control. Pam's story is an interesting example of how powerful this can be:

> Pam, an only child, came for counselling with her husband Clive after they had been married for four years. She had never been able to allow consummation of the marriage but they now wished for a baby. Pam was a dominant personality, who had identified with both parents, being a mixture of butch and feminine. For years her parents had bickered and fought and she took a position of mediator and believed they needed her in their relationship. This caused her to resist other relationships. Her mother then died and Pam took the role of caring for her father. During this period she met and married Clive, but did not completely give herself to him.
>
> While Pam was having counselling she was very shaken to find her father taking an interest in another woman. The combination of this shock and psychotherapy caused her to take a more realistic view of herself and her power. She came to understand that she was denying her husband and herself sex and a child in order to maintain a fantasy about her father's need of her and a position in his life she did not really have. This insight freed her to make love and she quickly conceived and was delighted with her child.

Persistent ideas of omnipotence can greatly affect the way anger is dealt with in relationships. In any long-term close relationship there will be some anger and disappointment with the partner. Anger means that an unpleasant feeling is being produced. As we saw with parents, if there is a wish, however brief, to be rid of the irritating loved one, the individual with strong feelings of omnipotence will have correspondingly strong feelings of anxiety. This person feels that their anger is very dangerous and that they may cause damage, and so they withdraw from their partner both emotionally and physically. Many impotent men are, consciously or unconsciously, angry with their partners and afraid that if they were potent they could cause harm.

Puberty

The emergence of testosterone causes sex to intrude in a much more physical way on adolescent boys than girls. The young man may find it hard to think of anything other than his embarrassingly arousable penis and the uncontrollability of it (as described so eloquently by Adrian Mole following his visit to the swimming pool). To be so sensitive to arousal, and thus to the potential embarrassment of unbidden erection and ejaculation or obvious non-arousal, is a burden from which women are spared. Because of this vulnerability, men tend to like situations which allow them to be in control. For example, the essentially male development of the computer, with its exact output controlled by men's input, has provided an ideal consort which men can rely on to give a satisfactory response.

The young woman also undergoes physical changes and is concerned about sensations in her body. She may allow herself to become conscious, for the first time, of pleasurable feelings from her genitals. However, she is likely to be more concerned with the effect her hormones have on her body generally. Female hormones are mainly concerned with achieving and maintaining pregnancy rather than stimulating sexual feelings; indeed oestrogen tends to have a dampening effect on sexual desire, and in some countries it has been given to male sexual deviants in order to dampen their arousal. The female hormones can produce troublesome mood swings together with menstruation, which not only has a physical effect in causing discomfort and sometimes pain, but has huge emotional significance because it compels girls to recognise the great difference between themselves and boys.

Until adolescence many girls can, and do, deny gender difference. With the development of breasts and the onset of menstruation they are no longer able to maintain this denial. Most adjust and accept a change of goal, but some resent the role to come, and this can cause physical and emotional distress, as it did for Monica:

Monica had an older and a younger brother. She saw herself as one of the boys, always played with the same toys and was as good at games as her brothers, and shared their interests in every way. She felt her father, who was a surgeon and full of interesting stories, saw her as another boy and she did not identify with her mother who waited on them all equally.

When Monica was 13 she started to eat less and became rather thin. She began to exercise more and while those around her began to menstruate and develop breasts, her figure did not change. She did not remain childlike but she was not becoming a woman either.

At 17 Monica's periods started and were rather erratic. She remained slim and looked boyish. She got into university to read engineering and got on well with the boys but always as one of them. When she was thirty she began to realise that she was missing an emotional relationship and started coming to me for psychotherapy because she wanted to understand why she could not allow herself to be a woman but could not, of course, be a man either.

Young women, therefore, are essentially concerned with change. They are also concerned about the significance of the physical changes they are experiencing and their new feelings about the opposite gender. With the advent of periods comes the need to adjust to the obvious differentiation of their reproductive role from that of young men; some young women welcome this while others see disadvantages which make them resent the changes. They may worry about sexual pressures from the opposite sex.

Because women lack the pull of testosterone, they depend upon emotional and social drives to pull them into the sexual field. Young women long for a 'relationship', unlike most young men, and usually believe that they need to please their boyfriend sexually to ensure this. To have a boyfriend also means social success, which is particularly important for the vulnerable young woman, and these two factors combine as strong Pro-Sex team members. Where the young woman's Basic Insecurity about sex is not too strong, fears of pregnancy and worries about contraception do not have too great an effect. However, where the Anti-Sex team anchor combines with low self-esteem, insecurity about gender and worries about image, there is nothing to offset the early anxieties about sex so they hold the girl back.

Love

Much of what has been discussed so far has been about the desire of the individual to be safe. Under the influence of healthy parental love, however, a child learns how to love others. This leads to the problem of not wishing to hurt the loved one by doing what may cause pain. The act of separation from parents that sexual intercourse heralds is often difficult for this reason. Frequently those who come from close loving families have initial difficulty in breaking away. Once they have done so, however, the prognosis for future relationships is better than those who broke away easily from emotionally cold families.

This difficulty in breaking away from a loving family could be described as a healthy difficulty. Another sort of difficulty, which might debatably be called healthy, is where someone behaves in a way of which not only would their parents disapprove but of which they themselves disapprove. Valerie's story illustrates this:

Valerie, an intelligent young woman of 28, told me she had been diagnosed with vaginal thrush four years previously, and although she had received treatment, the symptoms had never gone away. Numerous tests showed no sign of infection but she was sore and itched day and night and was unable to sleep without pills.

Valerie told me of her rather casual sex life and her difficulty in settling down with any particular man. She had had a strict but loving upbringing and when describing her sex life spoke as if she was justifying and excusing herself. She very tetchily denied having any feelings of guilt or anxiety. However, when describing an affair with a married man, she gave so many explanations and justifications – the wife was abroad, the husband did not get on well with his wife, she had never been with a married man before, she never would again – that the guilty feelings shone through.

It turned out that Valerie's original infection came when she was having this very affair. I told her that I thought the problem came about because she was feeling guilty but could not face her guilt, so unconsciously she was both punishing herself and preventing herself from carrying on with sex by being too sore to make love. I explained how originally she had managed to rationalise her behaviour as being acceptable in order to protect herself from having to experience the pain of guilt and enable her to continue with the forbidden activity. However when the infection struck it felt as if she was being punished; she maintained the punishment as a penance and a protection.

Valerie was very irritable and did not appear to accept any of this, and I wrote in her notes that I wasn't hopeful of a good outcome because of her attitude. However, on her return visit three weeks later, she described how she had gone home and told her mother about her affairs and said that I had told her she was guilty about her sex life. Her mother had replied, 'Well, if you weren't, you should have been after the way I brought you up', and the itching disappeared from that moment. In religious terms this was confession and acceptance by her mother being good for the soul. In analytical terms it is the catharsis of Valerie facing the truth about her feelings. What was not healthy was the way Valerie hid her true feelings from herself.

Whether or not to cause pain to our loved parents in order to find adult love for ourselves is clearly a very difficult tug of war. The issue arises in reverse later in life when we, as parents, often have to cause pain to a loved child. This can be physical pain, such as injections for their health, or emotional pain, such as by sending them to school or not being unable to devote as much attention as the child feels it needs. We have to face, therefore, that there is no love without pain. Unless we can recognise this we will not see love when it is there because it will always be rejected as not good enough.

Risk

We have seen that we feel we are taking a risk when we make love for the first time. We feel we risk loss of love and security from parents. A person who takes this risk without difficulty seems able to do this for one of two reasons. First, they may have a great sense of security and optimism generated by loving and non-judgmental parents. This person has always known that although parents disapprove, they will not stop loving. Secondly, they may have low self-esteem and emotionally cold parents, and may take risks very early in an attempt to find love. This person has always felt that its parents were so unloving that there would be no hope of pleasing them or gaining their respect, so any relationship may seem better than the relationships at home. This person is usually a girl, who may react by starting to have sexual intercourse at puberty, seeing sex as security and because of this often remaining unable to experience true passion or orgasm.

Most people cope with the anxiety of risk-taking by a serious weighing of the situation. The daughter of loving parents, raised with a strong sense of personal and moral value, will not take thoughtless sexual risks. Once she meets someone she loves enough to take the various risks involved in a sexual relationship, one of which may be a fear of losing her parents' love, she will detach herself from her first loves and put her partner before them. The young man may experience the same anxiety as the young woman, but his Pro-Sex testosterone competitor is usually strong enough to win against parental influence. Where testosterone is not a strong enough competitor there will be a sexual problem.

In the early days of sexual permissiveness many young women were pulled both ways, and in the tug of war between family and partners they ended up sacrificing their own feelings. They would have intercourse with their boyfriends, but would fail to become aroused or enjoy the process. In this way they were unconsciously trying to accommodate their internalised parents, or consciences, by reassuring themselves that as long as they felt no pleasure they were not really doing wrong, and they also accommodated the demands of their partners by agreeing to intercourse. Thirty years on there are still many women using the same mechanism to resolve their conflict over their sexuality.

It is obvious that guilt is an important human attribute and there are things we should feel guilty about. Except for deliberately hurting others, these things are usually debatable, and this then requires us to have faith in our own opinion. The art is to be able to distinguish between those things about which it is reasonable to feel guilt and those which come from misunderstandings in the past due to the gullible and primitive fears of the child and its parents.

In the last two chapters we have explored the importance of security in our earliest development and seen how much this depends on the sort of relationship we have with our mother. We have seen that this is the background against which our sensuality emerges. As young children we experience feelings of power and helplessness, security and insecurity, anxiety, guilt and omnipotence. The balance of these feelings, and the defences we develop for coping with threat, all contribute to forming our personality and the attributes we bring to adult relationships. In the next chapter we go on to consider how specifically sexual feelings begin to emerge.

Key Points

♦ We have the evidence in our behaviour as adults which allows us to link with and reconstruct the past for ourselves

♦ The genital phase of sensual development is a complicated, paradoxical time, full of potential emotional difficulty and conflict with mother

♦ Guilt is an intensely unpleasant feeling associated with a failure to behave as we believe we should

♦ Psychological freedom from the trap of guilt is achieved when individuals are able to make judgments that they deem appropriate and accept the consequences

♦ Psychological prison exists when it is felt that for the sake of safety, change must always be resisted, however appropriate it might be

♦ In any long-term close relationship there will be some anger and disappointment with the partner.

- Under the influence of healthy parental love a child learns how to love others
- There is no love without pain
- It is important to be able to distinguish between reasonable guilt and guilt driven by unconscious associations.

PART III

Love and the Family

7

Drawn to Love

What is Love?

This chapter is about the origins of 'falling in love', the possessiveness of that love, the problem of rivals and the excitement and anxiety which surround these feelings. Love is a vast and complex subject and this is about one sort of love which, because of the great 'high' its presence engenders, is wonderful, addictive and dangerous. It can overwhelm people, preventing them from making proper judgments, and sometimes inciting them to cause pain to others whom they also love but in a different way. For example, a mother may leave her children because she has 'fallen in love'.

We are all aware as adults that 'falling in love' is both wonderfully exciting and relatively fleeting. We seek this type of love desperately, not only because of the delightful feelings it produces, but also because of the unpleasant feelings that it overcomes. Failures and frustration are forgotten and the loved one can be carried around in our thoughts like a talisman. It is like magic, a miracle, out of our control, and an illusion which quickly fades in the light of reality. Because of its fleeting nature it is tremendously seductive, but as novelists repeatedly show us, it can only be maintained if the security of the relationship itself cannot be maintained. People stay 'in love' with their partners only if they feel insecure and unsure of the partner or if they are prevented by the world from fulfilling their love. Thus the power of the story of Heloise and Abelard stems from the terrible frustration those lovers experienced. This unhappy paradox, that passionate love endures only if it is not fulfilled, is denied by most people in their quest for a mate. The idea held by most is that to find the right person means there will be elation for life. This notion is fanned by many authors who kill two birds with one stone. They satisfy the quest for love in themselves by writing romantic novels for the general public who pay for the quenching of their own thirst for magic love.

The fact that feeling secure in a relationship heralds the loss of excitement is, of course, unwelcome news. Sometimes people's inability to cope with changing from the marvels of being 'in love' to the mundane preoccupations of sharing their life with another ordinary person leads to relationship breakdown. Commonly heard phrases such as 'it just didn't work out' or 'I fell out of love' usually mean that for one or both partners the magic didn't last and the everyday wasn't an acceptable substitute.

Where did the phenomenon of being 'in love' originate which makes it so universal that literature of any country is so much concerned with it? Even more important, how do we turn illusory love into real love?

First Loves

Returning to our exploration of the development of sexuality, the next major influence affecting sexual attitudes is that of the inherent interest of the child in the parent of the opposite sex. This begins to emerge at three to four years of age, the exact age depending on the intelligence and maturity of the child, when a new quality of feeling begins to develop towards the parent of the opposite sex.

Up to this point in its development the child's main interest has been in its mother, as a provider of security and gratifier of the primitive sensualities of feeding and excretion. As we have seen, these early pleasurable sensualities are concomitant with security. Now a subtle excitement and tension towards the parent of the opposite sex develops, an emotional 'falling in love' which is powerful enough to cause guilt and anxiety because of the possessive fantasies that inevitably go with this sort of love at any age. The main problems of this phase are that the child recognises the authority of its parents and their relationship, but wishes to have an exclusive relationship (like theirs) for itself with the parent of the opposite sex. It partly recognises that this is forbidden yet dares to fantasise about the situation, and the extent to which it does this can determine whether a problem will develop. (As we will see later, the extent of the child's fantasy is not the only factor in the production of a problem, and the personality and contentment of the relevant parent will also make a large contribution.) The pleasure of such fantasies is offset by the fact that they involve displacing or even getting rid of the rival parent and this produces much discomfort. From this moment on the child is emotionally destabilised by a conflict between maintaining its security and status quo, and having exciting thoughts that cause anxiety – another tug of war.

While the child may feel very secure in the love of its same-sex parent, the development of a more passionate love towards the parent of the opposite sex produces a sense of insecurity. By definition the child cannot have the parent as its unique partner because that person clearly belongs to the other parent. This frustration is a major factor in maintaining, at an unconscious or even a conscious level, the longing for this parent which is the first experience of being 'in love'. Other loves are a reflection of this and are sought as a replacement of it. Seeking a lover is universal because we endlessly look to satisfy the original frustration, and when we think we have found the right partner it is because there will be some important characteristic of the parent which gives hope that at last the childhood object has been achieved.

Because the original condition of being 'in love' with the opposite-sex parent was inevitably doomed to frustration, the adult state of being 'in love' requires some frustration in order to be stimulated. Thus the unattainable married person may be much more interesting than the available person. The partner who is difficult to get or who refuses to make a commitment becomes utterly desirable. If the heart's desire is achieved, however, anxiety creeps in. Is this really the one? Alas, it is not, and can never be, because unavailability is an essential requirement. The excitement lessens, faults begin to be seen, the relationship does not feel as it used to feel. This did not happen in the original version because the taboo against actual incest kept the love endlessly frustrated and therefore endlessly alive.

Many years ago, two young women coincidentally came to my clinic in the same week complaining of inability to enjoy sex. Both were secretaries 'in love' with their married bosses; both had striven to break the marriage in order to get the man for themselves. The striking thing was that although both had achieved their objective, neither actually wanted their man once he had been won. The psychological point was that unconsciously they were seeking the father who had been denied them by their mother. To win their man meant symbolically beating their mother, which produced guilt. Also, actually succeeding broke the fantasy, and the consequent recognition of their lover as just an ordinary older man made him undesirable.

To understand this phase we must once again study the environment of the child. Today's society produces many more complicated situations than the neat nuclear family, but since the issues are themselves so difficult to understand, it is easier to start from this traditional position and examine the effects of variations later. Also, since the reaction to this new development is so different in the two sexes, it must be dealt with separately. First, however, there are a number of general points to be made.

Jealousy

In previous chapters we have seen that the sort of relationship we have with our parents and siblings affects our expectations and behaviour in later relationships. Understanding our early relationships will provide clues to our current relationships. Equally, our current relationships give clues to the past: if someone is very jealous in the present you can be sure they were very jealous in the past. As we shall see, we are all jealous, but some have more problems with it than others.

To understand this phase we must imagine the child's perception of its world, which is likely to be quite different from the way in which adults perceive the child's world. The child feels immensely aware of and totally controlled by the two powerful adults with whom it lives and on whom it depends. It is also aware that it can exercise control itself, by rage or seduction, and it is endlessly experimenting and juggling between these two extreme poles of helplessness and control. Dominating the situation for the child, however, is the fact that it is excluded, by language, secrets and private activities, from the parental relationship. This exclusion is particularly obvious at bedtime when most children resist for as long as possible the isolation and rejection that this separation brings.

Many of these issues are particularly powerful for the first-born child who will experience the isolation and loneliness of being alone in a bedroom separate from its parents. The parental relationship can arouse great envy in a child at any stage, but during the phase we are dealing with, when the child becomes aware of its special interest in the parent of the opposite sex and experiments with its powers of seduction to see if it can compete with the parent of the same sex, envy turns to jealousy.

Hostile feelings towards the same-sex parent cause great discomfort and anxiety for the child and also have emotional repercussions for the parents. The child feels guilty and anxious about hostile feelings towards a loved and powerful parent. The parent who is the rival feels suddenly rejected, finds it difficult to understand what is happening and may also react with hostility. The parents and the child seek ways to defend themselves against the pain of the situation and, as usual, the defence mechanisms themselves cause problems.

In exploring these matters further, we need to consider:

110

- ◆ Anxiety about seeking the forbidden parent
- ◆ Conflict about getting the forbidden parent
- ◆ How to resolve that conflict
- ◆ Uses of defence mechanisms
- ◆ Problems arising from unresolved conflict

Specific defence mechanisms will be discussed in Chapter 8 as we are looking at general points in this chapter.

These matters affect the two sexes very differently, so they will be dealt with separately. For both sexes, however, serious problems will only arise in adulthood if the anxieties of dealing with these inevitable phases of development are more than usually intense due to particular circumstances.

The Boy's Experience

Up to this time mother has been important as a powerful security figure, creating a mixture of contentment and awe in the child in different proportions depending on the mother's personality. Now this new feeling, with its prototype sexuality and consequent new anxiety, creeps into the situation. The anxiety for the boy is that he is now 'in love' with his mother, feels totally possessive about her, can no longer tolerate his father's prior stake and would therefore like to be rid of him. He may daydream about this, creating dramas which fill him with guilt. For the boy, therefore, his father comes to seem merely a threat and of little value or interest, and his mother is everything. We have to be in no doubt that the issue is one of fantasy destruction of his father and the consequence of such fantasy, however fleeting, is a great fear of his father's rage should he gain an inkling of what is going on inside his son. This is the beginning of a sense of absolute need to hide certain feelings from the world, and of an uncertainty about personal goodness. It is also the basis of the classical castration anxiety which is that out of revenge, his father will cut off the boy's genitals and thereby destroy his manhood.

The intensity of the anxiety is affected by the personality of the father who may show quite clearly his jealousy of his partner's love of their son, giving the boy the sense that he cannot hide and all is already known. With a mature and tender father the anxiety is predominantly a feeling of guilt and betrayal. Some defence against these anxieties is always necessary. Problems arise when the defence is too strong or absolute, involving a profound suppression of feeling. The strength of defences is always important. They may, if too strong, distort our personality while, if more appropriate, they contribute usefully to our individuality.

The Boy's Defences

Detachment

Here the aim is for the boy to conceal his real feelings which seem dangerous and reveal those which seem safe. He will hide his feelings towards his mother and act out a scenario to convince his father of his lack of interest. To buttress his position he turns his attention towards his father, identifying with him, sharing games, interests and attitudes, and reassuring himself by his good relationship. This is the most satisfactory way of dealing with the anxiety since it helps the boy to develop, push out his horizons and shift from the predominantly female influence of his mother to develop the male influence of his father and thus become a more rounded personality. It is the normal resolution of this phase.

Obviously the boy's rejection of his mother must not be too great or he may find it difficult as an adult to dare to value a woman too much without feeling anxiety. A problem arising from this defence, therefore, is an unconscious resistance about making a relationship with a woman, particularly one who in any way resembles his mother. He may, if too defended, avoid women; he may feel he has to choose a woman from a different race who seems unlike his mother; he may partly neglect his partner under the socially acceptable flag of playing sport or being very successful at work, either of which can necessitate long absences from home. Alan's story shows an example of this:

> Alan was the only child of very academic parents. He too was very academic and enjoyed doing well at school, and his main recreation from an early age was books. He managed to avoid hearing anything about sex or masturbation and so was terrified when, after walking home from school with the girl next door, he was doing his homework when he had a sudden erection and ejaculation. He was very scared and thought there was something badly wrong with him but could not bring himself to mention it to his parents. This innocence and fear had such a serious effect on him that he was aged forty before he had another ejaculation.
>
> Alan was always friendly with the opposite sex and in particular he admired women who were like his mother. However he avoided any sexual encounters with women and indeed with anyone as he had no interest in members of his own sex. He went abroad in his work a great deal and always felt more relaxed

in a foreign environment. At the age of 45 he met an extrovert Italian lady who was unlike anyone he had met before. This time he allowed sex to enter the relationship. It became clear that his sexual anxieties were centred around his childhood experiences and were only freed by a woman who was totally unlike his mother.

Attachment

Less satisfactorily the boy may decide to throw in his lot mainly with his mother, suffer the anxiety towards his father and deal with it by denying his masculinity and demonstrating that he is not competing with his father because he is not really a boy. Some take this further in actually trying to become a girl. This is much more serious because it involves a distortion of the idea of gender and propels the child along a path which leads to confusion about sexual identity in later life. This distortion may be done with varying degrees of intensity resulting in problems in the adult from some actual transexuals, through a spectrum of homosexuality and bisexuality, to apparently exceptionally masculine men who have endlessly to prove their virility because of their hidden sense that they threw their masculinity away when they were young. This latter man usually has a very strong Sex Drive, which at first sight makes it seem likely that his Pro-Sex team would win the tug of war. However, his fear of rejection and his expectation that someone will see through him and know that he is not really a man adds much weight to his Basic Insecurity. As a result he is often impossible to satisfy, and makes a hard taskmaster as a partner, as he seeks endless reassurance.

This defence is often used where a father is away a great deal and the boy works out that since he has to rely on his mother for his relationship most of the time, it is worth taking the risk of allying himself with her and thereby possibly offending his father. It is also more likely to occur where the mother seems particularly powerful and able to protect her son. This involves the boy believing that his mother loves him more than she loves his father, which situation is frequently found in reality. The amount of distortion of gender is dependent on these two circumstances as well as the degree of fantasy in the boy.

This alliance with his mother is often found in the first-born son who, if he is an only child, may be doubly anxious in later life. His anxiety comes first from the problems that follow being too much in the thrall of his mother as a powerful security figure, and secondly from the problems that follow expecting and fearing resentment from his father.

However, particular problems may arise if the next sibling is born after the boy is about five, when his expectation of sovereignty with his mother has been well established. The boy experiences rage and disappointment with his mother, who he feels has betrayed him, making his anxiety and sacrifices worthless. This can produce a man who is unconsciously very angry and who is both dependent on and yet hostile towards women. He often finds it difficult to make a commitment because he seeks the perfect relationship he remembers when he was the only child. When this cannot be found, he feels much of the resentment towards his partner that he felt towards his mother at the time of that first betrayal. This can have a serious effect on adult relationships, as Alistair's story shows:

> Alistair's father was in the Navy and away a great deal. The family moved around from base to base and making friends was difficult because they had to say 'goodbye' so frequently. Alistair and his mother compensated by being very close and even the birth of his sister did not disturb him too much – he thought she was 'only' a girl and of no importance. Alistair's father was not too threatening when he came home and accepted their close relationship. However, when he was 17 his mother became pregnant again and had another son. This caused great upset. Alistair could not bear to stay at home and was still angry with his mother twenty years later. He left the base and came to England where he looked after himself, which caused him a lot of anxiety as he was not really ready to survive in a strange country without back-up, but he managed. What he had to live with was very mixed feelings about women. On the one hand he wanted a strong woman to look after him, but on the other hand he would become angry and hostile the moment such a woman failed in any of his quite extreme demands for attention.

Denial

Denial, which we met in Chapter 2, is a very common defence mechanism. It is used in numerous situations by children and adults but for the moment we are looking at the defence of denial at this particular point in a young boy's life.

Denial is particularly likely to be used in this context by the youngest boy in the family. During his formative years he will be the least capable, knowledgeable and trustworthy member of the family. This makes it very difficult for him to feel as adequate as other members of the family and he is used to using his mother for protection. There are, of course, many examples of a very bright youngest child fighting to be as adequate as their siblings and managing to overtake them, but many youngest children have problems with taking responsibility and feeling like a 'grown up'.

In the phase we are looking at, taking responsibility for the new development and finding a way through is crucial. With the youngest son, since the family tends to see him as the baby, they expect him to retain his closer relationship with his mother and often deal with their envy by insisting on his inadequacy. The boy responds by denying and suppressing his new sexual interest and keeping his mother as a security figure. His mother often colludes with this when she finds it difficult to let go of her last 'baby'.

Problems are caused in adulthood when the youngest boy has retained his relationship with his mother to the extent that he often finds it difficult to disappoint her and ''jilt' her for another woman. When he does find an adult partner he may unconsciously demand the same relationship as he had with his mother, thereby unconsciously placing his partner in a parental role while at the same time consciously resenting her dominance. The result is often a diminution in virility because his mother is sexually taboo and the boy will be unused to taking a thrusting role in life.

Many boys find it difficult to tell their mother that they have found someone who they are going to marry. Their mother has held the position of first lady so completely, by being needed and desired for so long, that they fear the loss of love that may follow their transfer of needs and desires to another woman. Often there is actual loss of love as the mother tries to come to terms with her envy of her daughter-in-law. Angus's is an interesting story:

> Angus was the youngest son and very close to his mother. His family moved abroad when he was 8 years old and he was devastated when his parents decided to send him back to England to boarding school. He did not fit in and did not, as many of the other children did, find compensation in the companionship of his mates. His relationship with his mother changed and he was distant to her and to everyone else. He was referred to me when, after twenty years of attaching himself to other families by being the friend of both husband and wife, he found a partner of his own. However he could not live with her and easily became very angry if she made any demands on him. His partner Millie was 37 and desperate to have a baby, and he agreed to this as long as he was allowed to stay in his cottage in the north while Millie and baby daughter stayed in London. This unusual arrangement was working well according to the last postcard I received from them.

The Girl's Experience

The sexual and emotional development of the girl is quite different. Her new passionate feeling is invested in her father, which results in different problems in childhood and has different sexual repercussions in adulthood. In this phase her father becomes the interesting and exciting parent who the girl wishes to be with, yet she usually has relatively little access to him. She spends most of her time at home with her mother and may not see her father during the week if he works late. She is, therefore, in a way that a boy is not, a frustrated person with little opportunity for the emotional satisfaction which is on offer to a boy. She has to face the fact that her loved one belongs with her mother, who has much more contact, control and power than she has herself. This leads to the recognition, where the parental relationship is good, that she cannot win in any competition with her mother. This is, of course, complicated by the fact that she loves and needs her mother who has suddenly become to some extent a rival.

Particularly in well-organised households where the daughter is in bed when her father gets home, the girl feels great pain at the lack of communication as well as the knowledge that her mother spends the evening and the night with him and that she is not welcome in their bedroom. This situation makes for an unhappy child. Sometimes she is only angry with her mother and able to maintain some relationship with her father but she is often angry with both parents, feeling jealous of her mother and wishing to punish her father for not returning her love. The universal evidence of this phase is the four-year-old saying that she is going to marry her daddy when she grows up: a comforting thought to help deal with the frustration.

The way a girl resolves this emotional problem will determine how she resolves such triangular problems for the rest of her life. Somehow she has to maintain a relationship with her mother-rival because she loves and needs her and has to spend a lot of time with her, but how is she to do it?

The problem for the girl is not only her frustration about her father but the envy and subsequent hostility she feels towards her mother. It makes a child very anxious to feel hostility towards its powerful security figure, and the girl will feel the need to try to defuse this. Like the boy, she has several options, and the option taken will depend on her age, her personality, the personalities of her parents and the quality of the parental relationship.

The Girl's Defences

As with the boy, the girl has a need to hide her real feelings, but the feelings concerned are different. Where the boy fears for his manhood, the girl fears for her general well-being. She develops hostile feelings towards her mother as she comes to envy her and to recognise their rivalry, and she fears that her mother will feel hostile in return and that love, and therefore security, will disappear. This is not always merely a fantasy, because if her father demonstrates more affection to his daughter than to her mother, the mother may well feel hostile. Many families have a situation rather like Elizabeth and Mr Bennett in *Pride and Prejudice*, where father and daughter share a closeness, often based on some sense of intellectual superiority, denied to the mother who is patronised, ignored and slightly sneered at.

Identification

One way of dealing with her anxiety is for the girl to over-compensate for feelings of hostility by becoming even more attached to her mother than before, neurotically demonstrating her love and devotion. She may find difficulty in being parted from her mother, and in order to feel even safer, she may act by seeming to reject her father. She may deliberately refuse to allow her father to have a relationship with her and he may become hurt and retire, not understanding what has happened to his little girl.

This is an unsatisfactory defence mechanism because it distorts the truth so totally and leaves the girl (and, later, the woman) unsure of who she wants or who she can have without anxiety. She may continue to use her defensive behaviour against men and is likely to be emotionally and sexually immature. She may be unconsciously seeking her lost father who makes all other men seem undesirable, which can lead to frigidity. She will probably choose a maternal type of man to look after her and be undemanding sexually and thus, by not putting her under any pressure to change, help to retard her development. She is likely to be attracted to someone like her father, but will deny this to herself and the world lest it reveal her childhood passion. She may identify with her mother, but because she doesn't wish to be seen to compete with her, will choose to remain rather helpless and childlike. Hilary's story shows some of the possible effects of such a situation:

> Hilary was an only child and she had a very combative relationship with her father. She was a tomboy and would have nothing to do with dolls or home-making toys, liking nothing better than to wear the trousers and shirts belonging to the boy next door. She was very close to her mother, who was really her best friend, and she saw herself as her father's rival for her mother's attention.
>
> Hilary's father was a handsome man and she was attracted to film stars who looked like him, but in real life she was tongue-tied and awkward with this sort

of man. She married someone who was very maternal and looked after her well but she found that she had little libido and avoided sex as much as she could. This meant she did not acquire the taste for, and learn to value, sex. Once she could see that unconsciously she still hankered after the father she had denied having any interest in, and that this distanced her from her husband, she made efforts to bring sex more into her life. She eventually exorcised her denied childish longing for her father by taking these steps.

Rejection

Another defence against anxiety is for the girl to keep her relationship with her father but manage to feel safe by becoming in her mind a tomboy and thus no rival to her mother. She may take an interest in football or help her father to maintain the family car. This defence colludes with the gender issue (discussed more fully in Part IV) which increases its power. It denies femininity at an important time when this new quality needs to be explored and experimented with. Since this method of alleviating anxiety depends on the girl rejecting an important area of her personality by pretending to be a boy, it can be dangerous. If the defence cannot be at least partly relinquished, then it results in a woman who despises women, gets on with men but only by being 'one of the boys', and who may lose her sexuality and her female destiny, as happened to Dodie:

> Dodie was the third child in a family of four, her siblings being boys. They lived in the country and their father was the main vet to a large area and a well-known charismatic character. Dodie could see no advantages in being like her mother, who seemed to have a hard time looking after all the men and experienced no interest in life except through the tales the children brought home.
>
> Dodie, like her brothers, also became a vet. She found it difficult to see herself as anything other than one of the boys, but as she was approaching the age of 40, she found herself more and more desperate to have a child. She tried artificial insemination by donor, but felt a great deal of guilt about whether a grandfather and uncles were good enough father-substitutes for a child or whether her child would find it unforgivable that its father was unknown. The problem was solved either unconsciously or mechanically because many attempts at artificial insemination failed.

As long as rejection is not too total a defence and can be put into reverse at the appropriate time, it can result in a feisty woman who is an asset to herself and society.

Affiliation

In the third defence the girl maintains openly her affiliation to her father without needing to reject her femininity. If her mother has failed as a security figure the girl will turn to her father for security, whereupon the father becomes everything to the girl as the mother is to the boy. The girl, however, feels much safer than the boy because she cannot be castrated and believes her father will protect her if necessary. The girl rarely recognises her hidden sexuality because the security aspect dominates the relationship. Frequently this girl can find no man worthy to replace her father, which usually suits the father, and so she remains single. If she does find a man to have a relationship with she may well be frigid.

A mother who fails as a security figure may be inadequate as a person, may be an ambitious career woman who invests little in her children, or may be openly jealous of her daughter. However, this can also occur when a devoted and successful mother gives birth to a sibling, which can make the eldest girl feel desperate about her mother's apparent loss of interest in her. Depending on her age, the eldest girl often turns to her father for security when the sight of her mother's close relationship with the new baby becomes too painful and she feels she has lost her mother's love. She feels safer investing in her father, despite the associated anxiety, than feeling distanced from both. Her relationship with her mother is spoilt because she feels angry and betrayed and, besides deriving comfort from the new relationship with her father, she wishes to punish her mother by withdrawing from her. Father is there, himself feeling rather bereft and displaced by the new baby. There can, therefore, be a uniting of two lost souls.

If this unity coincides with the stage of excitement that is under discussion, the resulting relationship can be too satisfactory. There may be a lasting sense in the girl that her father is her partner for life and no other is good enough or, in some cases, even allowed to compete. This can result in the same difficulties as experienced by the boy, who is in the same situation with his mother. However, it is even more difficult for the girl to relinquish her father for another partner than it is for the boy to relinquish his mother. You will remember that the boy has the very strong competitor, testosterone, in his Pro-Sex team. The girl has no equivalent hormonal push to drive her towards a mature sexual relationship and the consequent 'jilting' of her father. She often feels very satisfied with her emotional relationship with her father, and finds any idea of sex an unnecessary intrusion into her life. Later, with his death, she is likely to have the pain of realising the loss of her mature destiny, as happened to Annabel:

Annabel was an only child with an anxious unsupportive mother and she became very close to her father who she adored. When she was 14 her father became ill and died and she was not able to get over his death. She and her mother could not support each other and resented each other's pain. Annabel was a violinist and worked very hard at her music; she saw this hard work as being for her father. She began to get over his death when she met a young man who reminded her of her father. All was well until she had to go abroad for three months, when he asked if she would mind if he had the odd affair while she was away. This was like another death and for the next five years she just worked very hard at her music.

Annabel came to me because she was not interested in having sex with her new boyfriend yet did not want to lose him. He was very unlike both her father and the last boy and was faithful and loyal but something was missing. It was as if excitement was likely to invite loss but safety was not sexually stimulating. As a result of our discussions Annabel decided to make this relationship work by introducing sex on a regular basis and making more effort to get involved, partly because she loved him and partly because she wanted a child.

As with all defences, it is the intensity of the use which will determine whether an actual problem is found in later life. The defence becomes the remembered situation: for example, a special love for her father comes to be denied by a girl who later would only be prepared to remember her love of her mother, or at most lump the parents together and protest an equal love of both. We can understand that many families experience a sudden change in relationships, when a child is going through this phase, which is hard to understand and is often distressing.

Childhood Gender Difference

To summarise so far, the great difference between the sexes at this stage is that the boy has all his needs and desires invested in his mother, while the girl has her investment split between the two parents, and this makes for a great emotional and psychological difference. The boy fears for the survival of his sexuality, while the girl suffers a loss of security which makes her personal survival seem to be at risk. So we can see that both sexes have to cope with fear of retribution for their new interests, and both fear for their survival. Both use defence mechanisms to deal with their anxieties, and the extent and intensity of these defence mechanisms determines whether there are problems in adulthood.

It is clear that some special quality of feeling is involved, which is linked to gender, and there are a number of questions to be asked about this mystery ingredient. The emphasis has been on the emotional aspects of this early relationship. However, it becomes increasingly clear that it is the difference of gender which is the attraction and the threat; in other words, it is the sexuality of the situation which adds the new dimension. Clearly it is important to try to understand what may cause a dangerous breakdown in the safety net of the incest taboo or the paedophile taboo.

It is safe to assume that we, like all animals, have a reproductive drive without which our species would not survive. There is, however, considerable debate over the timing of the development of a consciousness which links sexual role with physical attributes. In other words, how sexual are the love fantasies of childhood, and at what stage does the conception of adult sexuality begin? This is obviously an important question, particularly for those going through therapy who believe they have suddenly remembered being sexually abused.

How innate is our adult sexual knowledge? Is there an inbuilt wish, either to penetrate or to be penetrated, which is linked to the genital structure of the individual? We know there are a number of instincts which ensure the survival of the individual, such as the inbuilt drive to suck which ensures nourishment, and it seems logical that there are similar instincts for the survival of the species. Does having a penis make a young boy want to poke about, either with sticks or by transforming this instinct into, say, research or painting? Does having no penis induce a passivity in young girls which is only overcome by defensively keeping up with the boys?

If there is innate coital knowledge it is largely unconscious. At a conscious level, while children discover early the sensual pleasure of their own genitals, it is clear that most young children have no concept of sexual intercourse unless they are abused.

The way in which we acquire the so-called 'facts of life' is relevant here. The word 'facts' sounds so absolute that we forget how much depends on our interpretation of the data we receive, some of which has already been interpreted by those who pass it on. On being told 'the facts of life', children are often disbelieving, and have to be reassured that what they have been told is really true and that it can be pleasurable rather than painful. Equally, since so many adults with sexual problems seem to have no inbuilt sense of what to do in the sex act and require manuals and instruction, it is easy to assume that there is no inbuilt sense of sexual role and that these particular people have failed to glean in teenage years the necessary information to ensure denouement. The defences of the stage we are discussing may so cut people off from sexuality that they cannot learn about it. For instance, I have seen people like Luke, whose experiences were detailed in Chapter 2, who claim to have gone through their school days without hearing a dirty joke: they must have listened but not heard. Don was a classic example of this:

> Don was very keen to please authority figures, and had no conscious knowledge of masturbation until the age of 17. He went to a boys' school but heard no dirty jokes. There were no changes in his body or voice at the usual time, and he didn't have his first wet dream until he was 17.
>
> The interesting fact in Don's story was that his family were very open about nudity. His parents, his sister and Don himself walked around with no clothes on, yet he was 'blind' and 'deaf' to sex for so long.

How long, then, should our 'innocence' ideally last? Clearly, with more and more explicit television programmes, it is increasingly difficult for children to turn a protective blind eye for very long.

Results of Defences

We now need to consider in more detail a number of problems coming from the defences used in this phase which affect the personality and life of the adult.

Sometimes the individual may be relatively inhibited sexually because they retain a sense that they are not allowed to love someone who reminds them of their parent. Some people resolve this by choosing a partner who is very different from their parent. I have seen several people complaining of frigidity or impotence who become free when abroad and are quite uninhibited with men or women from a different country or race. It seems that the unconscious does not recognise, in the partner with different racial features, the symbolism of the parent, and this allays anxiety and allows the person to have a heterosexual relationship. The problem with this group is that while some anxiety is relieved, there is a greater than usual sense of dissatisfaction because the person is not like the loved parent.

Similarly, where there has been a distortion of the gender image such that a girl rejects femininity or a boy identifies with girls, there will be a necessity to deny interest in the opposite sex which will lead to uncertainty about what is really felt for that gender. The tomboy often feels at ease with boys and feels herself to be one of them but does not feel comfortable in a sexual relationship. The boy who has identified with girls often gets on well with them and feels threatened by other boys, so does not feel at home in a competitive male environment, particularly if girls and sex are under discussion.

Where the child is very anxious about their sexual feelings for the parent of the opposite sex, and has a strong need to hide their interest, these feelings will be consciously denied and will therefore float freely in the unconscious looking for a safe person to invest in. The safe person is someone of the same sex. This is a common way of dealing with this particular anxiety: it leads to crushes during early adolescence, which are transitory for many, but which for some become the permanent feature of their sexuality.

Many people, even when married, remain predominantly involved with their parent or parents. Sometimes both partners are failing to make the necessary step away from home and commitment, and this results in a 'them and us' separation between the two families which prevents the new couple from completely uniting and cementing their relationship. Sometimes only one is involved with the parents in this way, and then the partner will feel excluded and unloved, which will lead to unsuccessful sex and much resentment to be dealt with in the relationship.

One of the difficulties in a committed relationship is the question of the partner being second best to the loved parent. There are two possible outcomes. First, if the adult retains a close relationship with their parent and is felt to put that parent before the partner, the reason for the partner's jealousy is obvious. The second occurs where the adult has felt the need to suppress their interest in the parent, but the interest has been retained as an unconscious ideal which no partner can quite live up to. This is harder to deal with, because as far as the adult is consciously aware they may not even have liked the parent, and therefore they find it difficult to believe that they are unconsciously interested in the parent and that this can have caused a problem.

As we saw earlier, falling in love is probably the false sense that the perfect parent substitute has at last been found. The lover seems to produce feelings as good as those of an unconscious memory from this phase in the past, and disappointment inevitably follows as it is impossible for the loved one to fulfil such a fantasy for very long. The partner is then always second best, always being measured against a fantasy and always causing disappointment. When seeking a partner we are all looking for someone with our parent's good points and without their bad points. For example, as with the girls mentioned earlier, many women choose a passive man to 'correct' an active father only to complain that he is not decisive enough. Partnerships founder if the transition to a more pragmatic but ultimately more profound love cannot be made, and the individuals who can only form partnerships if they are in love must inevitably move from partner to partner.

A fear of having children can be the result of two kinds of fear coming from this phase. First, there is the fear of revealing to the parent of the same sex the hidden competitive feelings someone has had about that parent. It seems almost disrespectful to wish to take the parent role, and seems safest to remain their child. Also, having played baby for so long, the person does not feel powerful enough to take the parent role. Secondly, there may be a wish to remain a child, in order not to have to lose the permissible relationship with the parent. Irene had a problem with this:

> Irene had been married for four years when she became pregnant. She was extremely anxious about her father seeing her in this condition, because she wanted them both to be able to retain the fantasy that she was still his little girl. She had not had a good relationship with her mother since the birth of her sister when Irene was four years old. She turned to her father and had been very close to him ever since.
>
> Irene met her husband in her last year at university and they had married with parental backing and a large wedding. However, she managed to deny to herself that her father would know she had had a sexual relationship, and indeed convinced herself that he would assume she would not have sex.
>
> Irene felt greatly embarrassed by the obvious sign of her sexual activity in the pregnancy and had to work hard in her counselling sessions to face reality. By the eighth month she was able to face her father and all was well.

In a free society such as ours, people marry for many reasons. Money and status may be priorities for some, cultural demands for others. Predominantly we marry for love and that can produce its own problems. One form of 'falling in love' is attaining a feeling of contentment that is an echo of satisfactions from the past. As we have seen the past is full of defence mechanisms, and the satisfaction *can be* of a defence which may eventually no longer be needed. Jill's story is an interesting one:

> Jill selected as her husband a maternal man with qualities of her mother. This appeared to follow on naturally from her having in childhood formed a particularly close relationship with her mother. However, on analysis, it became clear that Jill's close relationship with her mother had concealed a strong interest in her father and had developed partly as a defence against that interest. As Jill grew older, she gradually gained the maturity and confidence to address her feelings towards her father and she became restless as she realised that she had missed out on relating to him or anyone like him. This in turn made her resless in her relationship with her husband who did not possess her father's qualities, and who she had chosen for that very reason. Ultimately, Jill was able to explore these issues and came to recognise that no one person could fulfil all possible aspects and needs within her personality. She was able to recognise that companionship, a shared history and some compatibility, along with an effort to keep sex alive and well, would allow her to weather this change within her.

However, for some people, the restlessness felt by Jill is interpreted as generalised dissatisfaction or boredom with their partner without any understanding of why they might have become dissatisfied. In some relationships, such feelings may become insurmountable and lead to the end of the relationship. For example:

> Emily had a romantic nature and found being committed to Harry restricting. She began studying fine arts and met a completely different group of people who seemed much more exciting to her. She left Harry for a painter, who in turn left Emily for a model after two years. Emily tried to find Harry again but he now had another partner. She became lost and depressed and had no sense that her exciting fling had been worth the losses.

Cultural Reinforcement of Defences

Each sex has its defences incorporated into the culture. Traditionally men have resisted marriage while women have wanted it.

Men

A man may have difficulty in finally putting another woman in place of his mother who at one time was everything to him, the source of his first sensual experience and his security. Once he has had the courage to relinquish his mother for an adult partner, he is more likely than a woman to be able to separate from his parents, hence the adage 'a boy is a son 'til he takes a wife, a girl is a daughter for all of her life'. Where his mother has been widowed, however, there may be much greater difficulty in separating from her as she now regards her son as a substitute for the man she has lost. This may put her son under great strain as he cannot deny his mother and often feels split between her demands and those of his partner. This can be dangerous to his relationship, as Carl's story shows:

> Carl was a young professional man whose mother was very demanding, partly because she had been recently widowed and partly because her traditions told her that her son belonged to her and was there for her to call on. Carl came to hate his wife because she refused to let him help his mother in any way and continuously fought against her. He felt constantly guilty and persecuted by his two women who caused a continuous tug of war within himself. He was offered a job abroad and told his mother that it was necessary for him to take it. He did not really want to go but thought it would save his marriage. Unfortunately his mother decided to follow him and at this point I lost contact.

Women

Women tend to remain more emotionally tied to the parental home and tend to look after parents more than their brothers. This is partly because of guilt felt towards their mothers. By doing this they assuage their guilt and are able to remain close to their fathers. Also when a woman marries she loses her own mothering person, and has to become that person for her partner as well as shouldering sexual responsibility. While she feels this loss of security she has a tendency to return home. Also she can feel more at ease with her mother now that they are not competitors.

By taking a partner there is also the achievement of a different sort of security. The small girl, forced to spend most of her time with her mother, feels deprived of the person who excites her, envious of her mother and determined to have what she sees her mother as having, even if it is only second best. The fulfilment of her reproductive role, and therefore her success, lies in having a child but she needs a man to provide the security for this success. Even in today's successful career woman there is often a longing, which may have been suppressed for many years, to have what her mother had: a man of her own and children. Evelyn's story shows an extreme version of this:

> Evelyn was a 48-year-old woman of considerable beauty, who had had many affairs but had never married. She wanted to be married but was extremely intolerant of her partners. She felt that her parents had had a perfect relationship and that no relationship of hers ever came up to the same standard. She was therefore deprived of a relationship because of a fantasy about her parents. She had a similar fantasy about her brother's marriage, and was very shaken when he divorced, because she had to face the fact that it was not as perfect as she had believed.

As we have seen, love is a simple feeling when we are very young and becomes more complicated as we develop. As a child, the very early demands we make on our first love are fulfilled, so we expect this to continue. The pain of childhood is the frustration of having to share love when what we want is to possess it for ourselves. With our fathers and, as we shall see in the next chapter, later with the rest of our family, the need to share is a frustration; our attempts to deal with this can lead to destructive defences that make later relationships difficult. Understanding these defences can free us to focus on our adult relationship in a new way.

The art of the relationship is to harness the joyful feeling of a sense of 'coming home', that falling in love gives as we re-experience very early love, to the disappointing reality that our lover cannot remain magical for ever. Understanding that this magic is bound to be fleeting lessens the disappointment as it diminishes. Less disappointment means that sex can continue to flourish and support the creation of a shared history of companionship and mutual support which can realistically make the relationship a 'coming home'.

Key Points

- Sexuality develops in our relationship with our parents
- This phase has a profound effect on our adult sexuality
- Feeling secure in a relationship heralds the loss of excitement
- Sexual and emotional development is very different for girls and boys
- Unconscious desires can dominate our intelligence and affect our behaviour, even when our intelligence tells us clearly that we would have a better life with something different
- When we are deprived of something important we tend to seek it
- The extent and intensity of the use of childhood defence mechanisms determines whether there are problems in adulthood
- Falling in love is probably the false sense that the perfect parent substitute has at last been found
- Disappointment inevitably follows as it is impossible for the loved one to fulfil such a fantasy for very long
- Partnerships founder if the transition to a more pragmatic but ultimately more profound love cannot be made
- Each gender has its defences incorporated into the culture.

8

Familial Situations

It is perhaps obvious that crucial factors in a child's relationship with either parent will be influenced by the parents' own relationship and their various relationships with other members of the family. Even grandparents can have an important effect, particularly in an 'extended' family situation or where grandparents are used for child care. Obviously everything that is said about the child in this book applies to everyone, including mothers when they were young themselves, so our parents may be understood best by looking at their relationship with their own parents.

Parents' Relationship

The quality of the relationship between the parents is of paramount importance. Parents who love each other, and show it, obviously produce a quite different environment from those who do not. It is clearly more pleasant to grow up in a harmonious atmosphere, and where parents love each other, the child eventually recognises that there is no real hope of turning the fantasies of this phase into reality. It will, therefore, gradually relinquish them and become free to develop and form relationships with its peers.

Less easily relinquished are those fantasies of the child who has been used by an unhappy parent to meet their needs in place of their adult partner. These do not have to be sexual needs (although we have only to read the papers to know that this happens), but it is generally the case that in an unhappy marriage, children are used as emotional partners for parents. When this happens a girl's fantasy of a life with her father, say, merges with a truth that the father is lonely and turns to his daughter for a relationship which allows the girl to imagine that her father loves her like a wife. Where later the parents divorce and her father finds another partner, the daughter will feel immeasurable pain and anger.

It is, of course, quite natural that parents may love their children more than their partner, since committed relationships are so difficult. If, however, this partnership is too obvious and the power of the child too great, dangerous fantasies are produced in the child allowing it to invest too much in the parent of the opposite sex. This can lead to difficulty in making the transition to investing in someone from the peer group later on. Peer group relationships are frightening because they have to be 'played by ear' and require us to take responsibility and deal with sexual anxiety. A relationship with a comfortable known parent, who is by definition a protector and who takes all responsibility, is easier but retards development and maturing.

The personalities of the parents can complicate the basic picture. For example, where the mother is benevolent and the father is difficult, there will be a tendency to wish to maintain the relationship with the mother which will affect the respect a child feels for the father. This will make the boy more inclined to stay with his mother, with the resulting problems as already discussed. For the girl, not only may this make it difficult to value her father but to value any man. She may remain greatly influenced by her mother which can later interfere with marriage, both because she allows her mother to play too large a part in her life and because she does not value a man enough to marry him. This is what happened to Hilda:

> Hilda did not feel attracted to a man until she was 26. She tried hard and went out with many boys but only when she met Bryan did she think that at last she had found someone she could marry. Unfortunately Bryan was offered a great career opportunity in the USA. Faced with the anxiety about going away from the mother she was so close to, Hilda chose her mother and parted from Bryan.

Depending on what the difficulty is with the father, there can be other problems. When I was working with a particular ethnic group where it was usual for the girls to have been beaten by their fathers during their upbringing, an interesting problem emerged. Many of the girls had become engaged or married to rather passive men from a different culture, determining that never again would they put themselves in a position where they could be dominated and beaten, only to find that their partners seemed boring and sexually unexciting. Their sexuality was unconsciously linked to the violent father and could not easily be evoked by the gentle man. This is an example, of course, of how dominant our unconscious desires can be, compared to our intelligence which tells us we would have a better life with something different.

Where the father is the more responsible and trustworthy parent, or has for some practical reason become the house-husband while the mother goes out to work, there will be more wish to invest in him. Here, for the girl, the repercussions of having a close relationship with her father (which combines security and excitement), are similar to the boy's with his mother. Father means everything and there is likely to be difficulty in 'jilting' father later and being prepared to invest in a more suitable man. One difference makes this dynamic more damaging for girls than for boys: girls don't have the testosterone competitor pulling for their Pro-Sex team. This hormone drives the adolescent boy to leave the mother with whom he has no sexual future and seek a more suitable partner. The adolescent girl has no equally strong impulse as her hormones are for 'nesting' and for the moment home feels like 'nesting'. She is likely, therefore, to remain emotionally bound to her father and sexually repressed.

Single-Parent Families

After reading about all the difficulties faced by children with two parents, it may seem as if it could be advantageous to have just one to deal with. Certainly, there is no jealousy involved, because the child does not have to share. However, it does mean that the intensity of the relationship with the one parent is that much greater, and therefore more difficult to extricate from later, particularly if the young adult feels extra responsibility for the parent.

An important factor in the development of the concept of an adult sexual relationship in these circumstances will be the reason why the parent is single. There are several possibilities here, each of which has a very different effect.

First, there is the man or woman who has been deprived of a partner by death, who has not chosen to be single, but who has to get on with the job of bringing up children in the best way possible in the circumstances. Grandparents, uncles, aunts and eventually another partner will provide some of the necessary identification for the child. However, besides the idea of death and loss which is not usually faced so early, the main problem here is that the child has no jealous triangular situation to be met at a time of inculcation and flexibility. This means that the very strong one-to-one bond becomes entrenched and later the young adult may expect and demand the same total attention from a partner as it has received from its parent.

Another problem may occur after a divorce or abandonment. In this case the deserted parent will have feelings of antagonism towards the deserting partner which will affect a child of either sex, making it feel guilty for the mixture of love and resentment it feels for the deserting parent, which in turn will affect its later relationships. After divorce or abandonment a child will live with one parent, becoming the surrogate partner for a time, only to feel rejected when the parent finds another partner. This undermines the child's solo position and cannot easily be tolerated. Intense depression, and jealousy at what feels like betrayal, may have to be coped with when this happens.

Death, divorce or abandonment produce a parent who is a victim, whether of circumstance or the opposite sex. This is not the case when the parent, almost invariably a woman, has chosen single parenthood. Increasingly in today's society women want to have a baby without a man. Some would like a man if he was 'just right' but nobody ever is; either way, the woman is prepared to go ahead alone and take the whole responsibility of career, home and child. This implies some personal difficulty in relating to the opposite sex, and she may consciously or unconsciously work out her own problems in that area through her child.

To the child concerned this must mean that the mother does not want a man. In the girl this may delay her own interest in the opposite sex as she identifies with and tries to 'play' her mother. In the boy, who has no wish for anyone else, this bond with his mother remains unchallenged and becomes entrenched, which makes separation difficult later.

A mother who is single by choice usually has a need to control her whole world, and is likely to be very controlling of her child whose need of another parent she has not considered. To have your father dismissed as of no importance clearly has a great effect. If her child is a boy she may be very pleased to have a male she can completely control, and adore him because of this, but it will be difficult for the boy to free himself from such a bond and to see himself as valuable to the opposite sex except as a possession. If the child is a girl the mother may be very pleased if she feels hostile to men, but is likely to pass on her prejudice to her daughter. She may suffer later when her daughter is likely to feel great resentment at being deprived of her father.

It is within the family that we have our best chance of getting used to the opposite sex and the way the sexes relate to one another. If we are deprived of this we are not fully prepared for the adult world. Only children find it difficult to relate to their peer group because they have not experienced competition with siblings in the family, and equally children deprived of two parents lose an important experience. In a fatherless family, the boy has lost the experience of dealing with competition, and may find it hard to cope with the cut and thrust of seeking a mate.

When we are deprived of something important we tend to seek it, and a girl seeking her father (or a boy his mother) may look for him too strongly in her lover to the detriment of that relationship.

Abuse and Incest

The fact that there is an incest taboo shows that there is a danger of incest. This is so shocking to most people that there has been, and still is, a resistance in society to believe that such a thing can happen.

Incest between adult and child is, by its nature, lopsided. The child, while sensually aware, is sexually innocent, while the adult is sexually knowing. It can be argued that a child's fantasies will only include actively sexual content if the child has actually been aroused by the abuse of an adult.

Young children can be very winning, even sometimes appearing to be seductive, and men may be put under considerable pressure to resist arousal. Later, the fathers of adolescent girls may suddenly become strict and aggressive and refuse to let their daughters go out to meet boyfriends, but few people realise that this reaction can be jealousy and repressed sexuality.

With divorce so widespread and family life often unstable, it is common for children to have to relate to a parent's new partner, which can cause many difficulties. A new stepfather is not protected by the incest taboo. It is rare to find abuse of a boy by his stepmother, or to find abuse of children by same-sex adults within the family, so the sexual implications are greater for girls, which once again emphasises the difference in sexuality between men and women. Sometimes the abused daughter tries to protect her relationship with her mother by not telling what her stepfather is doing, and sometimes the mother knows the abuse is going on and does nothing to protect her child lest she lose her new partner. There are also more complicated cases where the daughter colludes in the abuse, but denies to herself her own complicity and justifies it as being the only way to keep the family together.

Abuse varies from a light touch in a private area to extremely painful penetration by a large organ into a small orifice. It can be strongly resisted or easily complied with, either from fear, bribery or pleasure. Compliance causes intense shame, which leads to much of the guilt and distress in the aftermath of sexual abuse; this means that the abused person finds it particularly important to deny any sense of arousal they may have had. Denial helps to convince them that they were not to blame, but the defence is commonly continued beyond the point of usefulness and leads to inability to achieve arousal in non-abusive adult relationships.

One way to define the sexual abuse of a child is to say that it is an act that causes the loss of innocence and prematurely arouses the child's realisation of its sexual power to arouse adults and of its own possibilities of being aroused. Of course the child has felt sensual pleasure when being soaped in the bath, when urinating and when defaecating, but these are unilateral experiences. Most of all they do not involve the child's sense of sexual power over the adult, and it is the realisation of this power which is so potentially damaging to the child. There are two common results of this realisation. The first is for the child to become obsessed with denying sexual interest, which distorts their attitude in adult life making sexual relationships difficult. The second is for the child to become obsessed with pursuing sexual interest, which distracts it away from the other important interests in life. The exploration of the reasons for abusing children is not an issue for this book except to say that a small child is easy prey for the inadequate man, driven by his sexuality yet vulnerable to the power of the adult female.

There are many other senarios which I have not attempted to address including abuse between siblings. Clearly any abuse from within the family will have a psychological impact upon a child. It must also be pointed out that while women abuse their children in other ways, it is relatively rare for their abuse to be sexual.

Siblings

Another factor affecting the situation is the presence of siblings. Only the first child has had any real expectation of being able to have a one-to-one relationship with either parent. The others may naturally strive to be the favourite but, where there is less hope and expectation, there is less pain and disappointment and they weather this stage better than a first child. However, in a family with a child of each sex and divided parents, the family will usually split into pairs. This can happen naturally, with mother and son in one pair and father and daughter in the other, or defensively, with mother and daughter in one pair and father and son in the other. Each situation will have an effect. An older girl with a younger brother, an older brother with a younger sister, two brothers, two sisters, an only girl with several brothers and an only boy with several sisters all produce special difficulties.

Tug of siblings Position in the family plays a greatly underrated part in the development of the individual. This and genetic factors are the main reasons for siblings being so different from each other despite the same environment. A point that many people question in counselling is 'if the contribution made by my parents is so important, why does my sister not have the same problems'. Eldest girl, eldest boy, two girls, two boys, two girls and a boy etc., the permutations are endless. My aim is to show how to work out the effect of one's own situation. The fundamental factors to be taken into account are:

♦ Competition
♦ Parents' hopes
♦ Birth order
♦ Gene factor
♦ Death of a sibling

Competition We all want to be the best. Being in a family helps a child to accept that:

♦ we cannot always be best
♦ everyone longs for love and attention
♦ one winner means the rest are losers
♦ we all need to win sometimes and accept losing as well
♦ winning too much means the envy of the rest

As siblings, we all compete to be the most important child. We learn to deal with competition from our siblings, unless we are an only child. Depending on our temperament through the genes, and our place in the family, we cope with competition in different ways. As usual our defence mechanisms come into play. One way to cope is by striving to be the most studious, the most beautiful, the most helpful; parents often collude with this and label their children in ways that can be difficult to shed even as an adult, when the swan emerges from the ugly duckling but still feels ugly. If the competition is very strong we may choose to 'drop out' when winning seems impossible and there is some satisfaction and independence in showing no interest. We can go further and get attention and notoriety by being difficult, not eating or not working, and later by smoking, drinking or taking drugs.

Children who are not interested in playing games are usually refusing the pain of competing and perhaps losing. They will only join in an activity if they are sure to win. Games players are tougher because they learn to accept losing. The fact that a game produces a winner and a loser may seem almost politically incorrect, but it is an unavoidable fact of human nature that *everybody* is interested in winning whether they allow the world to see this or not. The result of this is a more or less concealed contest which affects all our relationships, from those with parents, teachers or bosses who may have favourites, to competing for and with our partners.

Because of the inevitable competition between siblings, we must find a way to deal with our hostile feelings which will emerge towards them from time to time. There are three main ways in which we may deal with this:

1. by being openly hostile and aggressive
2. by unconsciously denying our hostility and feeling only devotion
3. by distancing ourselves from the family

Despite the difficulties of the first, within reason this is the best reaction as it deals with the reality, allows everyone to recognise the situation and does not involve distortion of feelings that might leave the child not knowing what they feel. The second causes distortion of feelings, but can be useful if not too all-embracing, as part of a continuum of making the best of things. The last happens particularly when there is one child of different sex to the rest and when a single room and different toys and interests help the denial of hostile feelings but may leave the child isolated. Hermione's story is an interesting one:

> Hermione was the eldest of six. Her upper middle-class family had many servants and lived in a large mansion. The birth of her first sibling induced rages and temper tantrums in Hermione to the point that the staff of the house were told that Hermione must never be left alone with the child. This did not improve with the birth of subsequent children and as an adult she was both able to describe this situation and at the same time say that she still could not understand why they wanted all those children and thought that one should have been enough. She was still an angry woman who found maintaining a partnership difficult. She wanted no children herself.

Sam's situation was much more straightforward:

> Sam described how his older sister tormented him. He told how when he was small he had to sit down when she came into the room or she would push him over. He was a late developer who was dyslexic and a failure at school. Once free of his sister, when she went to university, he began to be able to study and belatedly became a successful lawyer.

There was no concealment of hostility here.

Jodie's was a very different story:

Jodie had a younger brother, Tim, whom she made her only friend. She followed him everywhere, to the extent that his friends became annoyed with him because she would always turn up and control their activities. She spoke of adoring Tim and could not accept for one moment that she was jealous and resented him.

This was their relationship until he was called up to do his military service in a particularly dangerous section of the army. Then she lost touch with him and only met him years later when they quarrelled over the furniture their parents had left when they died.

It was clear that while Jodie felt that she was in competition with her brother she denied her hostile feelings and turned them into devotion. When he went away, instead of feeling anxious concern for his safety, she lost interest because he no longer seemed to be a competitor. It was difficult for her to know whether she had any real love for him because she used love as her camouflage.

Charles's situation was different again:

Charles had two feisty sisters, one older, one younger. From an early age he had a room of his own and remembered trying to keep the peace between his sisters, which continued into adulthood. He was a quiet studious boy, never in trouble, although he always felt his 'goodness' and cleverness to be undervalued.

As an adult Charles retained the equivalent of a room of his own, as despite having many friends he had never been able to live with or be intimate with anyone. One clue to his hidden feelings was the fact that he liked to watch over and over again a film in which the mother was forced to choose between keeping her son or her daughter, and so revealed his interest and satisfaction in the fact that she chose her son.

The discussion of these negative feelings which are inherent in the family situation should not mask the fact that at the same time most siblings share very good feelings as well as defensive ones. Real brotherly and sisterly love develops out of sharing a unique history, in which they hold each other's secrets and may well form a group which will support and back each other against the grown-ups. However, it is important to understand the negative feelings, or we cannot understand what goes wrong in later relationships.

Parents' Hopes It can be said that siblings are rivals to fulfil their parents' dreams. We have seen how important our parents are to us and how important we are to them. We are important to them because we are theirs and part of them. This last means that we are then the vessels through which they can hope for recognition of their maturity and for the possibility of fulfilment of their own failed ambitions. One child may be able to do this while another may disappoint, causing some inevitable reaction in both the relationship with the parents and with each other. Depending on the degree of their own insecurity, our parents' demands on us to be perfect will vary. These are demands that can cripple our own potential because we need to please our parents, and because to disappoint loved ones is painful; hence their ambitions and prejudices can affect us greatly.

The eldest child is the first ambassador and most demand is made on this child. Of course, still in the twenty-first century, in aristocratic and royal families, there is a reward for being the eldest which compensates for later displacement. Titles, land and money are heaped on the eldest, and this can seem like a prize or a responsibility. Either way, the eldest must expect envy and resentment.

The youngest child has least demand made upon it unless the other children have disappointed the parents. If we look at the film *The Godfather* we see that his son Michael, as the youngest, has no demands put on him and is protected from the squalid operations of his family until the older brothers show lack of judgment and the whole family turns to Michael to save them.

As we shall see later, the only child is the first and last, and combines all the difficulties and rewards of both situations.

There are different considerations in respect of fathers and mothers, but both have fears that they may not share their children's interests. This can become a problem in a family if one child succeeds in fulfilling parental hopes while the others fail. Paradoxically one father whose second son had Down's Syndrome told me how much easier it was to love this child than the older boy on whom all the parents' hopes were placed and who much more easily disappointed them.

Father   Many men want a boy to carry their family name and also to follow them into the same job, club etc. Some men have expressed to me their desire for a boy who will play football, while others have expressed a fear that the boy will play football and not like classical music. Depending on their own inner security, some men are able to enjoy a child who is different and to see it as an enrichment, while others feel alienated and disappointed. Rory's father belonged to the second group:

> Rory had a tough father who was a policeman and ran his family as if they were constables under his command. His sister was able to weather this because their father did not expect the same qualities in her as he demanded in his son. Rory was worried about many things. He was unsure of his gender orientation, he wanted to be a painter and he was frightened of aggression, his own as much as

anyone else's, although he was very passive. Most of all he worried because his father regarded him as a complete failure and would barely talk to him.

While many men may enjoy having a daughter and dare to show their feelings, others feel they must conceal their love. This may be in case their wife is jealous but more often because they fear that overt affection will be interpreted as sexual interest. The distance that some fathers keep is felt as lack of love by their daughters. If, at the same time, a girl has to watch her brother having a close relationship with his father, she will feel that the only valued sex is the male sex. She may then become as much like a boy as she can but is likely to resent both father and other males for their preference for each other. Deborah's and Penny's stories show different manifestations of this:

Deborah only recognised the root of her deep resentment towards her father when she saw the delight he took in playing with his grandson. She immediately had the feeling that he would not have enjoyed the rough and tumble with her in the same way when she was young but remembered that he used to do this with her brother. She had found dealing with her male contemporaries very difficult, and from late teens was watching for evidence of unequal pay and any other sort of disadvantage for women that she could find, to justify the hostility she felt to the opposite sex. I found it difficult to discuss these issues with her at first, because while she often had a just point, her anger made her unable to take an objective view until she became able to see where her feelings stemmed from.

Penny's father, to whom she was very close, disappointed her by leaving his money first to his wife and then to his children with the larger portion in trust for his son who had a family. Penny had always known that her mother loved and her father valued her brother more than her. She had not fought this but had accepted that 'men were better' and she was expected to do what they wanted. She never married although she longed for children. Since she was very attractive she had always expected to marry, but no one was ever quite right. She began to understand what had gone wrong when she explored her hidden hostile feelings to her male contemporaries. Her anger towards men and her sense that she would have to live for them had prevented her making a relationship.

Mother Mothers have a very intimate relationship with both sexes but that with sons potentially lasts longer as the girl pulls some of her interest away to be invested in her father. Nevertheless she will find it unbearable to feel that her mother loves her brother more, as Myra's story shows:

Myra heard her mother say that a mother had a special feeling for her son and was naturally distraught to hear this. I suggested that her father would equally say that he had a special feeling for a daughter but she said her mother was the one who mattered most. For some time she distanced herself from her mother and adopted her father's interests, but when she became pregnant, the shared joy of the child reunited her with her mother.

A mother may feel quite mixed about her relationships with her daughter. She may feel jealous as the girl develops and forms a close relationship with her father, or she may want her daughter to fulfil her own lost career potential and may at the same time resent her if she does. A child may then bear the burden of the mother's ambivalence.

Birth Order The predominant referral to my clinic, in many hundreds, has been the first child. This would seem to reflect the greater burden that the first child carries, whether the eldest or an only child. The other explanation could be that the first child is more able to seek the help that they need. I suspect it is a mixture of both and that the ability to seek what you need comes from learning how to survive a parent's first attempts at their job of parenting and the problems that follow.

The oldest child is the only one to have the whole attention of the family for at least 10 months and to have the sense of being the most important thing in their parents' lives. The loss of this intense attention is therefore felt more keenly than by any subsequent child. None of the others have ever expected *all* the attention. The first child will react to displacement by a sibling by finding a defence which seems to work. Generally the child will either be extra-helpful or extra-difficult. Since these are defensive reactions, if they become part of the personality they may conceal in the adult their true feelings. The extra-helpful man will want his qualities to be recognised or he may become angry, and the extra-difficult person may reveal unexpected tenderness when they feel loved.

The eldest girl may deal with loss of self-esteem by competing with her mother and later by having more children and by delighting in managing the house better. This is one defence against the resentment that is often felt by the eldest of a large family because they have been expected to support their mother in her quest for more children, which results in their having even less attention. Another defence may be for the girl to determine never to be in this position herself and to completely reject the domestic role, as Ann did:

> Ann's mother had six children and as the eldest she was expected to babysit, bath the other children and be a mother's help. She resented this and felt that she was given no attention herself. Her father was in the army and away a lot. This story was complicated by the fact that her parents were Roman Catholics,

who brought her up to feel anxious and guilty about sex while at the same time producing all these children. She turned to her next door neighbours for love and attention and would escape there as often as she could.

As soon as Ann was old enough she left home. She chose a job which meant travelling a great deal and this proved a difficulty when she finally married. Her husband wanted her to settle, and for them to have a family, but she became anxious and depressed when she felt that he was imposing a dreaded role like that of her mother upon her and she always accepted assignments to the most far-off parts of the world. She loved and wanted to please her husband but her need to feel free caused much distress to them both.

Eldest boys with mothers who believe that boys should be boys may escape the domestic burden but where they do not, they too may be less likely to want children.

The youngest has the distinction of seeming to satisfy parents who apparently need no more children. The youngest is not displaced but has to deal with other difficulties. The child may face hostility and envy from siblings at the extra attention it receives from their mother as she drags out the last babyhood that she dreads to lose. The youngest must learn either to placate the others by relinquishing its mother or to remain protected and unconfident. Just by its position the youngest feels the least competent because for a time it is. Even when grown up it can never catch its siblings who always have more experience. It often remains inarticulate because all the others speak with greater authority. However a bright youngest child, avid to compete, can seem very threatening to the child above.

Middle children have to cope with abuse and domination from the older jealous ones, and loss of mother's special protection as youngest, and have to find a way to survive the feeling of being squashed from both ends. If they have a special talent they feel all right, otherwise they may retreat into themselves and are often the ones who distance themselves from the fray and eventually from life if they are not careful.

The second child who is the same sex as the eldest has a harder time in establishing itself later on. The eldest is used to being a leader and taking the responsibility of command, and the second is used to being led and tends to feel it must do as it is are told or get bullied. Both may find adjusting to different positions in life rather difficult. This can happen with twins. One set of twins found themselves in trouble because early on they had divided the responsibilities. One had never handled money and felt quite helpless in that area but did all the talking, so that the second twin found communication with strangers very difficult but could handle finances with no trouble. When they left school

140

and separated, both they and their parents were surprised by the difficulties which were suddenly revealed.

If the sex of the second child is different then there is a different issue to deal with. There is often a lot of joy in the family when the second child is of a different sex 'one of each' so that the eldest can get the idea that it would have been better to be a different sex.

Different sex children are less directly competitive and can make use of the differences in finding a place in the family. For example, Alistair (page 114) was able to deal with the birth of his sister by thinking she was only a girl. His sister may have had to put up with condescension and being put down, but where the brother feels secure in his mother's love he can enjoy looking after his small sister and she can enjoy being looked after. This perhaps is the best combination for all concerned. The boy tolerates displacement by a girl more easily because he can maintain the idea that his mother loves him more. The girl can enjoy the support of an older brother and can admire him and then other boys in her peer group. On the other hand, if she admires her brother and wants to compete she has the excuse that she cannot quite manage this because she is younger, and so she can maintain the idea that her gender is just as good as his.

Third children who are the same sex as the older ones have a problem that parents may now be quite severely disappointed and they may reveal this, depending on their character and maturity. It may be some time before this child realises they must have been a disappointment to some extent, or the mother may unconsciously punish or even try to clothe the child as if it was a different sex. This child is often very anxious to please and may show other signs of anxiety such as immaturity of speech. Later it may take on aspects of the sex it feels was wanted. Lesley was in fact an only child but her experience shows how a child can feel unsatisfactory:

> Lesley's parents were very involved with the Cub Scout movement. From an early age she was dressed as a Cub and taken to Cub meetings where she was a 'pretend' Cub, and her sense of being a disappointment to her mother continued through her teens when it seemed as if she turned the tables and set out to disappoint her by refusing her place at university and moving away from home as soon as she could.

Another child will react to rejection by being difficult and determined never to please, like Hazel:

> Hazel grew up with the family legend that her father had not looked at her for a week after her birth when he heard she was a second girl. Hazel was a rather pushy, attention-seeking person, and her family tended to be rather afraid of her.

There was an interesting revenge on her part. When she and her sister were in their teens their father, having been extremely wealthy, lost all his money. Their mother, who had never worked in her life, had to work in the local supermarket and they moved into a small house. Hazel would not speak to him and never forgave him; when he was dying she refused to visit him. Her older sister, who had managed to feel more valued, forgave and was kind to him.

The only child The only child is a first child who suffers from being the centre of attention, not only to parents but to grandparents as well. It continues to hold this position with parents and naturally assumes this is how its life is and that this central position will continue outside. At school it is a shock not to hold a central position and to be surrounded by competitors, an experience not encountered before. There is a natural tendency to try to be 'teacher's pet', which only alienates the other children more.

The only child often goes through life with a sense of isolation and learns to deal with loneliness by setting up defence mechanisms which may continue to operate in adulthood. Joining groups often accentuates the separate feeling and most only children want to create a family of their own with whom they feel completely relaxed, because it gives them the feeling that they belong.

The only child often feels an outsider at school, and at home where the others are adults. There is no place for it within the parents' intimate world and there is no one with whom to be intimate except the family pet. This introduces envy of the parents' relationship and highlights the difficulties of the phases of sexual development already described. The only child is different from other children in that it is often more immature because it lacks experience of competition. Parents also tend to solve problems that the child would be better solving itself, which contributes to its immaturity, yet at the same time the child often seems more sophisticated than others of its age as it spends so much time with adults who are also companions and playmates. It understands and knows how to play with the adults but is quite uncertain about how to play with its peer group.

Where parents do not get on well, the only child becomes the special companion of each and has to learn early political skills to keep both happy. However, where the parents do get on well, the only child feels excluded and even unwanted.

The only child's behaviour is always very important and it tries to behave like its parents. This means it has less chance to share its normal childhood anxieties about sex, bad behaviour and aggressive feelings. On the other hand, it has parents ready to control any tendency to bad behaviour, which they do with great power. Only children do not have the advantage of the family situation where they would see that other children behave badly yet continue to be loved by parents. They tend to be more afraid of their bad behaviour which seems worse than it really is because it is only compared with adult behaviour which they assume to be good.

The only boy is usually a happy child and does not long for siblings. He is content because he is at home with his mother who satisfies him completely. The only girl, however, is usually much more discontented. She tends to blame her restlessness on her lack of siblings, whereas really it is about being at home with her mother who does not satisfy her completely. Her father is often not around very much and so she feels frustrated. This causes her to look for other means of satisfaction but she may not find it easy to feel part of a group.

The positive factors of being an only child are useful for society in that, unless totally overindulged, only children are usually conscientious, faithful, sensible and self-sufficient. They make good employees, husbands, wives and parents.

Twins The subject of twins can only be touched upon because of the complexity of the relationship. All twins have the problem of an unusually long close relationship which, for fulfilment of their individual personalities, must at some time be relinquished. This tight bond means that for many, the usual competitive jealousies feel very threatening, and they have to deal with extra anxiety about the love/hate aspect of their relationship. Later, when one forms an intimate relationship with someone else, the twin left behind can feel distraught in their anger and sense of rejection. The one who goes may feel guilty and this may interfere with their new relationship.

There are many different twin combinations and many different types of parents. Some parents, sensitive to the problems, will make sure their twins are dealt with as individuals. Others, more seduced by the chic of twins dressed the same, may foster the worst elements of the situation.

The best combination is non-identical mixed sex twins who are likely to have less hositility and fewer problems with their sense of identity. Non-identical twins of the same sex have less problems with identity than identical twins, but may have considerable problems with competitiveness. Identical twins have the strongest bond to break, and one or other or both is likely to feel guilt and loss and difficulty in completely focusing on another partner. Brenda's story shows how this can work:

143

Brenda was the dominant identical twin throughout her school days. She was cleverer, more popular, and more loved by the teachers than her sister, who was naughtier and did not work so hard. Brenda went to Cambridge to do a degree while her less clever sister became a social worker. While at Cambridge Brenda became very anxious and was unable to fulfil her academic promise. She was unused to the strong competition at university and lost the comparison with her sister which allowed her to feel superior. She became very jealous of her sister who was doing well in her job and had met the man she later married. Their roles of success had been reversed and Brenda found it more and more difficult to tolerate.

It was made harder by the fact that while her sister had not been good at school she had always been happier with their parents. Now Brenda found herself unsuccessful both at home and outside. When she did eventually find a man herself, many of the tensions eased.

The Gene Factor   This is not a place to debate complex issues of nature versus nurture, however we can make a broad assumption that our genes will give a general structure to our body and also have a marked say in our temperament and the way we will tend to cope with things. This will obviously have an effect on the relationships we make, not least the first relationships. For example, you may look like your mother but have your father's temperament, with a sister who looks like your father but has your mother's temperament. If you are a girl in this situation you and your father may understand each other but not get on as well your sister and your father, since if your sister reacts to things like your mother, he will know how to deal with that because he chose your mother to live with. Some people are narcissistic and love a similar partner, but on the whole we get on with someone who offsets our qualities rather than shares them.

A boy who is temperamentally like his mother is likely to get on well with his father but have difficulties with his mother, while a boy who is temperamentally like his father will get on well with his mother but may find the relationship with father particularly difficult. If father and son are both aggressive there may be many fireworks, and if they are both passive they may never communicate. This idea applies to siblings as well. Siblings who are temperamentally different tend to get on better than those who are temperamentally alike.

Death of a Sibling   One situation which makes for more difficulties than all the rest is where a sibling dies. Many people who have experienced this have been left with problems that affect their later

relationships. Again we face a situation in which there are many permutations. The main issues involved are listed below:

1. Loss of a child is something parents cannot ever quite recover from.
    They will usually learn to deal with their grief, but they will be
    changed. Obviously this will affect the remaining children.
2. Where siblings have had a particularly difficult time with jealousy,
    they will have often longed to be rid of their sibling, and will there-
    fore have the problem of much guilt to deal with. For example:

> Amelia was a stiff correct girl who enunciated very clearly, dressed immacu-
> lately and was careful and wary about what we discussed. Her younger brother
> by three years was the 'star' of the family. He was recognised by his school and
> the local paper as a potential tennis champion at the age of six, but in the same
> year he died of encephalitis. Naturally his parents were distraught. Amelia, who
> had already chosen her defence of 'perfection' and helpfulness to her parents to
> deal with this favourite, found herself locked even further into this defence with
> the need to be satisfactory for her parents and of some worth. As she grew up
> her brother remained in the full glory of the six-year-old who would never disap-
> point, fail 'A' levels, take drugs, or smoke, and she was emotionally crippled by
> this icon. She went to university and married but stayed very involved with her
> parents, did not enjoy sex and felt very mixed about whether to have a child.
> After several years of these deliberations she found she could not get pregnant
> once she had decided to. She recognised that part of her was reluctant to produce
> another boy for her parents to idolize at the same time as she wanted to please
> them. Her inability to conceive then began to feel like another failure to achieve
> the recognition she longed for. However, finding that I could help her to face
> and understand the envy of her brother, of which she was so ashamed, freed her
> in many ways. Until then she was very tied to her parents, hoplessly trying to
> compensate for her bad feelings and to be perfect so that they would love her.
> She was able to separate more from them and even feel resentment that they had
> not valued her more. Her investment in her husband became proportionally
> greater and she started to get on with her life as a more relaxed person.

3. The lost sibling is likely to become idealised so that none of the rest
    feel they can compete. This may mean that remaining siblings sense
    that it is hopeless to try to make their mark by being good; as a result
    they will cause difficulties, be rebellious and have regular conflicts
    with their parents.
4. The grief of parents may have been terrifying and the need to try to
    make recompense may block a child's own development. For
    example:

> The death of Fatima's brother left a great burden for her to carry. Her parents had
> taken great pride in his entry to university to study law and she felt that she must
> do the same, both for their sake and also as she felt it would be the only way to

gain their attention. She did this but had many problems with personal relation-ships, as she felt that to get married would mean that she would not prosper in her career and that this must be her priority.

5. The loss of an older sibling, who has perhaps taken on a parental role and been a 'protector', can give rise to a relatively straightfor-ward grief reaction in a younger sibling. Other children, in dealing with their grief at the loss of someone who is also a friend, may be confused by an additional burden of guilt because of an element of satisfaction in losing a rival.
6. Early in life these siblings are having to question why their brother or sister has died and not them. Is someone being punished for something they have done – is it the parents or the child? How careful must they now be to avoid meeting the same fate?
7. Parents are usually preoccupied with fear of their childrens' deaths, and sometimes torment themselves about which they could bear the least or which could be tolerated the most easily. Equally, after a disaster when a sibling has died, the other children ask themselves if their parents would not have preferred the death to be theirs.

The effect of all these situations is that children may feel that they must be especially good, both to help their parents and to prevent anything bad happening to themselves. Fears about their sexual interest may be increased if they are in that particular phase of development. Fears arising from their emotional experiences may make it difficult for them to become too attached to anyone. Seeing so much pain at the loss of loved ones makes these children wary about life and their future in a way that most are spared until they are older. This can affect the invest-ment they will make in others as they go through life. Many who are brought face to face with death early on choose to protect themselves from further loss by remaining uninvolved, a defence which they are likely to suffer from later.

Key Points

♦ The quality of the relationship between the parents is of paramount importance to the child

♦ Position in the family plays a greatly underrated part in the devel-opment of the individual.

PART IV

The Gender Dialectic

9

Gender Roles

Problems of Gender

Usually we use the word 'sex' when distinguishing males and females; we talk of 'the two sexes' and 'the opposite sex'. By the term 'gender' I mean the inner feelings, ideas and attitudes a person has about membership of one or the other sex.

This chapter is about the conflict between the sexes caused by the difference in gender roles. It explores the development and reasons for this conflict, and traces the historical influences which persist in a destructive way in both society and the family. It examines the effect of gender conflict on sexual relationships and seeks to differentiate between good and bad ways of dealing with the issues.

Problems with gender roles emerge from a negative attitude formed in response to a natural circumstance. Most people satisfactorily adjust to their own gender, but for others the same universal facts seem more or less intolerable, with unhappy consequences.

Since dissatisfactions originate in early childhood we again have to put ourselves in the shoes of very young children of both sexes. We must try to understand how the painful emotions arise which lead a child to develop defence mechanisms to alleviate their unhappiness. As always, such defence mechanisms produce some immediate relief of unpleasant feelings, but often create problems in the long term. Since a sexual problem usually arises out of a defence mechanism retained from childhood, it is vital to understand what particular factors, both in society and in the individual, allow one person to mature contentedly in their gender while another is angry and rejecting.

The issue of gender causes more anger and resistance than anything else in sexual counselling. Hinting that someone might envy either the opposite sex in general, or a despised or idealised sibling in particular, can provoke considerable turbulence. On more than one occasion women have walked out of counselling sessions when I have merely asked them to consider the possibility that they might envy men. These women were so angered by and resistant to my suggestion that they were not even able to discuss it. Such force of feeling can be very destructive to a heterosexual relationship and in some cases can completely prevent a relationship with a partner of the opposite sex. It is important for us to understand where such a powerful feeling originates.

Noticing the Difference

In the child, before the act of sex is known about, the fact of sexual difference is perceived. The social significance of having or not having a penis is gradually assimilated through experiences in the society of the child's particular home, and determines whether the child feels positive or negative about its body and therefore itself. This will be discussed more fully in the next section. At this point it is necessary to emphasize that such feelings, and therefore the child's attitude to sex and gender, are all linked to a bodily fact: to have, or not to have, the penis.

There is a moment of perception during our early development when we notice for the first time the other sex, significantly named the 'opposite' sex. This oppositeness is of great significance in sexual problems. At some point there is a sudden realisation in the child that there are other children, similar in almost every way, but with one part which is very different. This involves a quite momentous act of noticing, which has great consequences because it poses the questions of 'why?' and 'for what?'. The age at which this happens varies according to circumstances of environment, culture and intelligence, but there is no doubt that for everyone there is a time when we recognise that there are two sexes and that they have an important anatomical difference. However, each sex has to cope with very different stresses arising from this perception.

Boys and Young Men

For boys, anxiety is the main issue. The boy suddenly sees a child, like himself but without the penis with which he enjoys playing, and it looks as if the other child has had its penis removed. The boy's logical mind assumes that this has been deliberately done by authority figures, usually parents, and he is concerned about how this occurred in case it should happen to him. Psychologists call this 'castration anxiety'. The boy will wonder if bad behaviour, such as too much playing with the penis, might have been the reason. An accident or even a war may come to mind as well. This last may seem rather bizarre, but one of my sons asked if his sister had been in a war when he first saw her without clothes. Even the idea of an accident is complicated by the fact that at a very early age the child believes the parents to be so powerful that they could prevent accidents if they wanted to, so if an accident occurs the parents must have allowed it to happen. Even in some adult minds this idea is retained, in a slightly different shape, when they feel that accidents are really punishments by God.

Wherever the boy's reasoning takes him, it leads to anxiety about the power of parents and his own vulnerability. As we have seen, this kind of experience leads to the formation of an attitude. In this case the perception of the vulnerability of his penis stays with the boy, in an increasingly hidden way, throughout his life. We will see later how castration anxiety can sometimes be so strong that it pervades his development, first under his mother's influence and later his father's. As a teenager, he fears his mother's distaste for his wet dreams and masturbation. As a young adult he fears that his penis may be unacceptable to women, which inhibits him from making or responding to sexual approaches. If his anxiety is confirmed by a woman's rejection, his confidence will be reduced further. This can make young men passive, unable to initiate and unwilling to persuade, thereby spoiling an important part of successful male sexuality.

As with all problems caused by emotion, it is the degree of anxiety which matters as well as the context in which it is experienced. In the context of a happy environment where all other feelings of value and security are strong, the anxiety will have relatively little effect. However, where parents are immature or over-dominating, the child feels fundamentally insecure and extra anxiety will have a powerful effect.

To sum up, the first sight of a naked girl creates an idea of the possibility of castration in the mind of a boy and thereby induces anxiety. The anxiety concerns what might happen to his penis if he is not careful. He develops defence mechanisms to relieve the unpleasant feeling of anxiety, which work so well that by the time he is an adult he is usually unaware of the anxiety's existence.

As always with anxiety, the attempts to relieve it can sometimes have effects which, in the long-term, are worse than suffering the original anxiety. For instance, one defence against a sense that parents do not like masculinity is to act in the most unmasculine way possible, because the reduction in masculinity produces a corresponding reduction in anxiety, so it seems best to be like a girl. This may relieve anxiety in boyhood, but if it becomes an entrenched part of an individual's character, potency as an adult will be lost. Depending on the strength of the defence the adult may be impotent, uninterested in sex or, in some cases, effeminate.

Girls and Young Women

A girl has a very different problem to cope with when she first sees a boy's penis. At one moment she is happy and used to her body, and the next moment she becomes aware that there is something missing. She wonders why the boy has something which she does not, and she tries to work out why she has been deprived.

The most common time for this to occur is when a girl first sees a small boy urinate. In the necessarily rather restricted early life of a child, with its emphasis on bodily functions generally, successful retention and elimination is rated highly by mother and therefore by the child. The ease with which a boy can urinate, compared with a girl's annoying need to partly undress, to be held over public lavatories or to squat and maybe wet her shoes, throws into focus the sheer practical advantage of the male anatomy in this respect.

The girl's first attitude to the recognition of gender difference, therefore, is a sense of practical disadvantage which leads to feelings of envy. This leads to the phrase 'penis envy' which causes so much misunderstanding and sometimes almost hysterical rejection as an idea among those adults who feel the need to deny any envy.

The defence mechanism of denial is a common response to envy, and denial is often fortified by investing the envied object with dislike and hatred. If this particular defence is used, young women will find it very difficult to see anything to admire in the male body. Their feelings may be concentrated on envy of his social status and resentment of womens' unfair position. I saw a very clear example of this when I was in a seminar for a group of psychotherapy trainees who were discussing the subject. One woman became very angry, and said 'Who would want that disgusting excrescence stuck on their body anyway?'; she then left the room in a rage.

The recognition of the fact of not having a penis has both short and long-term implications. In the short term, because children are very possessive and find it painful to accept that they cannot have something which others have, the girl feels envious. From this moment on she monitors the differences between boys and girls, weighs the advantages and disadvantages and potentially becomes disappointed with her position. Promises of breasts in the bush are no compensation for a penis in the hand! This affects her relationships with the boys she envies. From the symbolism of this small practical disadvantage can develop a long-term prejudice which slants the attitude of the young woman to the various social, biological and even spiritual differences which she discovers. After all, the Pope has ruled for ever against the ordination of women.

The girl looks for logical explanations and, in keeping with her experience of her mother as all-powerful, may feel that her mother deprived her of a penis and spoiled her chance of being a boy. There are four possible reasons for this which occur to girls. The first is that they have been punished for a known or unknown crime. The second is that their mother envied them because she herself had wanted to be a boy. The third is that the mother needed another female to help in the home, and this may be particularly felt by an eldest girl. The fourth is that the mother disliked boys and so forced the child into being a girl. Whichever reason is chosen, the result is some tension with the mother and a likely increase in the attention to the father, which as we have seen is just about to happen around this time anyway.

The Penis

Fifty per cent of the population have been endowed with this organ which not only differentiates them from the other half but has seemed, as far back as history records, to symbolise power and domination. It is, of course, this symbolism which reinforces strong feelings about what is otherwise just a natural feature with particular physiological functions.

The psychological problems which arise from the issue of anatomical differences come from the fact that these differences determine, to a large extent, physical power and activity, reproductive contribution and social role. Many women and men resent this fact, and in resenting it, may try to fight or even deny it. The differences between the sexes which are apparent at birth immediately determine differences in the way in which boys and girls are brought up and viewed in society. In this way differences of upbringing add on to inbuilt physical ones to increase the differences between the sexes.

It is a fact that a person's initial inheritance of certain chromosomes determines the development of physiological differences of genitalia, muscle, skin, bone and some brain factors between the sexes, by controlling the production of hormones which act on the foetus as it is growing.

Men are bigger and more powerful physically, their reproductive role is to penetrate and factors in their brain mean they are better at certain types of problem solving than women. Women are better at other types of problem solving, are less sensitive to pain and are more likely to survive both as babies and adults. They have to be strong enough to accept impregnation and the risk and responsibility of childbearing.

These differences produce different attitudes of mind. Men and women are differentiated by more than just anatomy. The penis is the totem of all the other differences and, like a totem, provokes an instinctive reaction as a symbol of authority. People in authority (whether men or women) are normally envied and will incite one of two opposite reactions: submission or revolt. The instinctive reaction to the penis, as a symbol of authority, is similar. Where either submission or revolt is too dominant, sexual problems arise.

These physical and attitudinal differences lead to a sense of unfairness, which is largely where the conflict springs from. Everyone is interested in fairness but each sex also has its own particular concerns which must be dealt with separately. These are anxiety, in the case of men, and envy, in the case of women. Of course men also experience envy and women also experience anxiety, but it is men's anxiety and women's envy which are at the root of most sexual problems.

Injustice

Families, as we have seen, are places of inbuilt unfairness where children each want the most love and the most attention for themselves. They watch like hawks for indications of what, why and who gets the best position or the best piece of food. The older child may do things that the younger child cannot, like staying up later in the evening, and the younger child cannot always be consoled by the thought that its turn will come. The younger child gets more nurturing than the older one on any given day, because its need is greater, and it is often no comfort to the older child that it used to receive as much nurturing when it was as young. Boys may be allowed more freedom than girls, and girls may be given more protection in disputes. The apparent injustices are endless. Children are very concerned with fairness generally for two reasons. The first is that, like adults, they want to have what they see that others have. The second is that parents and teachers teach social interaction through the idea of fairness, using methods like taking turns and counting out sweets to give equal shares.

We are concerned here with the particular injustices brought about by gender. If children feel unfairly treated or unloved because of their sex, this will affect their attitude to their own gender and to the opposite sex, which may lay the foundation for later gender-related sexual problems. Since parents were once children themselves, they bring into the family the remnants of their own experiences in childhood, which will affect their behaviour and may produce a particularly unfair situation for their children. For instance, a child may actually be undervalued by a parent because it is not of the desired sex, and in such a case the child would wish to be what they are not and cannot be.

There are many examples of parental behaviour leading to a child's sense that it belongs to the inferior sex. I have seen many girls who were brought up to understand that they were worth less than their brothers. One example was where a son had been sent to a private school and the equally intelligent daughter to the local comprehensive. In another case the sons in the family were given larger portions of food than the daughters, and one girl I saw had to do her brothers' ironing. One of the most famous examples of gender injustice was that of Vita Sackville West having to relinquish her family house at Knole, in which she was brought up, to a male cousin. It is impossible for a girl to avoid feeling less valuable than boys in such situations. Girls will develop defence mechanisms in an attempt to compensate.

On the other hand, girls may be valued more highly than boys, perhaps because either the mother or father finds girls less threatening than boys, or perhaps because the daughter is cleverer or more attractive than her brother. A boy who, rightly or wrongly, assumes that he would have been more loved had he been a girl, is going to have difficulty valuing his own gender. His resulting envy of women will lead him to develop compensatory defence mechanisms.

A longed-for boy with several older sisters can be in a particularly vulnerable position. Because of the delighted reactions of parents and family, the sisters have to cope with a sense that the awaited messiah has arrived. They want to punish him for this. Of course they are expected to be just as delighted as their parents, and to act like little mothers, with the result that a combination of bossiness, caring and viciousness is experienced by the young boy. Ian's story shows how this can lead to problems:

Ian saw his older sisters as so powerful that he wished to be one of them. The girls had a joint bedroom and Ian was excluded from the whispered secrets they were always sharing in there, and he desperately longed to join them. This resulted in his rejection of his body and the development of a phobia about taking his clothes off in front of others in case they should see his penis. This disrupted his school life and isolated him from his peers. He refused to join in games because of the customary communal shower afterwards. Later when other boys were going through puberty, he did not. He did not remember being concerned about this and he was 17 before he developed and accepted his masculinity. After this he changed in personality and became aggressively athletic and took up dangerous sports, probably to compensate for years of wanting to be a 'cissy'.

Gender differences are likely to be a source of tension to most people at some time. They will only lead to relationship or sexual problems if there has been significant unfairness of the kind described above. To understand more about the way in which such problems are experienced and express themselves, we need to consider in some detail two universal sets of factors which influence all of us. The first set is concerned with the way in which gender differences are first perceived by a child, and can help to explain why, on the whole, gender-related problems in women are experienced as envy and in men as anxiety. The second set is to do with the way that society defines different roles for men and women and the way in which these definitions have been changing over the last hundred years. Taken together, these factors create the mould which shapes our attitudes to differences between the sexes and shapes our gender itself.

Conflict between the Sexes

As we have seen, the gender issue begins with the realisation that some people have something which others don't have. As with the unfair distribution of money, social status, beauty or intelligence, some accept their lot but others do not and are determined to equalise or reverse the inequality. It is a fact that we are divided into two groups depending on whether we have or don't have a penis, and that we have no choice about membership of our group and no chance to alter our label (without gross distortion). This causes some resentment in most people and much resentment in those sensitised to the issue by events in their childhood.

The most physically powerful group has dominated society for centuries, with the result that they are seen as the first division. To be in any second division is obviously felt as less prestigious than to be in the first; some women, who find this an unacceptable pill to swallow, have a priority aim of altering the system.

It is perhaps obvious that women fear and resent being physically weaker and therefore more vulnerable to violence and rape. It is this sense of helplessness that causes the fundamental anger about the inequality, which tends to be dealt with either by fighting hard to be as tough as a man or by passively adhering to a man who will then do the fighting. Thus men find many women either aggressive or dependent and, in today's society, increasingly and confusingly, both.

On the other hand, men have had to face the fact that with strength and power comes extra responsibility: first, to control extra muscle power wisely, and secondly to accept social responsibility for biological acts resulting in children. Not all men have been willing to take on this burden, and some have envied women their apparently more protected role and have resented providing the protection that they feel is demanded of them.

Overall, compulsory membership of a group may confer specific advantages which, when viewed from the other group, become particularly desirable. This creates resentment which leads to conflicts or power games. Individual conflicts or games can have many different outcomes and it is not, of course, always sheer strength that wins. Skill and cunning, as in David's battle with Goliath, and less obvious tactics such as weakness and illness, can create very powerful game winners.

With all these very negative attitudes around, it is not surprising that it is difficult for people from different groups to form intimate relationships with one another. The factor which can neutralise these negative aspects of gender is sexual attraction and sexual fulfilment. This is why if there is a sexual problem interfering with this healing process, it is much more difficult to make the relationship work without a conflict or a game to be won being in progress. Where such a sexual problem is itself due to the gender issue, a vicious circle emerges, because resentment about sexual differences diminishes the sexual attraction and good feelings which are necessary for sexual intercourse to be successful. Avoidance of sexual intercourse because it evokes unpleasant feelings then prevents its neutralising effect from healing the resentments of everyday life.

The big question is how to take away the element of game-playing with its corollary of winners and losers. To do this we need to understand more about the power struggle.

Power

As we have seen, problems with gender arouse envy, particularly for women though also for men. The envy is of the other person's power. In other words, the gender issue is about power.

More women envy men than the other way around. Yet to some

extent this may be deceptive for two reasons: first, that women are prepared to voice their resentment about inequality, and second, that it has not been part of men's tradition to admit to emotional vulnerability in any form including envy. However, in respect of power a man may come to envy the power of a woman who can arouse him and therefore make him feel vulnerable, particularly if she denies him access to her. For instance, one of the most effective ways in which a woman can make a man feel powerless is to be sexually unarousable when he feels aroused by her. This is a common state of affairs due to his different hormonal drive, but it is clearly within women's scope to use it as a weapon of power, and it can be a way of emphasising that she is desirable and he is not. Traditionally this has been the only weapon available to physically fragile women, and it still seems to be operating despite changes in society.

The strategy is about how to feel less vulnerable by making the other person less powerful. The oblique approach I sometime take to make this point arises from people's frequent resistance to the implication that they want to be powerful. They feel as if I am accusing them of a kind of despotism and rarely recognise themselves that way. However, they usually accept the idea that they hate feeling powerless and are able to feel moral justification in fighting their powerlessness. There is an interesting illustration of this in the film *The Godfather*:

> The character Michael feels powerful enough to distance himself from the unsavoury aspects of his family, until he is enraged when his father is made vulnerable by being gunned down in the street. At that point he cannot tolerate his increasing sense of his own powerlessness and vulnerability. He compensates for it by developing a powerful defence: attack. By the end, this defensive power takes him over: he loses all judgment and seeks to destroy everyone.

This sort of shift can also happen in a sexual relationship. For example, many women who find their partner has been unfaithful cannot rest until they, too, have 'scored'. They often have to let the partner know of their infidelity whereupon the partner feels justified in punishing them as well. A deadly power game ensues, with no winners, as love turns to hate. For example:

> Wendy knew when she married Hugh that he frequently had to go away on business. On their honeymoon he told her that he wanted to feel free to have other liaisons on his trips abroad and that she was free to do the same. They were to regard their relationship as the secure foundation of their lives with the added bonus of a sense of freedom.
>
> Wendy had been very hurt when her father deserted his family for another woman when she was a teenager, and she had hoped to heal this wound with

her marriage. She was, therefore, particularly shattered by Hugh's proposal. She decided to 'beat him at his own game'. In fact he was largely loyal to her but she became very promiscuous.

Wendy felt that she had lost her love on her honeymoon and was seeking to regain it through her various affairs. She finally found love, but with a man who was married and had several children. Much distress was caused all round with the man having to decide whether or not to leave his family. Eventually he decided to stay with his wife. Wendy made a suicide attempt but was saved. Her marriage to Hugh ended.

There are many such games of attack and defence. They all show that each sex believes the other to be more powerful in some way and therefore feel the need to defend themselves against this power. The basic failure to understand that we may be seen by our partners as powerful and threatening, despite our own feelings of vulnerability, creates havoc by provoking inappropriate defensive reactions. All too often, as in Wendy's story above, the pre-emptive strike is the norm.

The mating process in birds brings home the power paradox very strongly. Beautiful peacocks, in all their splendid plumage, strut magnificently to impress the little brown hens. Other birds dance, sing, or demonstrate their nest-building ability to their potential mates. In these fervent seductions, who is the powerful one? Is it the dynamic male or the choosy female?

Social Roles

We have looked at the way in which the initial perception of gender difference can set the scene for later problems if it is accompanied by a strong sense of unfairness. We now need to look at the second major set of factors which affect all of us: the ways in which society defines different roles for men and for women.

Roles exist in every society and, like our remote ancestors, it is still necessary for us to use the skills of individuals to the best advantage for the survival of the species as a whole. However, as survival is a less immediate issue for most of us in the Western world, what constitutes 'best advantage' becomes more debatable. With more security and prosperity, individuals become more demanding and less accepting of social control over their lives.

In societies where survival is difficult and resources low, the allocation of work becomes crucial. The knowledgeable older people do the 'thinking' jobs and the physically fit younger people do the dangerous jobs requiring strength. At the heart of such a society lies the need to produce, care for and protect the children who are the new generation and represent hope for the future. A woman's biology demarcates her role: she has weaker muscles and is less physically suited to hunting and defence, but she is physiologically stronger, enabling her to take on the main internal danger of the group, which is childbirth. The man's role, therefore, is to impregnate his partner and protect her and their children. Men are precious because they can easily be lost in the dangerous pursuits of fighting and hunting.

The need for a constant stream of protectors and, later in history, workers on the land, meant that boys were valued more highly than girls. Indeed baby girls were frequently left to die because they needed to be fed and protected but were not useful in getting food or protecting the community. This valuing of boys over girls has had dire consequences, as we shall see below.

Where men and women need each other in order to survive, their separate and different qualities are highly valued. Thus resentfulness over role is in inverse proportion to adversity. In the past, men were revered because as warriors and hunters they were prepared to sacrifice themselves for the community; women were revered for the risks and pain suffered in childbirth. As women come to share the hunter function, and reproduction is less important because mother and child are more likely to survive so that fewer pregnancies are necessary, everything begins to change.

The anatomical features of sex had led to gender roles in our society which were traditional, expected and accepted by the majority. In the last hundred years particularly, and especially during two world wars, traditional roles have had to be relinquished. As always, when rigid rules are relaxed, it is difficult to put them back into force. Women were encouraged to do jobs which were previously only given to men, their self-esteem rose as their work was valued, and this experience changed both the way they were thought of by men and the way they thought about themselves. There was no going back.

Advances in technology have also brought about great changes in gender roles. Technology makes rigid role-taking unnecessary because men no longer have to be physically strong to do most work and women can do it just as well. Equally, with large families no longer necessary for security due to medical advances and better rates of child survival, the family can have greater prosperity if both parents work. Prosperity took over from survival as the priority issue as both men and women discovered the charms of a shared income and the luxury of vocation and inclination in the choice of work.

Thus anatomy, role and survival have, in our past, been inextricably linked. Many relationship difficulties in the present stem from the fact that they are no longer linked in this way. The changes that society experienced when immediate survival stopped being the priority and women joined ranks with men has led, to some extent, to trouble in those ranks.

When we felt we needed the opposite sex more, we valued it more, and we valued the differences which would ensure our needs were met. Independence reduces our need of each other and we desire, and are able to demand, the other role for ourselves instead of sharing in it through a relationship with a member of the opposite sex. Thus, once differences are no longer valued they become objects of envy. We saw in Chapter 5 that dependency can itself be a destructive force, where too much need prevents a person from knowing what they truly wish for. While freedom from dependency promotes freedom of choice, it produces a problem when a relationship gets into difficulties. This problem is that if the partner is not needed, too much effort to maintain the relationship is not worth it. The survival of relationships now depends on the individual recognising that, while they are free and able to exist alone, on balance it is better to put up with some frustration and compromise in order to gain all the new opportunities offered by a relationship. In this way we can value the partner again, and may even find ourselves able to admire rather than just envy the opposite sex because they contribute to our experience.

In our changed society a new understanding of roles is needed in order to understand as much as we can about envy, power, and how we cope with these central issues in relationships. In the attempt to establish greater fairness, a degree of equality is sought. It is important for the individual and society to distinguish between equality of worth and equality of role. Attempts to establish equality of role can introduce many destructive elements into a sexual relationship. Muddling up the issues of worth and role increases bad feelings. This is because the idea of equality of social role introduces the hope of a simple solution to the envy between the sexes. However, because there can be no equality of biological role, there can be no such easy solution.

We can speculate that sex is difficult for some women who achieve positions of great power and influence. The attitude necessary to dominate and control a commercial company or a government is rather different from that conducive to enjoyment of sexual intercourse as a woman. To be able to accept the man's power to penetrate her, necessitates some psychological gymnastics after a day of her own powerful drive. These gymnastics are quite possible but many powerful women do not realise that effort is required to make the adjustment.

Self-Esteem

Roles are about position, status, activity, potential and sexual behaviour. They can contribute greatly, therefore, to a person's self-esteem. Feeling good about one's role is of vital importance to a sense of wellbeing. As we have seen, self-esteem is developed (or not) early in life as a result of feeling loved and valued by parents. Those who have high self-esteem feel valuable by definition and have less need than others endlessly to prove their value. Those with low self-esteem suffer from a sense that their parents did not love them, and therefore did not value them, and that they are potentially worth nothing unless they work very hard to compensate.

Of course men and women can both suffer from low self-esteem. However, nearly all women suffer to some extent from a specific type of low self-esteem related to their sense, in childhood, of being inferior just because of their gender.

Those with low self-esteem, for whatever reason, are going to be very sensitive about their own and their partner's role. Competitive roles clearly make for tension within a relationship. In any partnership where a career is shared, a great success for one may cause difficulty for the other if their own need for success is very strong. I have often seen this with actors, whose lifestyle usually leads them to partner other actors, and who have, by definition, a need for centre stage which it is difficult for both to hold in the same measure.

Many people try to force their partner into a role with which they themselves can feel comfortable. This often produces great ambivalence since a woman with low self-esteem may try to relieve her problem by marrying a socially successful man, thus making her successful by association. Yet this highlights the problem of her need to feel personally successful: paradoxically, therefore, she is threatened by the success of her partner. We saw a similar process in action in Les's story in Chapter 5. In other cases a socially successful individual chooses a socially unsuccessful partner in order to enjoy a sense of superiority, only to find that their partner unexpectedly becomes successful and competitive. This happened to Edith and Ken:

> When Edith married Ken, she was a rather disorganised art student and he was an intellectual of some standing in his university. They had three children before serious cracks began to develop in their relationship. Edith resented the fact that Ken withdrew from her to his books while she coped with home, children and a developing career as a graphic artist in which she became much in demand.
>
> Edith's power grew and she began to earn more than Ken. Instead of being

pleased with the additional money, Ken grumbled that she did not charge enough. Her success in every field made him feel more and more helpless and inadequate and more and more angry. She responded to this by investing in all parts of her life except him and he started to 'drop out' of the family as he felt the children turning away from him.

The rot stopped when Edith and Ken examined together the issue of their power struggle. Edith saw that she had to concentrate on valuing Ken, and he in turn saw how his understandable distress caused him to react in a way which increased his sense of alienation.

It is not so long ago that women were thought to have no soul, to have greatly inferior brains and to exist solely to serve and comfort men. Women were virtually possessions and were therefore, depending on class, either slave or ornament. One of the problems of today, being so near to yesterday, is that many men and women still believe this to be the natural order of things. Most people at least half believe it, and very few are not influenced by it at all. There is, therefore, a constant struggle in society for women to prove, not just to others but also to themselves, that these remnants of past attitudes are misconceptions. The home-making role has come to be identified with the traditional image of women and has thus been devalued. Today it is seen as a less powerful role than that of the career woman because failure to earn money produces a dependence on the male provider which is very reminiscent of the woman's traditional role of bygone days.

It does not yet seem to be possible for people to perceive themselves as a partner equal in value unless they are also equal in role. While the traditionally female roles of home-making and caring remain devalued they cannot be seen by women or men as valuable roles which anyone may take up for part or all of their adult life. In reality these roles may be less or more powerful than traditional male roles, depending on the attitudes of the individual personalities involved and the satisfactions achieved. The perception is, however, still that the traditionally male roles of working and earning money are the most powerful and there-fore the most desirable. This leads to a tendency to believe that the most valuable people, whether men or women, are those who take up these roles.

This is obviously a complex issue. In terms of human rights, women have the right to take up interesting careers and to have the same influ-ence and power as men in the workplace. Equally, men have the right to look after children and elderly relatives, and to have the same influ-ence and power as women in the home. However, it is important for successful heterosexual relationships that the essential qualities of masculinity and femininity do not get lost in the pursuit of equality.

Masculinity and femininity are emotive words and are not mutually exclusive in terms of individuals. I am using them here solely to refer to the characteristics at the core of each gender which must be valued by the other gender if sexual relationships are to succeed.

Clearly, it is not easy to resolve the contradictory pulls of home and workplace, and simple solutions to complex issues rarely work. However, unless a role in the home is seen to be of value, nobody will be objective in deciding their priorities. Women's need to prove their parity with men may lead them to choose traditionally male roles for that reason alone. Thus the pursuit of free choice of role hides a trap in the need to reject traditionally female roles because of their second-class associations. If a woman's need to achieve in this way is very powerful, it will dominate her nature and divorce her from the unique satisfactions of the female role.

An inevitable sequel to women's demands for equality of role is that some men, seeing their sovereignty slipping away, hang on tightly to the traditional role which they feel is theirs by right. This situation is bound to cause conflict with any partner, especially one determined to show that men have no special rights at all. Sensitivity and overcompensation on both sides make it all too easy for a couple to throw a relationship away rather than throw away a defended principle. For instance, getting a meal for a man can seem, to the woman, too demeaning and slave-like, while for the man to iron his own shirts can represent the loss of all power and authority. The result, for such a couple, is that every issue becomes a point of honour to be fought over. This can have disastrous consequences for a sexual relationship, as Tracey's story shows:

> Tracey was born in the 1960s but was still expected to iron her brothers' shirts and be in by 10 p.m. while the boys in the family were allowed to stay out until midnight. This mixture of domestic slavery and overprotection, while submitted to as a teenager, produced much conflict in adulthood. Tracey had a mixture of guilt if not playing the full domestic role and rage if she did.
>
> In her conversations she constantly deferred to her husband's opinion and dared not stand by her own – yet she was rejecting sexually and always slightly cross with him.

In a situation like this it is difficult for the partner ever to get it right.

Power and role, then, are of greater importance for those with low self-esteem. Since gender is so closely related to power and role, then conflict over gender is likely to be greater for those with low self-esteem. We have seen that women's self-esteem is lowered by their sense of being inferior just because of their gender, so women have extra resentment to start with. So, fundamental problems in sexual relationships result from three things:

- Our early experiences of the attitude of our parents to gender
- A sense of personal vulnerability created by the first perception of anatomical difference
- Changes in social roles

These have three main consequences:

- A feeling that the opposite gender is powerful and needs defending against
- Power games within relationships
- Changed expectations about social roles, particularly for women

All of these situations can manifest themselves as gender conflict within sexual relationships.

Gender Conflict and Sex

Although men and women can sometimes now seem to get on better than they ever have at a social and professional level, due to greater discussion and understanding, there is still a long way to go. For those who are sensitive to gender issues, sexual activity can be particularly troublesome. This is because defensive attempts to deny difference between the sexes, which may be effective at other times, fail when individuals are confronted by the act of sexual intercourse. The reason is that intercourse exposes anatomical difference and any defensive attempt to deny gender difference will be thwarted. Apart from being pregnant, giving birth and breastfeeding, the act of sexual intercourse is the only one which clearly and unequivocally demonstrates the different role that anatomical features impose. Heterosexual intercourse, therefore, is the experience which confronts adults most powerfully with the reality of gender difference.

Since sexual intercourse requires us to reveal and use those parts of the body which determine gender, this means having to face an emotional issue which can be an irritant. Angry feelings about gender difference may be suppressed most of the time if during the day the person feels valued or does an important job. For those who wish to see it that way, it is nowadays possible to be convinced that there is virtually no difference between the sexes and, therefore, that all is fair and that the partner can be enjoyed as a companion. However, when that partner introduces the idea of sex, the sense of difference and therefore unfairness immediately appears with crushing force, and the act of sexual intercourse is found to evoke unpleasant feelings instead of the loving feelings which are expected. For example:

> Lola was representative of many women I have seen in the way she responded to pain from past hurts to do with the opposite sex. Before marriage she was very sexually responsive to her partner and had many 'clitoral' orgasms but she could see no point in actual intercourse since she felt entirely satisfied with the sensations she achieved through the clitoris.
>
> In the past she had had many friends who were boys but tended to be one of 'them' rather than relate sexually to them. When she met Eric things changed but although she loved him she now found she could not allow herself to be penetrated. She sought help after three years of marriage when Eric found he could not tolerate this situation.
>
> Lola had had a hard time as a child, as her mother had committed suicide when she was two years old and her father remarried four years later. She had got used to feeling very important to her father, and to 'looking after' him and her older brother, and felt displaced by her stepmother, Sarah, who seemed to dislike her. She had anxieties in her teens about whether she had caused her mother's death but her main problem was her stepmother's attitude to her. Her father and Sarah had a son for whom Sarah showed great preference; Sarah seemed threatened by Lola's relationship with her father and forced Lola to leave home at 16; her father was not strong enough to resist Sarah.
>
> Despite Sarah's rejection of her, Lola continually tried to please her, and even 15 years later seemed ingratiating. Sarah was very puritanical and this need to please her, together with Lola's resentment towards her half-brother and father, had caused her to resist complete commitment to her female role. She was angry with her father for letting her go and not fighting for her and she was angry with boys because she felt they were more important than she to the people she cared about.
>
> Eric was a caring man who for a long time tried to understand and support Lola but in the end could not accept her unwillingness to have sexual intercourse. By the time they came for counselling all sexual activity had ceased because it caused friction. After a few months it was reintroduced, which improved the relationship, but she still had to make the final acceptance.

Successful penetration requires some daring and confidence on the part of the man. Where conventional morality dominates, an inexperienced young man, faced with a scared young woman, will find it difficult to develop the necessary confidence to reassure both himself and his partner that pleasure is possible from this improbable act. Indeed, in the past, there was a tradition in some countries to send young men to experienced women, allowing them to learn their role in a way which would otherwise be difficult to achieve. At the beginning of his sexual career a man has to overcome fears of hurting his partner. He may also have fears about being hurt himself when he has to 'lose' his penis inside the woman's body. Apart from all these fears there is the difficulty of the sexual act itself.

At the risk of stating the obvious, I will reiterate that the man must first feel aroused before he can play his role. The arousal gives him an erection, which he must maintain while arousing his partner. Having aroused his partner, the man must penetrate her and maintain his erection for long enough to give her satisfaction through orgasm, but not for so long that she becomes bored by his own difficulty in reaching orgasm. Should he fail at any point, his failure is obvious to himself and his partner.

The woman has much more physical control of herself. Her sexual organs are largely hidden and she has the ability to reveal as much of her arousal as she chooses. She can choose to show pleasure she does not feel or lack of interest even when she is aroused. This all gives her a powerful advantage. However, she has this mysterious passage, may be unsure where it leads, and in the context of a committed relationship is expected at some point to allow the man's rather weapon-like organ to penetrate into it even if she doesn't really want to. She usually needs time to 'acquire the taste' before she can enjoy penetrative sex. Goodwill and trust are necessary for this to happen, and to learn to enjoy being penetrated requires an ability to be receptive, which is not easy for a woman who is otherwise defensively aggressive. Any envy she has of the man as someone who penetrates rather than being penetrated will affect her response to his penis.

Human beings are sensitive to their emotions and easily disturbed by anxiety, anger or fear. This makes sexual intercourse potentially a very difficult process. Each sex believes it is easy for the other, expects to be judged on their performance and starts off feeling anxious. The attitude of each to the other can make the difference between pleasant and unpleasant feelings and therefore between pleasurable or distressing sexual intercourse.

The Need for Conquest

Both sexes may be drawn to sexual intercourse by the need for conquest before or during a committed relationship. Many men raise their self-esteem through sexual conquest because for a man, persuading a woman to have sexual intercourse is a sign of his desirability. The more conquests he makes, the more valuable he feels. Similarly, the woman with low self-esteem may seek the triumph of conquest, just like a man, to right the wrongs of the past. However, the man's historical 'hunter' and 'seed sower' stereotypes still in some cultures sanction his sexual exploits, while the woman's needs are for security and a partner, and sexual intercourse may at first be payment for that. As she matures, if she continues to have sexual intercourse, she will 'acquire the taste' and learn to enjoy it.

Many women today deny this and insist that they want sex just like a man. No doubt in some cases this is so. However, it is difficult for women to be sure of what they really want while they are so determined to act the same as men. I have seen so many women over the years who have lost interest in sexual intercourse as soon as they have made their conquest and the ring is on their finger that I am sure that some, at any rate, do not have the same sexual drive as men who usually maintain their interest in sexual intercourse after marriage.

Conquest is largely achieved by making the other person feel valuable. The well-adjusted person who can genuinely admire their partner finds this easy to do and easy to sustain. For the envious person, who finds it difficult to be admiring because it seems, by comparison, to make them seem weak, this is necessarily a temporary strategy. The envious person withdraws admiration once the conquest is made, stops valuing, and punishes the partner for being powerful by withdrawing sexual favours.

Women Who Envy Men

If the envious person is a woman, she is often consciously unhappy and guilty about the sexual failure which motivates her to seek help, but she rarely realises that what she is coping with is anger at the exposure of her partner's symbol of superiority: his penis. Also, unconsciously, she wishes to avoid confirming the worth of his penis by allowing it to give her pleasure. One might say that she cuts off her clitoris to spite her vagina. Thus envy can kill any pleasure which would otherwise be there for both partners.

This produces the unbalanced situation where a man feels admiration for, and interest in, a woman while she apparently feels no interest in him and lets him know it. Showing her lack of interest is, of course, a very important part of the game, as it reduces his power by making him feel undesirable. If she lets him be desirable to her, she feels she has further lost status and reduced her own power. Angie and Dave's story shows how this can develop:

Angie had strong feelings of anxiety about sex. She had two brothers who were given freedoms which she had longed for and been denied. They were also encouraged to take up professions, but Angie's parents felt she should be a secretary while waiting to get married. This left her with a sense of being second class which she fought bitterly.

When Angie met Dave she used her religious beliefs to justify not allowing actual penetration before marriage but they made love regularly and she expected all to be well on the honeymoon. They were dismayed to find that starting on the honeymoon she was very resistant not only to penetration but to making love at all. As she no longer had any reason for denying penetration, her fear of it meant avoiding foreplay as well. Dave became angry and frustrated about the fact that he found his wife desirable and that he thought she also felt the same about him only to find she avoided him.

It took some time for Angie to explore her deep feelings about sex. She had grown up with a sense that sex was something to be done for the sake of the man and that there would not be and should not be any enjoyment in it for her. Unconsciously she rejected the female role because of this. Gradually she started to accept and develop her own sexual identity and lost her fear that in accepting the female role she would lose self-esteem and status.

In such a relationship the man is always pursuing and feeling rejected and the woman is always feeling persecuted and resentful of his overtures. It is interesting, however, that of hundreds of women in this situation who I have asked if they would prefer their partners to be impotent, never has the reply been 'yes'. These women are frequently mystified by the illogicality of their own reply, but the reason is that their partner's impotence would preclude their satisfaction in denying him their arousal. There is nothing more flattening to egos or penises than genuine lack of interest!

Men Who Envy Women

If a man has a problem of impotence related to the gender issue, he is unconsciously denying the woman the ability to affect him and therefore control him. This is likely to be a man who was particularly dominated by his mother or sister as a child, was afraid of the aggressive feelings he had towards them, and who dealt with his anger in the safest way he knew: by withdrawing and becoming passive. He may well choose a dominant woman as a partner, partly because of his love for his mother, and partly because that is what he is used to and may have come to need. Unfortunately, in doing so, he recreates the need to be passive and withdrawing. If his partner becomes particularly controlling or disappoints him, he knows of no way to assert himself without showing his aggression, and so he repeats the defence mechanism of his childhood and withdraws. He may seem to be emotionally unmoved by whatever is upsetting him, but be unable to get an erection. It seems very non-aggressive to be impotent, but it manages to leave the woman helpless and frustrated by denying her the power to arouse him. Consciously he tries very hard and is extremely distressed for his own sake as well as hers, but he is nevertheless being aggressive without appearing to be. Bob's story shows how such a passive reaction can permeate life completely:

Bob, a passive man who never showed anger, married late at the age of 40. He chose Abigail for his wife, a very attractive but deeply neurotic woman who was unable to tolerate frustration and was permanently on anti-depressant tablets. He rapidly became impotent and completely uninterested in sex and this was why, ten years later, he was referred to me. Unfortunately, Bob didn't really want to improve the situation and only came because his wife wanted him to, so success wasn't very likely.

During the course of counselling Bob and Abigail came to tell of a big upset the previous weekend. Bob had taken their young daughter to the park and returned late, 30 minutes after he was due to leave with Abigail for a social event. After ten years together he knew that this would cause her great distress, and it did. I asked him whether he wore a watch and he told me that he had stopped wearing one two months before. He told me that he always knew the time to within ten minutes anyway and turned to Abigail for confirmation. He then realised that he was saying he had been late even though he knew the time. Although Bob didn't express his anger outwardly, his behaviour could still cause havoc.

Jack's story shows how effective passivity can be in controlling relationships:

Jack was a very attractive, passive man in his late thirties who had never actively sought a woman. He was always pursued by women and always potent until, for the first time, he became deeply involved with Nadia, a woman he loved. She wanted commitment and marriage from him whereupon he suddenly became impotent and remained so until the relationship ended.

Nadia became engaged to another man but, as she and Jack belonged to the same club, they met frequently and remained very attracted to each other. They could not resist making love when they met at the club and under these conditions Jack's potency was restored.

It became clear that Jack feared the power of women and had avoided commitment all his adult life. Nadia had a more than usually powerful effect, which had made him anxious, and which he had to try to control by making himself impotent. Once she belonged to someone else his anxiety was reduced and his potency restored.

Selection

Individuals with a particular set of attitudes to gender issues may well select partners whose attitudes are complementary, and provided that the polarisation is not too extreme, the union can work well. Thus a woman with a relatively strong masculine element in her personality will be attracted to a man with a relatively strong feminine element in his personality. Similarly, a man who is comfortable with his feminine side will be attracted to a woman who enjoys taking charge. However, where this process of selection has been controlled by the envies and resistances already described, problems will arise and vulnerabilities show through. Both partners contribute to the ensuing struggle.

The militant feminist is likely to feel ambivalent about sexual intercourse and want to have it only on her terms. She may, therefore, select an apparently controllable man who is relatively fearful of women and their power and who may seem less sexually demanding. What she will not immediately realise is that beneath his submissive persona he will have a lot of concealed aggression which will be difficult to deal with. Since he has submitted to an apparently dominating personality, he will have to suppress any desire to have things his own way, and store the resulting resentment. He will therefore tend to express any aggression passively. He may do this by letting his partner control everything and take all responsibility. This often produces confusion in his partner, as Charlotte and Richard's story shows:

> Charlotte got engaged to Richard when she was 28, but she was worried because her sexual interest had waned to the point of non-existence. She had had several committed relationships in which this problem always occurred; she had also had several casual partners with whom the problem never happened, although she had only ever had an orgasm through masturbation.
>
> It became clear that Charlotte's problem was not just loss of interest but the development of active resistance to sex. Her history was of a parental divorce when she was eight, an alcoholic mother and an extra-close involvement with her father. She had already had a considerable amount of counselling.
>
> Charlotte described her love for Richard and her appreciation of his tender loving nature, but also complained that he was passive and let her arrange everything. She was quickly able to see her ambivalence about her long-term partners. On the one hand, she wanted to have everything her own way, and her inability to achieve orgasm with a man expressed that controlling part of her. On the other hand, she wanted her partner to respond to the part of her which longed for a strong man like her father. After a few months in a relationship she unconsciously realised that by choosing a man she could control she had lost the possibility of an exciting partner who she could not control, and the result was

disappointment. In fact Charlotte didn't just lose interest. Because she had not developed a mature sexual need of a partner, she became hostile and resentful of having to do something which seemed to be merely for her partner's benefit. This hostility caused her to withdraw from him sexually, but her need to have a man she could control kept her with him.

Charlotte could see she made it impossible for Richard to 'win' with her. Despite her level of insight, she came to see me on her own, hoping to control the counselling without his input.

A man in such a relationship may also withdraw sexual interest. He not only seems to lose interest in sexual intercourse, but if he uses this strategy as a habit, he is actually likely to lose potency earlier in life than other men. This situation is often hidden for some time because early sexual attraction to the woman will have been strong. However, when this sexual attraction diminishes due to the friction of living together, his unconscious aggression expresses itself through lack of sexual interest. While the militant feminist does not want to have sex if she does not want it, she certainly does not want her partner to have no interest in her and feels very angry and frustrated when this happens. Lack of interest in sex in either partner is very controlling and completely dominates the couple's life in a hidden way.

In a less neurotic way a man may be content to share, rather than relinquish, power if he feels secure about himself. He may find a feisty personality more stimulating, knowing that he can stand up to her if necessary. Obviously such a secure person makes a better partner because he is less sensitive to insult and will need to play fewer games with his partner to deal with his unconscious anxieties and inadequacies. But where there are problems of the kind being considered, with unconscious emotional factors interfering with the expression of sexuality, the notion of the 'power-sharing couple' is helpful in promoting understanding.

The Power-Sharing Couple

The power sharing couple can be defined as a couple who each have a strong seam of the opposite sex in their character. They are likely both to be successful in their chosen professions and to recognise each other's independence.

My observation is that the most interesting and talented people tend to have more of the opposite sex in their character than the norm and therefore have more complicated ways of relating to a partner.

Put simply, sex in a power-sharing couple stands a varying degree of success depending on what is happening at the time. There are four possible permutations of masculinity and femininity which have different effects on the sexual and emotional relationships of a couple:

1. When a man is comfortable with his dominant masculine side and a woman is in tune with her receptive feminine side, sexual intercourse and their emotional relationship will function well.
2. When a man is feeling less like taking the masculine penetrative role and a woman is feeling less receptive, sexual intercourse will not be so straightforward but the emotional relationship will still be good.
3. When both the man and the woman are feeling dominant, both sexual intercourse and their emotional relationship will be a battle.
4. When both the man and the woman are feeling receptive, their emotional relationship will be good but their sexual relationship may fail.

Being in tune with these aspects of the self helps to make sense of the otherwise inexplicable fluctuation in the pleasure of sexual intercourse. In the power-sharing couple all four permutations will be found at different times. Understanding this underlying ambivalence shows what can help. For example, there is often the need for managerial women to 'change gear' consciously in order to make sexual intercourse more successful. A company director returning home after a day of management might have to make a special effort to change her attitude in order to allow her partner to be sexually effective. After a day in power, the acquiescence necessary for sexual satisfaction may be difficult to achieve. It also shows the need for a man who tends to be passive, to make efforts to take the sexual initiative. Carrie and Reuben's is an interesting story:

> Carrie and Reuben were doctors. They had married late because she was very career minded and he was shy and retiring. She was a surgeon with a driving active personality and he was a medical academic whose shyness caused him to avoid contact with patients whenever he could. They were obviously a complementary couple in many ways except that the 'wrong' person carried the sexual drive.
>
> When they came for help Carrie was continually angry and frustrated by Reuben's passivity, and the more angry she got the more passive and uninterested in her sexually he became. They obviously had a difficult problem to resolve sexually although they 'fitted' well in other ways.
>
> I pointed out to Carrie that she could not have lived with someone like herself, so it was someone like Reuben or no one. In order to improve their relationship, he had to understand her need for his interest in her, and she had to understand that she must encourage rather than bully his fragile sexual activity. Taking it in

turns to initiate sex helped and they succeeded in learning to operate in a way which was good enough for the relationship to survive.

Power-sharing couples are often couples where both lead busy career lives and have less energy to invest in sexual intercourse with each other. This may be complicated by the fact that successful people are often attractive to others, and with increasing power in careers, the temptation to have sexual intercourse outside the relationship grows. It is also likely that because affairs are more exciting and less emotionally complex, they provide an easier alternative to the effort required within the long-term relationship. There has been a tendency by some to promote the idea that affairs actually help a relationship by making the partner more interesting. There may be some who are more interested in constant excitement and danger than in anything else. However, working from basic principles, I can say that everyone fears loss and few feel entirely secure. Therefore almost everyone will feel angry and threatened at the unfaithfulness of a partner. The relationship will depend on the way this anger and threat is dealt with: some kill, some pretend not to care and some get satisfaction from beating the partner at their own game. As we saw in Wendy's story on page 158, such strategies can go wrong.

Today's gender problems are a result of the fact that there remains, in the unconscious of all and the conscious of many, a valuation of men which was associated with their original role in society. With the evolution of society, that role has become less valuable, but it is still maintained by men and challenged by women. Complicating matters is the fact that men's sexual role requires qualities of assertiveness and confidence to bring about penetrative sexual intercourse, and it is in women's interest to be able to accept this with enjoyment. While women are increasingly sexually assertive, those who have a high degree of defensive aggression about their 'inferior' role find sexual enjoyment difficult to achieve. Where this is the case for a woman, there is a danger that her partner's assertiveness will be lost between her envy and his anxiety. Sexual intercourse needs assertive men as well as secure women who can tolerate such assertiveness. The question is how both sexes can develop the sense of security necessary to be sexually and emotionally flexible, so that each can be assertive when necessary and also allow the other to be assertive when necessary. Only with the diminution of anxiety and envy will the sexes be able to truly admire and respect one another, which would seem to be the best way of dealing with gender difference.

Key Points

♦ Problems with gender roles emerge from a negative attitude formed in response to a natural circumstance

♦ Men's anxiety and women's envy are at the root of most sexual problems

♦ The first sight of a naked girl creates an idea of the possibility of castration in the mind of a boy and thereby induces anxiety

♦ The first sight of a naked boy creates a sense of deprivation in the mind of a girl and thereby induces envy

♦ We need to remove the element of game-playing, with its corollary of winners and losers, from relationships

♦ Where men and women need each other in order to survive, their separate and different qualities are highly valued

♦ Once differences are no longer valued they become objects of envy

♦ Roles are about position, status, activity, potential and sexual behaviour

♦ Heterosexual intercourse is the experience which confronts adults most powerfully with the reality of gender difference.

10

Gender Conflict

Gender conflict is the inner tug of war over accepting the deficiencies of one's own gender enough to be able to enjoy a relationship with the other gender. Where there is difficulty in doing this a number of defences are employed to try to reduce the inner tension.

As we have seen, defence mechanisms created to deal with conflict have, like drugs, side-effects. An individual's problems will be due as much to the distortion caused by their defence mechanisms as to the original issue itself. Consequently, problems in relationships are mostly due to disturbances caused by individuals defending themselves.

We looked at three important unconscious defence mechanisms in Chapter 2. There are many other defence mechanisms which adults employ, some of which fall outside the scope of this book. Five important defences, which clearly fall within the scope of this book, are those most commonly found within heterosexual relationships. These are perhaps best called strategies as they are designed to manipulate the feelings of the opposite sex rather than to manipulate our own feelings.

These are:

1. Destruction of Power
2. Demand for Freedom
3. Denial of Difference
4. Forming Same-Sex Groups
5. Transformation of Envy

It is helpful to consider the relative merits of the different strategies to see how we might discourage the more damaging and encourage the more beneficial in ourselves.

Destruction of Power

The first strategy uses various methods to destroy the power of the opposite sex. This strategy is used differently by women and men.

Women

Traditionally women have 'used' the power of men and by seeming weak have controlled them by making them do, and be responsible for, everything. This was largely due to men's control of society and finance, and this strategy is still employed by many women who feel that they cannot compete in the outside world through lack of talent or desire, or by those brought up to think that a woman's proper place is in the home. Needing to be cared for by a man, and adopting the passive role of critic, compensates for the dependency in such a situation.

Where women have gender conflict there is envy of men because of their perceived advantages. One strategy used against this envy is to try to 'destroy' the man's power by metaphorically castrating him. This is done by making him feel undesirable and therefore sexually helpless. A woman does this particularly effectively when she fails to be aroused by her partner. A woman with inexplicable pain on penetration, fatigue, headache or any other type of sexual resistance is, albeit often unconsciously, controlling the sexual activity of the couple.

One of the most common complaints I see is that of vaginismus, which is severe pain on intercourse for which no physical cause can be found. In my experience it is always a symptom of the woman unconsciously not wanting intercourse and, when it develops during a relationship in which sexual intercourse has previously been satisfactory, indicates some anger or disappointment in the woman. This anger is usually not spoken of or even recognised consciously by the woman. This is because she is afraid of the significance of her anger, fearing that it means she no longer loves her partner, and so she tries to limit the damage by using that most widespread defence mechanism: denial. Her vaginismus deals with both her anger and her resulting loss of desire for intercourse by making her partner unwilling to cause her pain. She is frequently wringing her hands over her guilt about the unfair strain on her partner that her vaginismus evokes, but because her motives are unconscious, this condition is often difficult to treat, as was the case for Abby:

Abby had been married but was now divorced and was involved with Jerome, a married man with two young children who lived with him. Sex went well until

Jerome moved into Abby's house with his children, when she started having severe pain on penetration which prevented intercourse and eventually led to no sexual activity at all.

There were two issues at play here which combined to produce this state of affairs. First, Abby was a career woman, used for several years to doing things and having things as she wanted them. Two children played havoc with her houseproud ways. Secondly, she had felt guilt about her father's disapproval of her divorce. She had been very strictly brought up and he was unable to forgive her for this. When she started to live with Jerome, a married man, she knew her father would be appalled.

Abby was in a great deal of conflict. She loved Jerome but not his children; she loved her father but felt cast away by him; she felt out of control of her life and unused to sharing. Her unconscious rejected Jerome because of the difficulties, but consciously she was desperately trying to keep and please him. She accepted and understood these interpretations, but because she could see no way out of her situation, she did not come for counselling again.

Other women are more direct and just say they do not want sex because they do not feel like it, or because their partner fails to arouse them. The unconscious aim of these women is to allow themselves to feel less vulnerable and more in control, but of course it may also be a conscious strategy used to punish the partner for some failure to please. In any case it has the effect of diminishing the man's self-esteem by destroying his sexual power. Indeed, the strongly 'castrating' woman is likely only to consort with a man who has relatively low self-esteem and will allow her to dominate. The issue is complicated by the fact that if the woman succeeds in feeling too powerful, she comes to despise the man for letting her beat him, thus putting him in a Catch 22 situation where he cannot please her whatever he does. For example:

Betty felt herself to be the least attractive of her siblings and had tried very hard to be valued by being useful. She had idolised her father, and married relatively late because she looked after him until he died although she had started her own business and was extremely successful as an entrepreneur.

Betty's husband Alfred was ten years older than her, and reminded her of her father in some ways, but she was disappointed that he was not more active and successful. He was out of a job and she took him into her business, made him a partner and generally felt herself to be indispensable. She was undoubtedly bossy but he seemed to like that. She was not very interested in sex, liked to have it occasionally when she wanted it but never at Alfred's instigation.

Betty was appalled when it came to light that 'after all she had done for him' Alfred had an affair. He did not want to leave Betty, but she was quite unable to forgive him or see that she might have failed him in any way.

Sexual problems clinics are filled with people caught up in this strategy. In the context of her battle to undo gender-based prejudice, a woman has to understand that if she insists upon competing and winning, she will always end up in a relationship with a *losing* man.

Another of the most common phenomena met by counsellors is the story of the middle-aged man preparing to leave his home after a life of endless frustration with a sexually uninterested wife who has controlled their sex life and occasionally doled out sexual favours as a reward for good behaviour. On suddenly being faced with the loss of her under-valued partner, she miraculously recovers her sexual interest just as he is about to leave her. She is likely to respond in one of two ways. Some women, faced with loss, naturally make a greater effort to try to keep their husbands, and the fright can make them realise their husbands' needs for the first time. Other women make no such effort. While distressed and angry, these women are also excited by their husbands becoming valuable again through the eyes of others, while to them their husbands had come to seem about as valuable as a single old sock. Their sexual interest will be completely rearoused and now that they no longer have the sexual control, they are inspired to try to recapture it. However, they are now vulnerable where before they were impreg-nable, and they experience the role of supplicant as they seek sexual reassurance. The men who hitherto have been the supplicants now have the sexual power. For some men this change in their wives encourages them to stay, but they frequently find that once reassured of their power, their wives lose sexual interest again. Donna and Sammy's story illus-trates this dynamic, and their problem was essentially similar to the problems of hundreds of couples I have seen over the years:

> Donna chose to stay at home and bring up their children herself, but as the chil-dren became more independent she found herself rather bored. This developed into mild depression and complete loss of interest in sex, which in turn devel-oped into a phobia and she was unwilling to make love at all.
>
> Donna didn't like Sammy very much. In fact she didn't like men in general very much and was not interested in anybody except her children. Sammy was a pleasant and rather passive man who took part in their counselling sessions, but it was difficult to persuade Donna to make much effort sexually, and he felt – and was – totally helpless to change anything.
>
> During the course of exploring this problem Donna discovered that Sammy was having an affair with his secretary and she became distraught as she feared to lose him. Suddenly she valued him again, rediscovered her sexual interest and her boredom and depression were relieved. She succeeded in keeping her relationship with Sammy and putting an end to his affair.
>
> After a few months of feeling in control again, all Donna's problems of loss of libido returned. She did now recognise, however, that the problem was in her, and she started to work to free herself from the trap she was in: that her sexuality was only available when she was insecure.

Men

Men will use various strategies of their own to reduce female power. Men who have already had early experiences of a dominating mother or sister are particularly likely to be sensitive.

The safest and most natural way is for the man to seduce a woman into a relationship and achieve sexual penetration, thus neutralising any negative feelings and proving himself valuable. If he is frustrated in this he becomes more affected by a sense of women's power and is likely to become resentful of it.

As with women, a powerful way for men to diminish the opposite sex while retaining personal dignity is by withdrawing sexual interest. Some men may do this consciously by being deliberately elusive, which will create some satisfaction at the retrieval of power. Men may openly look to male friends to provide alternative sporting or other interests. They may openly or secretly find another woman who will value their sexuality. Other men with more passive natures may employ the defence mechanism of denial and deal with their anger at an unconscious level, becoming depressed, suppressing sexual interest and finally becoming impotent. As Kinsey pointed out nearly 50 years ago, if a man has to learn to restrain his sexual response too much he will lose interest just as his partner, who may have taken many years to develop hers, has become aroused.

The ultimate attempt to devalue the woman is, of course, in the act of rape. Here the need to overpower becomes pathological and exposes the man's emotional weakness as all attempts to retain his self-esteem are relinquished.

Women and Men

Some strategies to reduce the power of the partner can be used equally effectively by either sex. One which is particularly common is to invest very strongly in other interests, whether these be career, children or hobby. Whether it is the politician dining too much at the Athenaeum, the woman repeatedly staying late at work or the man spending too many evenings in the garden shed doing woodwork, it is a statement to the partner of their relative unimportance. Hélène's story is an interesting example of this effect:

> Hélène, a Frenchwoman, was married to Peter who was English. She dealt with her many resentments towards Peter by lavishing all her love on her sons. She was sensitive to the gender issue, having had three brothers who were highly valued and favoured by their parents. This caused her to reject her male compa-

triots and marry a foreigner. On the other hand, although she talked of loving Peter, she felt hostile towards him, and attributed her feelings to his foreignness.

What Hélène had failed to see was that she had a basic feeling of hostility towards all men except her sons. While they were young she could see them as part of herself and as controlled by her, and they were therefore not threatening. Hélène slowly became aware that she treated her husband quite cruelly. She was very rejecting of sex and told Peter she found him unattractive, she openly showed her preference for her sons and continually compared him unfavourably with the French men she had, herself, rejected. It was a shock to her to realise how badly she did treat him, and once she became aware of it she made a great effort to stop hurting him.

What made the difference for Hélène was the realisation that while she grew up feeling powerless with men, she actually had power as far as her husband was concerned: the power to make his life miserable or to make him happy. This double recognition, first that she was not vulnerable and secondly that she was herself being rather threatening, allowed her to feel – and be – much more loving towards Peter.

Demand for Freedom

Women

An increasingly prevalent power strategy used by women is to demand the opportunity to fulfil any role they choose at any time they want. There is the traditional male role, the traditional female role and a fairly new in-between role with a bit of both. Even those who manage, because of the type of work they do, to create this middle road with part-time traditional male and female roles, often find themselves discontented with the sense that they can do neither as well as they would like. This demand for freedom is quite understandable from a historical point of view, but the repercussions can introduce dangers into relationships.

For example, the situation now arises relatively frequently in counselling that a man is attracted to a woman who is an independent, self-sufficient, successful provider in her own right, only to find that she now wants to relinquish this role and become domesticated and dependent, and that she becomes angry if her lover denies her this privilege. He, naturally, feels threatened if it feels necessary to him to take the burden of financial responsibility.

These increased choices have fundamentally altered the power struggle between the sexes. In the past, women were economically powerful according to their ability to beg, bully or seduce their partners into giving them what they wanted. It is very different if the woman can give herself what she wants, as more and more women now can. This has inevitable repercussions for relationships. Kim and Matthew's story is an example of how this can distort a relationship:

> Kim told me that she no longer wanted sex with her husband Matthew. In the course of trying to understand what was wrong she revealed that she felt very resentful towards him because he felt that she should contribute towards the costs of running the home. Kim and her mother both believed that, despite earning a salary as large as Matthew's, this was her money and it was his duty to 'keep' her.

It was obviously unfair that Kim wanted to retain the traditional role while also enjoying contemporary opportunities. She had been conditioned by her parents' attitudes and fundamentally expected Matthew to be like her father while accepting her rejection of the role taken by her mother. This is clearly unjust and unrealistic, but nevertheless deeply felt, and so likely to cause trouble.

There are also repercussions for the present generation of children as more and more women prefer the idea of complete control over their lives and wish to have a child without the responsibility of a committed relationship. Men are held to be useful only for their sperm and many of these women are quite deaf to any suggestion of disadvantages for fatherless children or of unfairness to men.

Men

Men's demand for freedom can be equally destructive, and men, like women, can come to expect the best of both worlds. This is particularly likely where a man has been brought up to believe that women are solely responsible for domestic tasks, and therefore gives no help in the home even when his wife does a full-time job and contributes financially to the household. Clearly this is equally unfair. Many women who complain of loss of libido eventually reveal this situation as being the cause of hidden resentment towards their partners.

The sharing of financial and domestic roles with women may be seen in two ways. It may come from the open-minded recognition by some men that until recently social roles have been unfair for women. They recognise that for mutual happiness fairness is necessary, and that if their partner is happiest with a career, they themselves will be happier for having a contented partner. The extra income will be nice, too! Other men may conceal their fears of responsibility, their envy of the female and their wish to recreate childhood and stay at home, by latching on to prevalent feminist dogma and encouraging their partner to take all the responsibility. A certain kind of househusband may, then, be wanting to take the traditional dependent role of the former woman rather than to take a fair share of the responsibilities.

Denial of Difference

Women and men

The cry for sameness is an understandable attempt to deal with the basic fact that there seems to be unfairness in difference. However there are dangers in trying to solve conflict in this way.

While the demand that the sexes be treated justly because they are equally valuable is obviously crucial, many people fail to distinguish between equality of value on the one hand and sameness on the other. This failure leads to important losses. Problems develop because the distinction is not clearly thought through, with the result that many people exert too much energy trying to alter external circumstances and not enough on taking responsibility for their own unreasonable internal demands. As the saying goes, 'it is easier to put on a pair of slippers than to carpet the world', but we often think it would be easier to change the world than to change ourselves.

In some areas it is clearly important for the sexes to be treated equally. Equal pay for work of equal value is an excellent example of this. However, a demand for the sexes to be treated as if they were the same in those areas in which they clearly are not, invites trouble. A solution which requires denial of truth is always shaky because the truth will continually threaten to break through the defences. Also, the hope that the equality of sameness will remove difficult feelings is usually dashed. This is because where the two sexes have biologically different roles, an attempt to be biologically the same requires one sex to imitate the other. Imitation being, by definition, not the real thing, this action only confirms the difference and leads to the need to destroy the real thing if the imitation is to have any credibility. Thus women who want to imitate men must destroy men's power, or metaphorically 'castrate' them, in order to compete and win. Similarly, men who wish to imitate women must caricature them excessively through ridiculous camp behaviour in order to seem the more feminine of the two.

Since there can never be sameness of action when it comes to hetero-sexual sex, the obsessive quest for it outside the bedrooom needs to be scrutinized. Otherwise, in the struggle for an easy solution to the problem, more can be lost than saved. We can twist and turn as we will, but there is an inevitable difference between the action of the plug and that of the socket. The plug and the socket are equally important in creating a flow of electricity but they are opposite in action and the analogy with heterosexual sex is obvious.

Some people in heterosexual relationships are reluctant to take their full sexual role because of its symbolism. Here the need to try to be the same causes some couples to limit sex to foreplay in the form of mutual masturbation, because the necessarily different roles of copulation distresses one or both of them. So much is missed physically, emotionally and spiritually by devaluing consummation that all effort should be made to make this possible. In other couples the same issue is expressed by the woman only being willing to have intercourse if she is on top. There is, of course, nothing wrong with the woman enjoying this position, but if she is limited to it, lovemaking is diminished for both.

There are other discordances. The opportunity to do anything has given women the chance to do everything. The increase in choices, however, also produces a new and unexpected sort of anxiety, particularly in the woman with low self-esteem. Here, career opportunity can be seen as an antidote, and the pressure to take every available career opportunity in order to raise self-esteem can become irresistible. This produces its own stifling pressure if the woman feels she must endlessly prove her worth, either by having too many children, or by working too hard at her career, or both. Sylvia's sad story shows this pressure in action:

> Sylvia was seriously depressed by the desertion of her husband Ross. She found it difficult to accept that she shared responsibility for the disaster and had contributed to his betrayal.
>
> Sylvia's story was that after an insecure childhood with a younger brother who was adored by her mother, she had found that her cleverness compensated for her sense of inferiority by getting attention for her at home, and she became extremely ambitious. She qualified as a lawyer and worked full-time, had five children, persuaded Ross to leave his teaching post and supported him and the family while he took a law degree.
>
> Sylvia was very controlling and, because of all she had done for Ross, believed that she had a right to his devotion however she behaved. He, however, felt continually diminished by her and her need for supremacy, and when he met a woman at work who was able to make him feel more valuable, he left his wife.

This story illustrates that while absolute rigidity in society is not good, total flexibility produces its own difficulties for those whose goal becomes to do everything.

Forming Same-Sex Groups

Men

The formation of same-sex groups has been around for a long time. Historically, in this country, men's clubs have protected their members through exclusivity which has kept out the power and distraction of women. While these clubs have had obvious professional and social purposes as well as a hidden emotional purpose, they have nevertheless been a divisive factor in the family. Clubbing together can be, on the one hand, a positive sharing of experiences unique to that sex. On the other hand, it can represent a defensive attitude of exclusion towards the opposite sex. Where a man spends his evenings at his club, be it the Garrick or the local working men's club, the energy left over from his work is not being invested in his family.

With the demystification of women, both through the sharing of the workplace and the general exposure of their bodies by the media, some of their sexual power should have been diminished and the need for men to protect themselves should consequently have been reduced. However, the new competitiveness of women seems to require the retention of the escape into exclusivity, as there is clearly great reluctance to break the tradition.

The three main reasons men historically gave for belonging to clubs were:

1. To escape the restrictions to their behaviour made by their family. For example, drinking, gambling and sexually available women were looked on with disfavour by the family yet often seen by society as normal male activities.
2. To feel free to use whatever language and share whatever jokes they pleased, without having to worry about offending others.
3. To talk about how the country should be run.

Women

With a few exceptions such as the Soroptimists, women have not formed clubs in the same way as men because their needs have been different. Traditionally women have either not wanted to escape because the men were not at home a great deal, or could not escape because they had to care for their children. Talking with men has always been valued by women, because until recently men's experience has been broader and more interesting. Unless an issue such as Greenham Common arose to unite women in a 'cause', their tendency has been to want to be with men and join in discussions on how the country should be run. In recent years women's determination to have equal value with men has meant they have been more likely to join evening classes and to enrich themselves in other independent ways.

Transformation of Envy

Everyone knows that there is a great deal of potential for conflict between men and women. Every member of each sex feels some envy of what they perceive to be the advantages of the opposite sex. Whether it is a man who is envious of what he sees as a woman's right to stay at home with her children, or indeed of her ability to bear children in the first place, or a woman who is envious of what she sees as the comparative ease with which a man can climb the career ladder, or of his ability to earn more than her for doing the same job, the same principle applies.

One of the great appeals of falling in love is our ability to transform this envy for the opposite sex in general into admiration for one of its members in particular. The difficulty is in retaining this admiration once the person becomes a familiar part of our life. In another field such as sport, untalented people envy the talented and transform this envy into admiration when they become fans. Again, in some societies the rich are envied and wealth is seen as something to aspire to. The less well-off may deal with their envy by working hard or buying lottery tickets in the belief that they too can become rich if they try hard enough or get lucky. Other societies fail to transform their envy of the rich and deal with it openly by trying to destroy them, whether through a nationally agreed policy such as communism or an outbreak of anger in riot or revolution.

This strategy can seem on the face of it to be largely positive. The danger is that we demand a great deal from someone in whom we have invested admiration, and the higher we place them the farther they can fall. As we all know, anger and disappointment are generated when the football team fails to win, or when having idealised a leading family such as the American Kennedys, we find we have been misled into beliefs about them that are totally wrong. We feel we have been conned. But then the tendency to want to destroy our heroes reveals our ambivalence about the whole issue.

Admiration is very different from loving someone 'warts and all', which is probably what we should all aim for and is certainly what we all demand for ourselves.

The above section has been about dealing with tensions caused by differences between the sexes and the way in which our inability to sympathise with the other's position can lead us to take action which is destructive to our relationships. The next section is about people who have chosen, for one reason or another, to avoid the problem of difference and who feel more comfort with, and interest in, members of their own sex.

Homosexuality

This book is based on my own experience as a therapist and counsellor and although the problems of homosexuality have come up over the years, they have not been central to my work. This is not, then, a detailed exploration of the subject but highlights some of the important issues.

This book can be used by homosexual and heterosexual people because it sets out to show the links between childhood experience, biological programming and contemporary problems. Fundamentally these are universal. Nevertheless there are problems unique to homosexuals which are not shared by heterosexuals, and vice versa.

Much of the debate about the contribution of nature and nurture to homosexuality is unresolved. It seems most likely that a genetic tendency towards homosexuality combines with the individual experiences of the child to produce this particular effect. In other words, a genetic tendency alone will not necessarily produce homosexual behaviour.

We have seen that anxiety, guilt, jealousy and fear of retribution about desires and loves during childhood cause defensive measures. These can lead a child to turn its attention away from the parent it naturally loves and desires because it seems safer to pay attention to the other parent. In doing so the child may split off their developing sexual interest and invest it where it will do least harm. For example, male homosexuals usually revere their mothers and love mother figures while keeping sexual interest away from them. This may be because of childhood fear, either of father's jealousy or of mother's punitive attitude to sex. Once this choice is made it is very difficult to change back without a great deal of anxiety. Also, at some point physical expression is shared with a desired person of the same sex, from which satisfaction is received, which adds weight to the choice and helps it to become the norm for that individual.

Another childhood experience which can lead to homosexuality is the excitement of childhood sexual arousal focused on an adult or another child of the same sex. This can set in train a fantasy life which may become entrenched so that adult sexual arousal is also focused on people of the same sex.

The sexual orientation of heterosexuals as well as homosexuals is formed in childhood, and the result for most of us, whatever our orientation, is that we feel we 'have always been this way'. However, some people's sexual orientation is not so fixed. Some homosexuals have sought help from me because they wish to change their orientation. This may or may not be possible depending on the individual's circumstances. There is no general answer to the question of the ability to change because everyone has their own personal history with a unique outcome. There are, however, some relevant points to make. First, the fact that many men have married, had children and then reverted to homosexuality means that we have considerable power over our behaviour. It is probable that if the opportunity were not given, many men with a tendency to homosexuality would lead straight lives and never give their homosexuality expression. Secondly, many married women, disappointed by life with a man, turn to a woman who they feel understands them better. Thirdly, homosexuality flourishes where there is only one sex available, such as in prisons. There is, therefore, some flexibility, and where opportunities for homosexuality exist, more people will choose that option.

It is harder for men to repress their desires than for women because of the power of the testosterone competitor in their Pro-Sex team. Sex is, therefore, more likely to become addictive in men than in women, and we all know how difficult it is to change an addiction. This means that men are generally less flexible about their sexual orientation than women.

People in homosexual relationships have to deal with a number of problems which are different from those faced by people in heterosexual relationships. The most obvious problems are those created by the fact that homosexuals are in the minority and therefore defined by the majority as different from the norm. Young homosexuals who are open about their sexual orientation while still at school are likely to face persecution due to the prejudice that they are a threat. Their persecutors will consciously feel more comfortable with people they assume are heterosexual, who they expect to encounter and understand, than with openly homosexual people who appear to them to be unnatural. Unconsciously, however, they may be fearful of their own homosexuality, particularly in adolescence as it is a phase of development experienced (but usually passed through) by most. Parents of homosexuals may be disappointed that they are to be deprived of their expected destiny of the excitement and love of grandchildren and investment in the future of their family. After leaving school, homosexuals will find that our wider society feels threatened by a newly vocal and at times subversive group whose numbers are unknown and who recruit from the mainstream. The effect of all this prejudice being aimed at the homosexual is usually to lower their self-esteem, leaving them to deal with the consequent anxieties this will create.

Another problem homosexuals face is their own loss of family, future and regeneration. Many homosexuals love and long for children. Very few are able to create an alternative parenting arrangement such as a lesbian bearing a child fathered by a gay man; most homosexuals never get the chance to encounter the indescribably awesome experiences of parenthood. They also, therefore, never undergo the process of feeling more grown-up because there is another generation below. Nevertheless, as we have already seen, the mechanism for controlling our desires and behaving as society requires does exist in some people. Through the ages, with different intensity, people have conformed and produced children and concealed their hidden desires.

One problem of which everyone will be aware, still facing male homosexuals in particular in this country, is high risk from the AIDS virus. This has caused great change in the sexual behaviour of male homosexuals over the last decade or so as safe sex has become the norm.

The sexual problems faced by homosexuals are similar to those faced by heterosexuals in that they are mostly due to partial withdrawal from the partner due to conflicts within the relationship. In male homosexuals particularly this is usually a problem of relative impotence related to infidelity.

The conflict of the wishes for fidelity, commitment and freedom at the same time is common to all. In heterosexual relationships, while children can cause difficulty in the partnership, the sharing of the investment of a child which is of such importance to both partners is a strong bond. Another bond is created by sex, and these two bonds provide the glue which helps to stick together the parts of a relationship that otherwise may have a tendency to fall apart. Whether you are heterosexual or homosexual, it is clearly difficult to stay in a relationship with one person for 60 years or even five. Other siren voices call when the inevitable difficulties and disappointments of committed relationships begin to accumulate. However, where couples recognise that their family and shared history are the most valuable things that people ever have, they usually find a way to make their relationship work.

Homosexuals do not have such a bond and have to rely entirely on their relationship. This makes the cementing of the relationship by its sexual side that much more important. However, where sex is too important other insecurities arise. In male homosexuals the penis is of exceptional symbolic meaning and size and potency are of great importance. Insecurity is built into such a situation and in particular the older homosexual with the young partner is often in extreme anxiety about his ability to hold the interest of the younger man.

In women the sexual side of the relationship is less dominant and is not driven by the prowess of the penis. Very few lesbians have sought my help for their relationships, and for those who have, the emotional difficulties and the social anxieties of their partnership have dominated. This applied to Sophie and Nell:

> Sophie and Nell met when they were in their early thirties. They had both had heterosexual relationships and neither had had a previous homosexual relationship or considered whether they might be lesbians. Nell had had a long-term relationship with a man who was very keen to marry her but her attention had been held and frustrated by another man who had a male partner. Sophie had lived with a married man for ten years, also with no hope of marriage.
>
> They both suffered from deep insecurities founded in their childhood, for which they had each had individual psychotherapy, and despite being attractive, intelligent and sociable had not found happiness until they found each other. At their first meeting they were immediately attracted to each other and rapidly set up house together despite the fact that this meant Sophie leaving Canada and accepting a much reduced salary and status in England.
>
> In the course of Sophie's psychotherapy, she described occasional bouts of sexual disappointment which she ascribed to fleeting difficulties in their daily life. Sophie and Nell's main difficulty, however, was in their shared sense of humiliation at being seen as lesbians. They found it difficult to see themselves as homosexual and, as they were not interested in others of their own sex, saw their relationship as different, a 'one off'. Gradually they became more confident about themselves socially and managed to create a very successful relationship.

The difficulties mentioned above of feeling like a social outcast, failing to meet parental expectations and having to commit to a life of barrenness make many homosexuals struggle to be heterosexual. In particular those who are perfectionists and hate to be faulted make the decision to be straight. This is a major cause of relative impotence in men and dissatisfaction in women. Men and women with strong repressed homosexual tendencies will be more than usually vulnerable to the vagaries of a relationship, and any unhappiness with the partner will be more easily transferred into sexual withdrawal.

The relatively new publicity of dedicated homosexuals increasingly promotes the idea that homosexuality is as satisfactory as heterosexuality. It is true that sensuality and sexual arousal in the human can have values of their own apart from reproduction, but this does not invalidate the idea that the fulfilment of the reproductive function is of vital personal and social importance. It should be valued because it is, at the very least, one of the few purposes of existence of which we can be sure. If we accept this we must face the fact that, as homosexuality precludes the important experiences of parenthood, heterosexuality and homosexuality are not alternatives of equal value. This is why the potential for satisfaction offered by heterosexuality goes beyond mere acceptance by society.

Homosexuals have been discriminated against for centuries and it is completely understandable that they should wish to promote their own position. The swing against bigotry may, however, lead to a situation where children passing through a normal homosexual phase and unready to accept a heterosexual role are seduced by an illusory idea of escape. We have seen that sexual orientation is not always fixed, but for some people it is, whether homosexual or heterosexual, and this must be respected. It is important to reassure people that there is no sin in homosexuality, yet each of us has a personal obligation to understand that we may use homosexuality as a haven from the difficulties of heterosexual sex and development. Adolescents in particular are often worried and confused about sex, and therefore vulnerable, and those with flexible orientations may choose homosexuality if it is offered to them in an acceptable form.

To make this choice is an individual's right. As well as rights, however, we also have responsibilities. It is our responsibility to try to understand anyone we encounter who defines themself as homosexual, rather than to accept the view that homosexuality is wrong. While unorthodoxy in individuals undoubtedly enriches society, such individuals are paradoxically limited by their unorthodoxy and cut off from valuable experiences by the very freedom they seek. Young people deserve protection while they develop and adolescents may be lost to the satisfactions of heterosexuality if there is no social pull towards it.

It is clearly important to have a society which is tolerant of those whose predilections and problems preclude them from orthodoxy, and indeed, the civilisation of a society can be judged by such tolerance. However, there is danger for many if tolerance leads to a situation where people are encouraged to follow the easiest path without any struggle. The question is how to introduce the opportunity for these issues to be understood without at the same time seeming reactionary and intolerant.

To summarise, the male homosexuals referred to me have been mainly for two reasons. First, where they are unhappy with being homosexual and have wanted to explore the possibility of change. Secondly, where they are committed homosexuals having problems with impotence. The difficulties of the few lesbians who have been referred to me have been more to do with their relationships and less with specifically sexual problems. Many of the homosexual people referred to me have previously had disappointing heterosexual relationships, and conversely, others have moved from homosexuality into heterosexuality. It can be seen, then, that some people can use homosexuality as a defence against difficult heterosexual experiences, while others can use heterosexuality as a defence against their own homosexual tendencies.

Key Points

♦ Some people can use homosexuality as a defence against difficult heterosexual experiences, while others can use heterosexuality as a defence against their own homosexual tendencies

♦ There can never be sameness of action when it comes to heterosexual sex

♦ There is a great deal of potential for conflict between men and women

♦ If you insist upon competing and winning within a relationship, you will always end up with a loser.

PART V

Fertility and Infertility

11

The Quest for Fertility

The greatest dilemma for women today is the conflict between their demands for equality and the biological fact that they alone bear children. This issue deserves further discussion and illustration.

Choice

Too much choice is always difficult because commitment to anything means the loss of so many other options. Making a commitment to a partner means giving up the others who might have been available. Women are now more at risk than men because the world contains much greater choice for women as far as role is concerned, and their problem is how to cope with it. Of course what we all want is everything, and at first sight it seems as if this is now possible for women, but choices do have to be made.

There are four choices open to today's woman.

Choice Number One

She can reject her reproductive role for a career or because she does not want the responsibility of children. Deciding not to have children is a valid choice for a woman today, but problems can arise if she later changes her mind, particularly if it is too much later when she will be disappointed. The highly educated woman naturally gives career status a priority when young, which she might not value so highly when more mature. This can result in an appalling loss of satisfaction if it is not recognised until it is too late.

Many women who have only wanted a career, and actively do not want to have a child, suddenly change in their late thirties. At this age there is more likely to be difficulty in conception, and if this is so, panic often sets in. There is particular distress for the successful woman, who is used to being able to achieve anything she sets her mind to, if she cannot control this aspect of her life. Less achieving women usually accept their disappointment more philosophically.

It would be reasonable to assume that a woman who for years felt strongly that she did not want a child would take disappointment over fertility better than someone who had always wanted a child. However, my experience of infertility counselling has shown that the sort of person who feels grossly ambivalent has a problem with tolerating frustration, and is afraid of having to cope either without something they do want or with something they do not want. It is, therefore, the inability to obtain what is now desired that is the main frustration, rather than loss of the child about whom there were always doubts anyway. Most of the women referred to me for infertility counselling have been successful career women with feelings of this kind. This ability to control their world often makes them difficult to help because failure, or putting up with second best, is unacceptable to them and their frustration is extreme. Alison's story gives a clear example of this:

> When Alison was a child, her father was always going away on important business and neglecting his family. She assumed that the outside world must be much more exciting than home, and as soon as she could she followed in his footsteps. She rejected all ideas of home and family, travelled the world in a successful job, and had many affairs with men but always avoided commitment.
>
> At the age of 40 Alison suddenly became aware that there was an experience she had not had. She desperately wanted a child, but her current partner, Bernard, already had a family and didn't want another child. Much anguish was created by this situation and their relationship could not sustain it. Alison was so angry with Bernard for frustrating her demand for a child that life with her became unbearable and he was unfaithful.
>
> Alison now had to face the bitter realisation that she had lost both her partner and the chance of a baby. There was no possibility of a happy solution for this couple. Alison was obsessed with achieving what she had now set her heart on: a child. Bernard didn't want the responsibility of another child, and did not want Alison enough to sacrifice his wishes for hers.

In great contrast to the women who went through this phase of not wanting children is the group of women I have seen who always wanted children and yet who are able to accept, albeit with great sadness, that they will not be able to have their own child. They are much less likely to be angry and to cut themselves off from children or friends with children, and are more likely to seek to adopt or find other ways of fulfilling their maternal instincts. Zoë's story illustrates this:

> Zoë was in her late twenties. She had always loved children and wanted a family

of her own. She came to talk to me about her disappointment over her infertility, and having done all she could to have it investigated, she accepted the situation. She decided to take up a career involved with children and applied for adoption with the minimum of distress.

Choice Number Two

A woman can combine a career and have a family at the same time. She can employ a full-time child carer or place the child in a creche. In this case she must accept that her importance to her child is greatly diminished. This is particularly so where a full-time nanny is employed, as the nanny will have the important relationship with the child. The case of the woman forced to work and in a non-vocational job is different from that of the career woman who has given her work top priority and who inevitably directs much of her energy and interest, as well as her time, into her job.

Marcia was in her late thirties. She had always felt very mixed about whether she wanted a child and resentful of some aspects of her female role generally. She was an eldest child who had openly disliked her four siblings and so felt uncertain of her ability to love and care for a child. After only a short period of counselling she decided to conceive.

She was determined to organise away all possible difficulties and remain in control. A nanny was hired to start before the birth as Marcia had no confidence in her ability to care for her child. She arranged to return to work two weeks after the birth and was deaf to any suggestion that she might not want to do so when the time came. This was because she was convinced that she was supposed to stay at home with the child and that everyone was going to make her feel guilty because she didn't want to. Any attempt to talk about her feelings over this was rejected and interpreted as a pressure against which she must rebel.

By the time Marcia's son was a few months old, she became reluctant to leave him with the nanny, her work became less important to her and she very much regretted the time she had lost with him. She was anxious for another child with whom she could have a more total experience.

Caring for Marcia's second child was a very fulfilling experience for her, but she still felt the need of a nanny to provide backup, because of her sense that she could not be an entirely good mother.

By the time her second child was two years old, she had built up confidence and was able to look forward to the days when she had complete responsibility at home. What is more, she no longer experienced the female position as a loss but as a precious gift.

Many women are satisfied by the engagement of a full-time nanny and this was, of course, the usual custom in upper-class families where childcare was not valued as an occupation. However, the above example shows that it all depends on what you want. The problem is trying to find out what that might be and in Marcia's case only her personal experiences revealed this.

Choice Number Three

The woman can take the traditional role during her reproductive years and accept the consequent reduction in her career potential.

It is very difficult in a competitive society to take ten, or even five, years out of the workplace and then try to go back. There is always a loss of confidence if there is not consistent building each day on the success of the day before. Many women fear to go back to work because of this. They feel that the world has moved on and that their experience may no longer be relevant so that there may not be a place for them. In any profession it is impossible to leave and then return, unless the individual is prepared to stay in a relatively low status position, and even then some retraining will be needed. A great deal of career loss has therefore to be faced for a woman making this particular choice.

While the career loss may be difficult, most women who take this option feel that the rewards are worthwhile. They are saved from worrying about the suitability of carers, they have the closest bond with their children, and they enjoy sharing their childrens' experiences and giving them guidance.

Choice Number Four

The fourth choice is a compromise. A woman can work part-time and employ part-time help, again accepting reduction of her career potential but being more likely to retain a sense of confidence. The problem is that it is difficult in this situation to make a total commitment to either role. She may choose to mitigate this by pleading pressure from home when she is at work and pressure from work when she is at home. For the ambitious woman this can be stressful because she is likely to try to do both jobs full-time. However, if career allows it, this way allows fulfilment of both sides of her personality without too much loss in either.

These are the difficult choices that women face.

Although I have been mainly concerned with the dilemma of women, we should remember that men not only have their own conflicts but share very much in any conflict a woman may have. It is, of course, understandable that there is a special bond between mother and baby. However, we must also understand that the rights of women to have abortions that men may not want them to have, and the demands for maintenance of a child a man may not have wanted and which could have been avoided, put a huge strain on today's man. The failure of many partnerships, and the possibility that a man may lose his close relationship with his children if this happens, inevitably makes for wariness. Women are increasingly powerful in their ability to make demands and in any such situation increased power on one side reduces that on the other. As men feel more threatened in this field, their own tug of war between self-protection and a wish to fulfil their partner becomes more paralysing.

How to Choose

There is a tendency for militant feminists to feel that more women are not in top jobs solely because men keep them out. Many men do, of course, try to keep women from equalling their own power, but this is not the whole story. It ignores the fact that those women who are perfectly capable of fighting their way into top jobs may not want the total commitment this requires during their reproductive years and this may lead them to hold back. Others, who believe they will have no difficulty in doing both, find that they have an unforeseen problem when the experience of having a child reveals unexpectedly strong emotional ties. They do not expect to resent relinquishing their new-found bond to someone else, but may find themselves jealous of the other's importance to the child.

It is true that a woman can have the satisfactions of carrying, giving birth to and breastfeeding a child, which a man cannot. She can also become prime minister and take the highest roles in society. 'Winner take all' is a very seductive call for some women but, if indulged too much, it may leave their partners and their children impoverished. This in the end leaves the woman herself impoverished, if her family look elsewhere for attention.

A recurrent situation I have seen is where the very successful woman, who needs this high achievement for herself, is at the same time unreasonably angry and aggressive towards her partner. Bronwen and Oscar were in this position:

> Bronwen had a rumbling anger towards her husband Oscar because he neither earned, nor was prepared to look after the house and the children, as much as she. At first glance there seemed some justice in her resentment but looking more deeply revealed a complex situation.
> Bronwen was a talented creative artist who valued her work greatly and resented not working when first married, despite the fact that she had desper-

ately wanted children. She was very possessive of her four children and believed that only she, and not Oscar, had the necessary sensitivity to give them the best care and guidance. She adored her children, and not only excluded Oscar from their cosy group, but endlessly expressed her dissatisfaction with him. She never wanted to, and only occasionally would, make love.

Oscar did not feel valued in his home so he retreated and took more trips away. This resulted in Bronwen feeling very angry and envious that he had the 'freedom' to go away, and she convinced herself that she was indispensable. In fact Oscar was happy to look after the home but Bronwen was unconsciously unwilling to relinquish her power to him. She justified this by believing that the children would not really be happy with him.

The resolution of this unhappy situation depended on Bronwen seeing the 'games' she was playing with herself and with Oscar, and on her trying to see the situation from his point of view. After sessions in which these issues were confronted, she could see Oscar's point of view and things would go better for a while. However, because Bronwen was basically envious of men, Oscar found it difficult to please her for long and she returned to her original position of punishing him for being a man.

So, which choice is a woman to make? These options are complex and deserve careful consideration before a decision is made because, as we saw in Chapter 3, we mostly make our choices by unconscious prejudice rather than the reason we think we are applying. In order to get the best out of our circumstances we need to have thought through our set of priorities actively, both as individuals and as a society. Like town planners, we should decide what is important to preserve and to pass on to our children, and what should be rebuilt. For example, during our reproductive years we have to make choices and be concerned with roles and responsibilities which we can ignore at other times. Before and after our reproductive years, we have more freedom to choose our roles and way of life.

When considering our priorities we have to take certain facts into account. We have to recognise that, like one of Newton's laws in physics, to every action there is an equal and opposite reaction, and this also applies in emotional relationships. For example, if someone is cross with us we will feel cross with them, however justified their anger may be. Similarly, every action we take produces a reaction. This means that while an individual is nowadays free to choose their level of involvement in any relationship, the outcome of that relationship will inevitably be altered by the amount of involvement they choose. The greater the commitment by an individual to a person, a career or a cause, the more it will flourish. Therefore, if a mother is with her child for much of the day, she will share that child's pleasures and pains and will have fundamental experiences that she would not previously have been able to predict. If she is not with her child, she will not have those experiences but the minder will. Equally, if a father is to be of significance to his child, he needs to share in its day-to-day experiences or they will both miss out. Whatever choice parents make, children do best with a significant contribution from both parents, and ultimately parents will benefit more from their children if they make such a contribution.

The practical need of the child is that its mother should feel materially secure. It also needs a father to give support to its mother in times of illness and worry. Most importantly it needs a father in order to have the experience of relating to parents of both sexes who are its prototypes for all other people.

Traditionally there has been a sharp division of role and tasks between the parents. The contemporary ideas that we have been exploring have broadened this picture, and clearly power-sharing parents can fulfil these conditions. However, for this to work, both parents have to be prepared to temper their career ambitions in order to have the time and energy to invest in their offspring, and this may mean that the family unit may not be as economically prosperous as it might have been. Parents have to be quite strong not to be greedy if they have the talent to reach the top in their chosen career. It has become part of the ethos of society to put prosperity before family life because many a father has mistakenly thought that the most important thing is to provide prosperity. In deprived societies it may well be that the father has to be sacrificed in this way, but today we mostly have a choice. Yet that choice can itself give rise to emotional tension.

So why do people decide to have children in the first place? This decision can have complex roots in past experience. In a society which has contraception and therefore choice, there is great responsibility on potential parents to make a specific choice about whether to have children. While feeling broody may well represent a biological drive for the survival of the species, there are many personal reasons for wanting a family.

Children are seen as a part of the self. They are easier to love than strangers and, because of the bonds of family, are expected to give love in return. They are, therefore, a source of love, and for those who find loving difficult, this special love is very important. On the same theme they are more to be relied upon for loyalty than strangers. Indeed, one of the difficulties I have frequently encountered in counselling is that of people feeling disloyal when they talk about their parents in anything other than the most positive terms.

As part of the self, children are also looked to as a source of pride and to realise the failed hopes of their parents. They give parents the opportunity to experience things which were denied to them as children themselves, which vicariously satisfies past deprivations. They allow parents to pass on experience in the hope that a transmitted part of themselves will be more successful. Also children can be seen to justify the hard work and success of the parents, the fruits of which can be passed on. Death may seem a little less final knowing that a part of oneself lives on. Reproduction can give direction and a goal to many who would otherwise feel their life to be purposeless.

Many of these hopes will, of course, be dashed. Asking for so much from another often leads to disappointment. Such hopes can also put a terrible burden on a child.

In reality, the effect of having a child is usually to amplify the personality by the experience of deeply loving someone who, while seen as a part of the self, is separate and is more important than self. In this way, through the essential selfishness of having a child, a greater selflessness can develop. The infertile are, therefore, denied this experience and are not then stretched to the full emotionally in this way. Not everyone chooses to have children, but it is probably true that everyone expects the right to make their own choice, and people are shocked and distressed if the choice is not there.

Infertility

It is important here to enter a warning. It must be remembered that as a counsellor I have only seen those who seek help over their distress. The majority of infertility patients are not seen by counsellors, although it is well known that prolonged infertility is stressful to anyone who experiences it. This large group may or may not be coping satisfactorily. I am writing only about my personal experience of those I have seen and learned from. I should also make it clear that an overall account of the physical causes of infertility is outside the scope of this book, and I shall only mention physical problems in so far as they help to understand the psychological side.

Women's reasons for wanting children are highlighted in cases of infertility. There are three common reasons in such cases which have recurred regularly throughout my counselling experience. They are:

◆ For the child itself
◆ Tug of child and career
◆ To fill a gap

For the Child Itself

These women have always wanted children and have tried to conceive reasonably soon after marriage. They tend to be emotionally mature and are prepared to take responsibility and care for others. If they are infertile, the dominant feeling they express is sadness. They will usually be keen to adopt or foster, and often get a job with children to compensate. In time they are likely to accept the problem and will not be too crippled by their sadness.

Tug of Child and Career

This group is closely linked to the first because having a child is valued. Career women are torn between the achievement of bearing a child and the achievement of succeeding in a career. Many hope for both, and since the career often follows higher education, they believe that the role of parent can come later. However the successful career may be hard to relinquish, while work stress and delay may lead to mechanical or emotional types of infertility. The ability to deal with disappointment will depend on the security and basic personality of the woman. She is likely to find compensations for her disappointment in work, because her basic personality is less fragile than those in the next group.

To Fill a Gap

Paradoxically, it can be the woman who has apparently been least interested in having children who copes least well with the frustration of infertility. This woman may say she delayed having a child because she wanted to have her house first, or her career first, but this really hides some reluctance to have children, of which she may or may not allow herself to be aware. This reluctance may be for many reasons. It could be because she does not want to have the role she saw her mother having. She may feel inadequate and not sufficiently grown up to be a mother. She may have hated having a baby in the house when her siblings were born, and fears she would hate any baby of her own.

If such a woman changes her mind, she is likely to have been motivated by disappointment in other areas of her life. A search for a new goal becomes imperative. If the new goal is a child, it is the idea of a child and the possibility of a new way of being successful which is being used to make her feel better. This child will, therefore, be needed rather than wanted. A baby may then seem like a last resort for satisfaction, which if it were to fail, would be a disaster.

This woman is often angry and distraught because of her infertility. She has usually been unhappy as a child and has dealt with low self-esteem by fighting her corner. Her quest for control over events has often led to a substantial success which she then expects and demands. Failure to get what she wants, i.e. to have a child, causes fear and agitation that she will not be able to bear the frustration.

This same anxiety is likely to have caused trouble in her career and in her life generally, and has essentially become a personality problem. Her relationship suffers greatly. This woman is usually angry with her partner, and envies him because he doesn't seem to feel as desperate as her. He doesn't mind so much about not having a child because he has other ways of being successful. There is then no refuge or succour for her in the relationship as she has turned her partner into an irritant and even, in some cases, an enemy.

Such a woman refuses to give up and is the most at risk from the advancing technology that seems to offer endless hope. Her partner is likely to become anxious about the persistent financial and emotional cost of her obsessive quest, yet he dare not refuse her because he can see that frustration is so catastrophic. Emma's story is a clear illustration of this:

> When Emma was 37 she recognised that her career was not going as well as her husband's. She decided to try to deal with her envy and resentment by getting pregnant, something she had never previously considered. She was a very beautiful woman who had always succeeded in achieving what she wanted. Conception, however, did not happen and she became more and more angry and demanding of her parents, her husband and her doctors. She was unable to accept that there was an aspect of her life which she could not control. She was also unable to make use of her counselling sessions and so the outcome of her misery is unknown to me.

Kirsten's story shows a different reaction to a similar situation:

> Kirsten was equally beautiful and successful, a company director who always expected things to come her way. She felt very ambivalent about having to give up her job to have a family, but finally decided she would do this. When she did not get pregnant in three months, she gave up trying and then became very anxious about the whole issue. Part of her anxiety was caused by her tendency towards general doubt and indecisiveness about everything except work. The other part was a fear of being unable to have what she wanted. She preferred 'to decide not to want' as a way of controlling the situation, because 'to want and not to have' would mean she was helpless.

Such compensations as adoption are usually rejected by these women. They rarely want to adopt another woman's child because they generally doubt their ability to love and fear that they might reject the child.

Most of today's women want children for some combination of these three reasons. It is only when one is a dominant feature that the above groups emerge. It is important, however, to have analysed the differences because the prognosis of each is so different.

Like women, men are frequently confused about what they want, whether they really want it and when they want it. Rightly or wrongly they feel they carry the financial burden and this is often their justification for not wanting a baby now. This may, of course, conceal the fact that they do not want a baby ever but fear to admit it. Men can see that a baby means a great loss of attention from their partner and their own parents, so the less secure man may have many doubts about his ability to cope with this. For men, too, a new baby in the home when they were a child meant loss of attention and an on-going disruption of their life which they are reluctant to repeat. Against this is the excitement and rise in self-esteem both as a person and as a man that is commonly felt by new fathers. The hope that a boy will share his interests and a girl will adore him are felt by many to be more than adequate compensation for other losses of money and attention.

To summarize, the rather frightening decision to take the 'rite of passage' into parenthood and the attempt to hold on to the freedoms of the previous stage naturally cause problems for thinking, sensitive people. As usual it is, of course, very important for us to face our deeper anxieties, to share them with our partner and to make sure that the wrong reasons are not being used either for having or not having children.

Key Points

♦ The greatest dilemma for women today is the conflict between their demands for equality and the biological fact that they alone bear children
♦ Children are seen as a part of the self
♦ The dilemma for men is the knowledge of loss of attention from the partner
♦ Financial demands may control the decisions made.

12

The Impact of Infertility

In considering the issue of fertility and the choices women face, I have drawn on examples of those who are unable to conceive to help to highlight certain points. It is now time to consider more fully the problems of those couples who fail to conceive.

It is important to distinguish between infertility which leaves the couple with no choice about their own fertility because the problem is absolute and clearly understood, and the infertility of those who may spend all their reproductive years trying to conceive because there is hope. The first couple still have choices to make between adoption, no children, or, when the problem is with the man, artificial insemination by donor, but they do know where they stand. Hope produces a different problem.

The failure to conceive and the subsequent medical investigations are stressful for both partners, usually more so for the woman, and can damage their relationship. Many couples go through a period of fear of infertility on their way to parenthood, and when this is a lengthy period it can be very destructive. Each understanding the other's separate and different fears can make a great difference to whether a couple pull together or blame each other and fall apart. The way they cope with this adversity again reflects their previous adjustment and the defence mechanisms that they use.

Often there is a power struggle in the partnership if one partner longs for a child and the other doesn't want one at all. Clearly this is a difficult problem to resolve, and it may be made more difficult if the unwilling partner is concealing it in some way. Even when recognised, the problem is dire, since it is an issue with no possible compromise. Both partners have equal rights to their desires but one or other will have to relinquish theirs entirely. A price will have to be paid for such a power struggle and it is never obvious who should pay it or how it should be resolved. Partners need help to sort out who will be most distressed by frustration of their wishes and how this might affect the relationship. Lisa and Dermot's story shows how complicated these situations can be:

> Lisa came to me for counselling for a sexual problem, and revealed that she had married her husband Dermot knowing that he was unwilling ever to have children. It was never clear to me whether she herself did not want a child at that time, or whether she did want a child and thought she would be able to win Dermot over.
>
> Dermot's story made his reluctance understandable. His own life had been disrupted by his older sister bringing home an illegitimate baby when he was 14 years old. He was moved out of his bedroom and the only memory he had of this time was that he was taken to the doctor because he had a sleeping problem. His adult rationalisation for not wanting children was that a baby would be very disruptive and he didn't want to change his lifestyle.
>
> Dermot was very intelligent but extremely passive, apparently fearful of any aggression in himself. After several months of counselling he felt that since Lisa would probably not forgive him if he denied her a child, and having acquired some insight about his resistance, he allowed conception to take place.
>
> The twist in this tale is that the birth of the baby produced a profound and lasting depression in Lisa, while Dermot became a devoted father who has indeed found that his lifestyle has changed because his wife is so frequently ill.

Such a relationship may well run into sexual difficulties. Reproduction and sex are so inextricably linked, despite desperate attempts through contraception to separate the two, that a problem in one often means a problem in the other. Facing infertility may highlight previously hidden difficulties.

While the biological destiny of both men and women is to have children, and the burdens of infertility affect women and men and the partnerships between them, these burdens fall most heavily on women. The male and female roles in reproduction are so specific that failure is bound to affect the two sexes differently. Fertility is a very emotive word full of rich associations, and to be infertile or 'barren' or 'sterile' conjures up feelings of deprivation and desolation.

Effect on Women

If a woman is unable to conceive, this can be a major blow to her self-esteem. Behind their defences, most women want a child. Even those who think that greater triumph and self-esteem lie in a career usually begin to feel they have lost out if they fail to have a child.

Self-esteem has to do with a sense of being valued. I have earlier argued that all women suffer, to some extent, from low self-esteem

207

because of the greater social and physical power of men. Many women have particularly low self-esteem from childhood because they felt their brothers were more valued by parents or even that their parents had wished that they were a boy. To such women, having a baby is their chance to be valued. Pregnancy was traditionally described as 'an interesting condition'. The woman becomes very important because she has to go through an ordeal which men recognise as both singular and dangerous and which they admire. Also, she might produce a boy for her parents. Producing a baby is her job alone. A man, who so often seems to have the advantage, cannot do this and, apart from a bit of back rubbing on the day, he must stand idly by. From childhood, while the young boy has been showing off his penis and developing stronger muscles, the little girl has been hugging the knowledge that she has the ultimate triumph of producing a child and thereby becoming successful and powerful like her mother. The contrast in reproductive role thus becomes a major means of redressing the balance of value between the sexes. The man's role is brief and without risk to him. The woman's role is prolonged and dangerous, and has a profound effect on her body and her mind.

The inability to have a child removes this opportunity for success, importance and power. The more a woman unconsciously looks to her child to raise her self-esteem, the less she is able to tolerate infertility. In cultures where the traditional role is still the only role for a woman, or where, through lack of opportunity or ability, a woman cannot compensate for reproductive failure with a career, the infertile woman feels very desperate. Her sense of well-being is lost, and many women become obsessed with the need to put this all right and prove that they are not a failure.

There is much anger for such a woman to cope with. She may be angry with God or fate; with the partner who makes her feel guilty, however much he may reassure her; with the mother who continues to be all-powerful and with whom she cannot now compete; and not least, with friends and siblings who have been more lucky and have had children. Here there will be secondary anger towards any baby who now claims attention. At every visit the friend or sibling will now have one eye firmly fixed on their baby. This can sometimes have unusual results:

One couple I knew were very proud of their new baby and wanted to show him off when a friend came to supper. After they had eaten, the husband decided to photograph the baby. In the middle of this rather lengthy process, the friend, who could not take frustration easily, became so fraught that she turned the light off!

This is particularly liable to cause depression arising from a sense of badness or loneliness. If seeing the lucky friend or sibling produces envy, the woman may begin to avoid such meetings, which can lead to an almost phobic avoidance of situations where other people's children have to be held and played with. Unfortunately, mothers and their children are everywhere, and there is no escape from the daily injection of painful envy for the infertile woman.

These unpleasant feelings of envy and jealousy are particularly hard to manage if a friend or sibling has a miscarriage or even loses a child. The infertile woman may be appalled to recognise that part of her is glad about this. She then has a guilty secret to hide which separates her further. One of the major contributions of counselling in infertility is to give understanding and support to a woman who feels alienated from friends and family by her envious feelings. She desperately needs to be reassured that such feelings are inevitable and that if there is any uncomfortable gladness at a friend's loss, it is only due to the release from the burden of her envy. She may not have recognised that it is possible to feel relieved of envy and desperately sad for the friend at the same time. Of course, it remains a moral problem for us all to struggle with on all fronts, that the protection of self should be such a dominating feature of the human being and that therefore the relief of our own feelings is so important that we cannot wholeheartedly suffer at the tragedy of a friend.

Mechanical Causes of Infertility

There is a group of women with mechanical causes of infertility due to rare and incurable problems because they have been born missing some vital part of their reproductive system due to a foetal accident, chromosome irregularity or hormone over- or under-production. Their personalities are greatly affected by their disability due to intense early medical intervention or, in some cases, late recognition of their problem. Their parents' attitude affects them even more, and many parents are bewildered and feel inadequate to deal with the situation. Many doctors, too, feel at a loss as to how to explain, or suggest how parents might explain, to their child what has happened to them.

The extent of the effect on the child depends on a number of factors including the age at which the girl is told of her disability, the type of family she belongs to, the friends and doctors involved and her own personality and its maturity. The loss is likely to be coped with well by someone who feels loved and cherished and is therefore able to accept disappointment and find ways to compensate such as a career or adoption. Sadly, so often, parents are bewildered and helpless and cannot reassure their child because they have had no help in coping with their own disappointment. The only way they know how to deal with it is to avoid the issue, with the result that the child has low self-esteem, finds it difficult to make friends and impossible to find a partner. On top of her own pain she often has to deal with her parents' guilt, anxiety and disappointment.

Even when such a situation has been dealt with in the best way possible, the woman has the problem of deciding at what point in a new relationship she must explain that she may need further operations and that she can never have a child. It is obvious that the humiliation and fear of rejection involved will make the forming of a partnership much more difficult than it already is. Janine's story shows how far-reaching the consequences of this may be:

> Ruth's daughter Janine was born without a womb. Ruth was so depressed (and, presumably, guilty) about Janine's problem that she was quite unable to support her daughter or give her any hope about her future.
>
> Janine left home at 16 and turned to other women for support, always seeking mother figures. She identified as a lesbian, thereby avoiding the problem of the infertility, and acquired a mother-figure who seemed more loving than Ruth. She was, however, depressed with a poor sense of self-worth, despite the apparently satisfactory nature of her defensive relationships.

Phoebe had a similar problem, and her sad story shows other aspects of this issue:

> Phoebe was born with Androgen Insensitivity Syndrome. This is a complex problem involving failed reaction to hormones while still in the womb which essentially meant that she had neither ovaries, uterus nor a proper vagina. Her mother could not speak to her about this at all. Her father told her when she was 14 that she would never have children. However, even he failed to organise the operation which was necessary for her to be able to have sexual intercourse.
>
> Phoebe left her home in New Zealand and organised her own operation in London with no family support at all. She recalled the hospital discharging her after the major operation and how she left carrying her suitcase with nobody to meet her and nowhere to go.
>
> On the surface Phoebe seemed tough and in control, but ten years after her operation she was filled with anger and suffered bouts of depression. She expected rejection from people and, in her pain and defensiveness, elicited it and confirmed her fears. She found it difficult to trust a partner, partly because she faced the difficult judgment of when to say that she could not have children.

When a satisfactory relationship is made these women still carry the burden of low self-esteem and anger, which is often released towards the loved one as the only safe person to reveal it to. This obviously takes its toll and requires a partner who is able to take and understand an anger that is often discharged at, but not really meant for, him.

Effect on Men

Men's self-esteem is very much linked to their virility. This word conjures up the ideas of both potency and fecundity, and any attack on the fecundity strikes also at the potency. The infertile man usually has low self-esteem and his potency is often diminished as a result. Some react differently and need to prove themselves, compensating for their infertility by becoming promiscuous. Both consequences are painful and hurtful for his partner who is already having to come to terms with her mixed feelings towards him. He feels guilty at his failure to give his partner what she wants, yet is resentful at both the unpleasant feeling of failure and the fact that it means so much to her. He feels as if he, alone, is insufficient and that only a child will satisfy her.

There is a distinction to be made between the completely infertile man with no sperm and the subfertile man with hope and potential. In the first case the couple know where they stand and must solve the problems of whether to adopt or how best to come to terms with their loss. However, frequently the man feels humiliated, and is reluctant to discuss his failure with outsiders. If a child is very important to the woman, then it is vital to the relationship for discussion and problem-solving to occur, because the wife may be able to tolerate something the husband cannot help but she will not be able to tolerate any unwillingness on his part to understand her feelings.

Where the subfertility is open to treatment, the couple may be in for a much more protracted emotional upheaval, as hopes are raised and dashed and life centres on the sperm count. This can have devastating effects on a relationship, as Malcolm and Fiona's story shows:

> Malcolm and Fiona spent their early married life abroad, drinking heavily and living for the moment. When they decided to start a family they discovered that there were problems. Malcolm's sperm count was low, and despite giving up drinking and many visits to the infertility clinic, they failed to conceive. He lost all desire to make love.
>
> In counselling it became clear that Malcolm hadn't really wanted to change his lifestyle but had tried for Fiona's sake. Her failure to conceive had caused their relationship to deteriorate. He felt he had been constantly humiliated by the process of enquiry into the infertility. As a result he had stopped trying to please his wife and now he no longer cared whether he pleased her or not.

Effect on Relationship

If the woman is infertile, she feels humiliated by this, and will feel defensive towards her partner for the wound she has caused him and the reprisal she imagines he really wishes to make. This defence frequently takes the form of anger, and she is often bad-tempered with both her husband and everyone else as she struggles with her sense of failure. She has been the cause of his loss, she fears he will regret marrying her, she feels she should be grateful that he stays with her and she hates him for this. Bryony and Nigel's story shows how this can develop in a relationship:

> Bryony and Nigel were both musicians. Bryony was depressed and needed counselling. She was distressed because she could not have a baby, and couldn't forgive Nigel because he didn't mind. His lack of suffering and ability to get on with his work caused such a gulf between them that she wanted to leave him. Up to this point in their marriage they had shared everything as equals. Their careers, which were also their hobbies, had given pleasure and unity, but now Bryony's need of a child threatened to separate them. It made their lives unequal in satisfaction for the first time and she needed Nigel to suffer more with her.

As with Bryony and Nigel, the man is often resented because he has his career or hobby to compensate. This may go further, and many men are positively pleased that they will not have to share their woman with a child. However, his partner's depression makes him feel he is not good enough, that all she wanted him for was to make a baby, and that without a baby she will never be satisfied. He feels he must keep trying or else she will not forgive him, and he begins to feel persecuted and finally resentful. The result of such pressure may be impotence. This can be dramatically reversed when the woman reaches menopause, with painful results, as happened to Maeve and Gordon:

> Maeve was referred to me because intercourse became painful after she was told that she had suffered an early menopause at the age of 40. This was a terrible blow because she had always longed for a child and had had four miscarriages for which no cause could be found. Four years later she came for counselling because she feared her marriage was in danger as sex was now 'impossible'. Her husband Gordon was now wanting sexual intercourse, when for years he had not been interested and she had had to persuade him in order to try to conceive. He had told her that he did not really want to have a child because her passion for one left him feeling that he would be displaced.
>
> When Maeve realised she had lost her chance for a child she became angry and depressed and saw no point in sexual intercourse. She felt bitter towards Gordon who she felt had wasted vital years by working too hard and never

having time for sex. By the time she came to me she had withdrawn from him and could find no way back.

If the man is infertile the woman feels angry and let down. She feels guilty, because she knows he can't help it, but she cannot stop blaming him. She is afraid she will damage his self-esteem, and that he will not be able to bear the humiliation of being sterile. She therefore feels that she has to be very careful how she treats him. This produces a situation in which a couple can become distanced from one another for safety in case they hurt one another.

Most men are less affected by being unable to have their own child than most women. They are relieved of their inner fears of being displaced in their wife's affections by a child and can usually compensate. However, even when this is the case, the loss of self-esteem is very great. The humiliation of letting the woman down causes defensiveness, with the result that men become either angry and difficult to live with or apologetic and emasculated. There can be many anxieties to be faced in dealing with his infertility, as Denzel and Julia's story shows:

Julia's husband Denzel had had cancer before they married. He had donated sperm before receiving chemotherapy, which made him sterile but cured his cancer. Two attempts at IVF using Denzel's sperm failed, and they naturally had to cope with much disappointment.

Julia had many anxieties about the other alternatives available to her. However, Julia and Denzel had a great deal of insight and were perhaps more aware than most of the emotional issues to be dealt with. They realised that adoption would give them an equal connection to the baby so that jealousy might be reduced, but that it would also deny Julia the experience of pregnancy and giving birth, and that such a denial could have left Denzel feeling guilty and Julia feeling resentful. They were worried about their possible reactions to a baby by donor, and about what to tell such a baby of its history and the pain this might cause it. They were concerned about some religious members of their families who were likely to reject such technological help. They were afraid they might not like the baby, and they were aware of the risk of blaming problems on unknown genes.

Julia tended to feel pressured by the opinions of others, and was particularly worried about what she thought her mother would want her to do. Julia's anxiety about Denzel's feelings and reactions clouded the issue and made it difficult for her to work out what her own fears were.

It is possible that Julia's choice to marry Denzel despite his infertility reflected her mixed feelings about parenthood. There is another piece of evidence which supports this: she was a talented woman who embarked on a new career to take some of the pressure off the problem, but this also served to delay the decision-making.

Fears of being unable to value the child, who would demand so much investment of effort and care, are inevitable in such cases. Julia and Denzel's experience also highlights the difficulty of making choices between apparently unsatisfactory alternatives. The move they were finally able to make was to adopt two children and this may or may not have been the end of the story.

Part of the stress of infertility these days comes from the actual process of investigation and treatment, however well-managed it may be. There are continuous visits to the hospital with investigations, raised hopes and regular disappointments. Where IVF is involved the taking of hormones and surgical procedures are upsetting to most and terrifying to some. The sexual relationship is greatly affected by the need to have intercourse on certain days of the month, or for the man to masturbate as required to provide specimens, and couples feel all their early spontaneity has been lost. There are difficult feelings to cope with when monthly hope is followed by monthly disappointment, and the woman's period comes to represent failure. This cycle of hope and disappointment can be very compelling and addictive. Like many gambling-related activities, the obsession with technique is reinforced by the idea of 'better luck next time'. Also, like other compulsions and addictions, if it becomes too all-consuming other aspects of life may be missed in the quest. Many couples express their disappointment by feeling rebellious at the dictates of the treatment, and feel that to have to have sex on Saturday, for instance, ruins the sexual feelings. The only way through this is for people to be reminded that if they care about their partner it should be possible to have intercourse on any day, particularly if it is of such importance.

Defences

With all these problems to face, defences have to be built to hide the hurt. The particular defences used will be based to a large extent on the ones developed in childhood. Many women start pretending they didn't want children anyway, and thus present themselves to the world untruthfully. Such women often seem hard, brittle and unmaternal when in fact they are quite the opposite. In this way the whole personality can be deprived of its spontaneity. Yvette used this defence very strongly:

> Yvette had a particular problem with low self-esteem, which had come about through having two brothers whom she felt were valued by her parents more than she was. The boys were sent to expensive schools and allowed more freedom than she was.
> Yvette was understandably angry and frustrated after years of coping with her envy and trying to hide her hostile feelings. It is possible that the medical problem

causing her infertility was due to a disruption of her hormone balance through emotional distress, but unfortunately, the certain effect was to reinforce her sense of frustration and inferiority.

Her brothers soon produced families while she was unable to do so. To alleviate her feeling of humiliation, she developed the defence of telling the world that she did not want to have children. She gave the impression that she didn't even like children and avoided ever picking up her nieces and nephews or her friends' children.

Yvette was fully aware of developing this defence but was also aware that her defence was to hide her feelings of humiliation, and so was not quite sure whether she wanted a child for the 'right' reasons. She knew she wanted a child and yet was afraid of having one in case she did not love it. Her defence distorted her personality and did not allow anyone to know or understand her, and indeed she did not know or understand herself.

She sought help for her infertility secretly and surprised everyone when she finally got pregnant as nobody thought she wanted a child. On the evidence she produced in counselling, it is likely that she only allowed herself to get pregnant once she accepted that her envy was understandable in the circumstances. This freed her to believe that her hostile feelings did not make a bad person, and she could therefore be a good parent, so it was safe to have a baby.

Another dangerous consequence of prolonged difficulty in achieving conception is that the child becomes idealised and, increasingly as the years pass, seen as the only worthwhile thing in life. The lack of a child becomes the reason for all unhappiness and the idea of a child the fount of all happiness. This, together with progressive technology sustaining hope, results in an obsessive investment in conceiving which may last for years.

This kind of obsession is damaging on two counts. First, other experiences are lost, and horizons contract around the idea of conception. The person frequently forgets that they had lived contentedly for two or three decades without a child, and often had only recently wanted one. Secondly, if the longing for and subsequent idealisation of the child has been too great, there is often depression when a child is finally born. A burden has been put on the child to remedy lost years of fear and misery that the woman has experienced and to fulfil all her hopes. Since looking after a baby is difficult and demanding, the reality is bound to be disappointing if too much had been expected.

In the normal course of events pregnant women, while excited and pleased, are also worried and fearful of the great responsibility to come. This mixture of feelings reflects the reality of the difficulties to be expected with a first baby and prepares the woman for what is ahead. The infertile woman who conceives after many years has become increasingly distanced from any worries about having a child because the quest to have it and the fear of not having it has been so strong. She is, therefore, less well prepared for the reality than her worrying sisters, and may even develop strongly rejecting feelings towards a difficult baby. Needless to say this is unexpected and feels very frightening.

It is important for us to remember that infertile people may be very sad and sensitive. Their need for the medical profession makes them especially angry and vulnerable, and they are frequently demanding and critical. They often blame the doctors for failing to put them right and even for their need to be there in the first place. Many people, even their partners, fail to realise how they suffer.

Psychological Factors in Infertility

There are, of course, many causes of infertility. Some of the most obvious are because the hormonal system is not working properly and the woman's eggs are not being produced, or because there is a blockage of the tubes so that the eggs and the sperm cannot meet. Some are due to very rare conditions. In many cases, no specific cause can be found.

If a specific cause is found, this may bring its own particular psychological problems. For example, a common form of infertility is where, following an infection, the fallopian tubes become blocked. Such infections are often linked with sexual intercourse, and sometimes with termination of a pregnancy, either of which may lead to guilt and anxiety that it is a punishment meted out for wrongdoing, particularly if the person is predisposed to think in this way. However in this section I want to examine how psychological factors may be involved in the failure of a couple to conceive.

We have to remember that, as we saw earlier on in this book, many people have been conditioned in their childhood to believe that interest in sex is bad and if they are bad they will be punished. The result of such conditioning is that if punishment comes, in the form of infection, there is the unconscious assumption that the individual must somehow have been bad. Where infertility follows infection, it becomes a second punishment. These punishments seem to prove that parents were right and sex is dirty and dangerous. So the person may shun sexual intercourse and blame their partner.

If someone feels doomed in this way, problems arising from an infection come as no surprise. I have seen many infertile people who never expected to conceive because they have never felt adequate to have a child. They do not feel in the same league as their mothers or maybe their peers. Megan was strongly affected in this way:

Megan was depressed and desperate for a child, but despite this she found it difficult to follow the guidelines for conception. She would avoid having intercourse,
even at the most fertile part of the month. Even after an operation to unblock her
tubes she seemed reluctant to try hard to conceive.

The reason Megan gave, once her passivity was pointed out, was that she was
protecting herself from further disappointment by not really trying. In her mind
this left some hope that there was a possibility of success if she did make the
effort.

For Megan, therefore, the most important thing was not the child but the fear
of frustration. She was afraid that she could not face failing to get what she
wanted. Exploration revealed that she felt she was being punished for an earlier
pregnancy termination, and was afraid that if she failed to conceive another
child, this would confirm the fact that she was unforgiven and still being
punished. She did not really want to put this to the test.

There is a further interesting topic to be explored, and this is the fact
that psychological factors may actually cause infertility.

Psychological Causes

Most people understand that infertility can have psychological results
in terms of personal unhappiness and emotional difficulty between
partners. Many people, however, find it hard to believe that infertility
itself can be the manifestation of an unrecognised psychological
problem. A suspicion that an emotional disturbance concealed in the
unconscious of the patient is actually causing the infertility is a difficult
issue because the infertile individual, whether a man or a woman, often
consciously believes that they are desperate to have a child and are naturally indignant at any suggestion that this might not be unambiguously
so. For those who have no understanding of psychology, it is understandably annoying to have suggestions made that seem contrary to
everything they know about themselves. If you are moved to tears by
small socks in shops and are jealous of every woman with a baby, how
can you be expected to accept and explore the idea that a part of you
does not want a child because of fear or some other reason?
Nevertheless, if this is the truth, then it is vital to tackle the situation
because a strong unconscious resistance can be totally powerful in
thwarting the conscious wish to have a child.

There are two ways in which hidden anxiety causes failure to conceive. The first is where a man or woman, consciously or
unconsciously, fails to do what is necessary for conception. The second
is where a hidden fear operates in a physiological or medical way and

conception fails to occur, and usually a reason for this cannot be found.

In the first category we have a group of people in whom a sexual or some related problem is the reason for their failure to conceive. I have seen many such women whose longing for a child has been crippled by fear of pregnancy and childbirth. Avoiding intercourse because of pain clearly protects them both from their fear of childbirth and from acknowledging this fear. Others just say they are afraid of having a child and have come for counselling to deal with this. These fears obviously frustrate the part of them which wants a child. It is interesting how often the fear is more powerful than the desire. These women often have a heightened fear of pain, both from sexual intercourse and from giving birth. This may be because of the reponsibility involved in being a mother, it may be because they resent being women and having to allow penetration and thus try to 'seal' their vaginas, or it may be associated with guilt over childhood abuse. In these women, it is what the fear of childbirth represents that needs to be dealt with. This is not always easy because, of course, it is reasonable to fear the inevitable pain of child-birth. Concentrating on the reasonable aspect, however, rarely relieves the anxiety, while analysing what lies behind it often does.

In some cases sexual intercourse is not taking place at all. It seems extraordinary that even in today's society people seek treatment for infertility without first revealing that no penetrative sexual intercourse is taking place. Several cases have been referred to me in which a couple have been thoroughly investigated for infertility over a number of years in more than one hospital, only for it to be revealed that penetration is not being, and never has been, achieved. Doreen and Joseph's story is typical of this group:

> Doreen and Joseph had been married for 15 years when they were referred to a gynaecologist because they wanted a baby. For several months they omitted to mention that they had never consummated their marriage. When this was revealed they agreed to be referred for counselling.
>
> They were a most charming and co-operative couple, but nevertheless they proved impossible to help. During the session Doreen would be prepared to explore and expose her anxieties, and seemed involved and interested in the understanding she gained. Unfortunately, each session would be followed by two or three which had to be cancelled because she developed severe migraine on the day of the appointment. In the end we all agreed that the resistance had won and they gave up their quest for a family.

A less obvious example of psychological factors contributing to infertility is when treatment is in effect being sabotaged. It is frequently possible to recognise that people who seem to be desperate to have a child in fact are failing to take the necessary measures to ensure conception. They don't read the literature they are given, they don't want to bother with taking their temperature and they say they 'want it to happen naturally'. Mandy's story is a characteristic example of this:

Mandy's husband was sterile. She had at least 20 tries at artificial insemination by donor. Various things went wrong: sometimes she was unable to read her ovulation detection kit properly, at other times she would have a cup of tea before measuring her urine when this was expressly forbidden, and each month she would have 'just' missed the day.

These small resistances are the tip of the iceberg of much larger resistances, and much time and money can be wasted if they are not picked up.

In the second category we see that psychological factors can directly affect the man's or the woman's reproductive physiology. Psychological distress can cause periods to stop with failure of ovulation, or it can reduce the production of sperm to the point of infertility. Many kinds of emotional distress can operate in this way, and Imogen's story shows just one example:

Imogen was referred because of distress associated with infertility. She told me that she had become pregnant at the age of 15 following a rape by a boy of her own age. The termination which followed, without any alternative or any counselling being offered, was a very traumatic affair dealt with insensitively by both Imogen's mother and the male gynaecologist. After the termination her mother saw a psychiatrist for six months, but no such help and understanding was offered to Imogen.

Among other consequences Imogen didn't ovulate for twelve years. She avoided her planned university career, left home and struggled to come to terms with her guilt and pain. During this time she developed blocked tubes from a pelvic infection, which reinforced her fear that she was to be punished for her part in the rape and the resultant death of her foetus by being denied another chance.

Imogen regained her ovulation during psychotherapy, but despite tubal surgery and two IVF attempts she still failed to conceive.

Ben and Cheryl's case was a good example of what can happen to a man and it shows how emotional factors can dominate outside chemical aids:

Ben and Cheryl were married with a young son named Zak, but had failed to conceive again after trying for four years. Their problem was that Ben's sperm count now fluctuated between low and non-existent and all hormone treatment had failed to alter this.

Cheryl was an attractive motherly part-time nurse and Ben was a rather dependent man with depressive tendencies. At first I saw them together but after a few sessions I started to see Ben alone, and he continued to see me monthly for about two years.

Ben's depression followed a very disturbed childhood. When his sister was born he was put in the care of the local authority who moved him around a lot as he grew up. As a result he had a very ambivalent relationship with his mother. Much of the time he treated Cheryl as if she were his mother and was very sulky and difficult to live with. This was partly to punish her in place of his disappointing mother, and partly because he wanted her to be a good mother and put his past right which was totally unrealistic. When Cheryl failed to be perfect Ben felt angry and let down all over again.

After two years of counselling Ben brought Cheryl back into a session and said he was ready to acknowledge something that he found very difficult. He told us that he had gradually come to realise that the suggestion I had made, that he did not entirely want another child, was true. He was terrified of it because after Zak's birth he had experienced very hostile feelings towards the baby, so much so that he had been frightened to be left alone with Zak lest he harm him. His fear was that he would punish Zak who now took Cheryl's attention away from him, just as he had wished to punish his sister when she was born for causing him to be sent away. Cheryl was astonished by Ben's revelation but was totally accepting of it and supportive of him.

To my amazement and theirs, the next time they came Cheryl was pregnant. We all believed that for Ben to be able to externalise his fear and have it understood reduced its power. Counselling reassured him that such feelings from his childhood were understandable and could be forgiven. It allowed him to understand the feelings he had had since childhood and have the confidence to know he could contain them. At first it seemed as if the catharsis of telling Cheryl was the freeing component, but it turned out that she had conceived two weeks before his disclosure. This suggests that his increased insight had already made him feel safe enough to recommence the production of sperm.

While it is clear that no conscious alteration of the sperm count is possible, Ben's case is particularly interesting because it implies that unconscious control of it is possible.

Serious overweight and underweight can make conception difficult because they interfere with ovulation. The former is often a reflection of anxiety about life, and the latter is often linked with a resistance to being adult and taking the inevitable responsibilities of child-rearing. Both these extremes operate physically to prevent conception, but they have strong psychological roots. Sylvia's story shows this in action:

Sylvia was referred because she had decided to have a child but was not able to conceive. She had been anorexic for years and was very keen for me to take responsibility for her eating by giving her a diet and demanding that she stick to it, yet she was obviously a rather controlling and rebellious person. I felt it was a situation where this would result in a struggle, as she would want to rebel against advice, and would not accept analysis of her problem. I suggested to her that she was sufficiently intelligent to read and understand a diet book, and if she wanted a child enough she would eat properly.

A few months later her gynaecologist let me know that Sylvia was pregnant.

I think it likely that if I had allowed her to give me the responsibility, she would have thereby remained the child and failed to eat.

The underlying anxieties are often deeply hidden and affect men and women differently.

Women

In order to explore these questions we need to understand further the circumstances in which there may be a strong unconscious wish in a woman not to have children. There are many natural reasons to feel anxious about the responsibility of having children. Where a girl has been anxious about growing up and has attempted to stop the process by remaining childish, she has a deep fear that she will not be capable of motherhood. Her intelligence may tell her that in fact she is capable, so she acquires a baby by adoption with which she can reassure her unconscious.

As we have seen, the birth of a sibling can induce strongly hostile feelings towards the baby who has stolen the mother away. Crying babies are associated with loss of mother's attention, and therefore feel very threatening. This means that there has actually been a real experience of a baby when, day after day, resentment had to be swallowed and life was turned sour by the advent of the child. As far as infertility goes this can mean that this early experience of a baby not only causes pain and irritation at the time of the baby's arrival, but can be buried in the unconscious as a negative feeling associated with babies that resurfaces when it is time to consider a baby of one's own. In a corner of the unconscious, therefore, there is a powerful resistance to, at the same time as there are other parts of the unconscious and conscious which are strongly wanting, a baby. Because it used to be so, such a woman may unconsciously fear being trapped at home with a baby she hates. She is now likely to reject this proposition consciously at the same time as she unconsciously tries to prevent another unpleasant experience. It is vital, however, that she faces this past hostility in order to reassure her unconscious mind that, if she has her own baby, she will be powerful when before she was helpless over her mother's baby. This reassurance will make all the difference.

There are other clues to the possibility that unconscious factors may be at work in producing infertility, and they need to be detected and evaluated before any judgment of their importance can be reached. As we saw in Chapter 8, the position of the child in the family often has a significant effect here. The eldest girl, for example, has had the traumatic experience of being displaced by a baby. Her experience is to have had her security shattered by the imposition of a crying demanding baby who never goes away, and she never wants to experience this again. She often builds strong defences of denial and believes that she is longing for a baby.

Sometimes the youngest girl, if unable to relinquish her role as a baby who must be looked after, retains a feeling of inadequacy. Unconsciously she doesn't want to have to grow up and so she doesn't feel capable of being a mother. She knows that she wants to be mothered herself. This can be quite a problem because her whole personality may be quite immature, and while she consciously wants what her friends are having she unconsciously fears that she could not cope.

Women who have a prestigious and interesting job while holding the idea that being a mother is a second-class social role may be vulnerable. If they have grown up seeing a woman's role, as exemplified by their mothers, as inferior, there will be a corner of resistance which in some is powerful enough to avoid the demands made by the conscious mind. The woman may reason that a baby is what she needs now, but unconsciously she still has the underlying fear that having a baby is a 'second-class' thing to do and she therefore fears it will take over and kill off the successful part of her which she values.

Another clue is to be found where there has been a deep reluctance to accept femininity. Conception is the ultimate expression and confirmation of femaleness. Yet in some there is a reluctance to face, once and for all, that their gender is female. Those who had strong girlhood ambivalence about gender often retain a remnant which hopes that they are really male and is reluctant to surrender that hope.

While there is plenty of conscious rationalisation for delaying conception, such a delay often represents the fact that at present the woman doesn't want a child but has a fantasy that sometime in the future she will feel more like it. It may be an expression of her overall situation, which is that she is not entirely sure that she wants a child. Of course age and circumstances are relevant factors, but, for example, a woman of 30 who says she will be ready to have children in a few years is, by implication, saying that she does not want children now. In another example, a woman of similar age who wants to get her three piece suite before trying to conceive is demonstrating where her priorities lie.

The way someone tells their story, and the way they talk about their partner, can be more revealing than any of the above categories. Some people can tolerate frustration much more than others, are more open-minded than others and are more prepared to take responsibility than others. Where an infertile person is self-justifying, self-pitying and blaming everyone else, it is likely that they have some hidden resistance which makes them block the process in ways that are obvious when discovered but may not have been obvious to them at the time. Perhaps they accidentally miss the important dates, or they forget the important pills. Often they have always felt some discontent and infertility seems to be just another example of the bad luck which seems to dog them. They may not even want to work at solving their problem. All they want is what they want, and if they cannot get it the way they want it, nothing else will do.

Men

Men may also be infertile for psychological reasons. The two main reasons for men resisting conception are fear of responsibility and fear of displacement. While the reproductive destiny of the woman is to grow the child inside her body, that of the man has been to be responsible for providing for the family. To many men this burden seems too heavy to carry. Particularly where the woman is very eager for a child, the less mature man sees a baby as a potential rival and already feels rejected by his wife. Some men are quite open about their fears, but I have found that in infertility the anxiety is usually unconscious and completely denied. Men, like women, have plenty of conscious rationalisation for delaying or refusing conception, including not wanting a child for economic reasons or because they fear a change in a happy lifestyle. Problems arise when these conscious fears disguise other unconscious fears so that the conscious fears can never be allayed.

Psychological factors causing men to be infertile mostly manifest themselves as impotence. This can take the form of failure to get an erection, premature ejaculation or failure to ejaculate. Where a man has been impotent throughout the relationship, this must be investigated as a sexual problem and may or may not be due to an unconscious fear of creating a child. I have seen many men, however, who mysteriously become incapable of getting an erection or ejaculating when the decision to have a child occurs. The juxtaposition of these two events makes it more than likely that the man is unconsciously resistant to having a child.

These symptoms usually reflect a deep anxiety about introducing a child into the relationship and the man is likely to be highly defended against conception. He may be quite unaware of his anxiety, or he may know he does not want a child but does not dare to say so. The sudden onset of his impotence, just as the woman wants a child, produces a lot of anger in her. She often feels that her partner has more control over his problem than he actually has. This anger in her incites anger in him which combines with the original anxiety about conception to increase his impotence. This situation, naturally, is extremely frustrating, both to the man who believes he wants a child and to the woman who feels her partner is deliberately thwarting her and that he could function properly if he really tried. In my experience, the woman is usually right that he is thwarting her desire but wrong that it is deliberate. He cannot perform, however hard he tries, if part of his unconscious mind has decided against it. The partnership in this case is very much under threat and the quality of life of the couple is diminished by the continuous threat of the woman's anger. This is very difficult for the man who, because he clearly does not want to face the truth that part of him does not want a child, feels quite helpless and yet is unwilling to accept counselling. Often, he will come along to please his wife, but he tends to remain withdrawn. Ali was such a man:

> Ali and Jasmin were under pressure from their family to conceive. They had been married for 10 years but had never achieved full intercourse. Originally Ali seemed potent but Jasmin suffered pain and tightening of the vagina and could not allow penetration. After many months of counselling she was able to relax, allow examinations by her gynaecologist and to accept penetration, but Ali now found himself unable to penetrate.
>
> They achieved conception by AIH (artificial insemination by husband) as Jasmin's age was beginning to cause concern. AIH meant that Ali had to produce a specimen of semen which was then injected into Jasmin's womb. Despite the fact that they agreed it was important to continue the counselling to improve the sexual side of their relationship, predictably they did not return after the baby was born.

As we have seen, a man is not usually as distressed as his partner by infertility. Exceptions occur when the idea of a child symbolises the healing of some lack in his own life. Paul's story is an example of this:

> Paul was so desperate for a child that even though he disliked his partner Sharon enough to refuse to live with her, he wanted her to have his child. His case was very complicated because he was unable to ejaculate except by masturbation and wanted artificial insemination.
>
> It was difficult to be sure of the origin of Paul's fear of ejaculating inside a woman, but one strong possibility was that he felt more ambivalent about having a child than he thought. The unconscious controlling part of him feared a child, but consciously he was desperate for one, and tried to override his unconscious resistance by mechanical means.
>
> Paul had been adopted, and seemed to be desperate to give himself a 'natural' family. At the same time he recognised some incongruity in the fact that he was reluctant to make a commitment to Sharon, with whom he wanted to found his dynasty.

There are a number of other factors that can be at work in infertile men. Lien's story is an interesting one which shows several factors in action:

Lien was a charming man who had had a very strict upbringing. He was forced by war to leave home when he was barely an adult, which meant that he did not have time to shed his inhibitions before survival became his top priority. The result was that he remained sexually innocent and did not marry until his late forties.

Lien's wife Mia complained to me that he was uninterested in sex and reluctant to have sexual intercourse. She was 38 and as she very much wanted a child this was causing a great deal of difficulty in their marriage. I saw them for several months. He was most co-operative, but under stress because his strict upbringing had instilled in him the belief that sex was not good, and he strongly wished to be good. He now felt that he was letting Mia down, which made him feel bad, but his older anxieties seemed to dominate and he still made little apparent effort to have sex.

I finally told Lien that I felt I could not help him and the only thing I could suggest was a particular drug which I had found could be helpful in the sort of phobic anxiety which I thought he had. I told him the name of the drug and said that next time I would prescribe it if, after thinking it over and discussing it with Mia, he wanted me to.

It was a delightful surprise when they returned two months later and Mia was pregnant! When I asked why they thought this was, Lien admitted that he had gone to the library to look up the drug and had discovered that it required certain food restrictions and might have specific side-effects. He then felt so afraid of taking it that he was pushed into taking sexual action which seemed the lesser of two evils.

Such factors are not always unconscious, and may in some cases be completely conscious. Pierre and Eileen's story is an example of this:

Eileen was 40 when she suddenly lost her job and decided she wanted a child, having previously been adamant that she didn't want one. Her husband Pierre lived in his native France during the week but came to England at weekends. I found it a curious marriage because Eileen had refused to sacrifice any part of her life to commit herself to him and join him in his own country, and to keep the relationship going he had to make many sacrifices to meet her demands.

Many investigations took place with this couple and much time was wasted until the first revelation which was that Pierre could no longer ejaculate. At this point they were referred for counselling, and at first Eileen came alone. After she had had a few sessions Pierre asked to see me, also alone. He revealed that he loved his wife dearly but thought her incapable of looking after a child, because in his view she was too immature for this responsibility and would become depressed. He knew that if he said this to her she would never forgive him, and he felt that his only way out was to be unable to ejaculate while apparently trying very hard to resolve this.

Pierre's position was understandable, but he had allowed an immense amount of NHS money to be spent on fruitless tests in order to protect his marriage. It reminded everyone involved that where sexual problems are concerned, all is rarely as it seems. It also raised the difficulty for me of whether to condone his lie or risk their marriage. Since nobody could make Pierre ejaculate if he did not want to, and his loving understanding of his wife rang true, the best way forward seemed to be to concentrate on helping her accept her disappointment.

Two other interesting examples are those of Melvyn and Noel, who were both adopted as children. They shared a tendency to deny that learning about their adoptive status bothered them in any way. They were both unable to explore any difficult feelings in this area, which gave me some clues to the causes of their infertility.

Melvyn had a strong desire to have a child but he had a problem with his erection. Before he could penetrate he lost the erection. He had ejaculated only once when with a woman, in a casual relationship ten years before I saw him. He was burdened with a mixture of guilt about sex and a strong history of obsession with pornography from which he would masturbate satisfactorily. He was, however, desperate to have a child despite what appeared to be a very unsatisfactory relationship.

Melvyn's partner Stella already had three children by another man and did not particularly want another one, but was willing to bear one for him. However, there was friction in their relationship, because he lived at home with his mother and would not commit himself to Stella. She was quite unpleasant to him, and it was difficult to know whether this was because he wouldn't commit himself or whether he wouldn't commit because she treated him badly.

For Melvyn, his obsessive wish for a child was the dominant issue and the fact that he could barely get on with Stella was secondary. It seemed likely that at the same time that he longed for kin, he felt himself to be unfit as a father and was unconsciously protecting a child from himself.

Noel and his wife Debbie came for counselling together. He claimed never to have ejaculated, although Debbie thought there was a small amount of ejaculate during oral sex. He had had a thorough investigation of his hormonal, nervous and cardiovascular system and no reason could be found.

Noel was very difficult to communicate with and looked to Debbie to answer any question. It emerged after several sessions that he had been reluctant to marry and there were many rows over his freedom to play football and other sports. They both seemed immature in different ways: Noel was a kind of Peter Pan figure while Debbie, who had put on several stone in weight since her marriage, was very dependent on him. She had no life of her own and tried to deal with her dependency by controlling Noel.

Unfortunately Noel and Debbie could not use counselling, because he could not speak with her there and she was unwilling for him to come alone. They were not prepared to face any emotional basis to the problem. While protesting strongly that he wanted a child, it seemed likely that Noel feared the extra responsibility and the further curtailing of his activities that would ensue. Since he could not confront Debbie and say that he was not yet ready for a child, his unconscious mind found a passive way to remove the threat.

Liz and Ray's story had a happier ending:

Ray was aged 37 and had never been able to ejaculate. His wife Liz was very frustrated. He was a charming, non-assertive man, who was an artist by nature and inclination but was struggling to make a living in insurance. He had been brought up by a nanny who was very restrictive in her attitude to the body and had tied his hands in mittens so that he could not touch himself.

Because the foundation of Ray's problem was in the conditioning of his upbringing and not in the present relationship he was able to respond to counselling. Ray and Liz were proud and happy to have a son two years after I first saw them.

To take a situation which many people recognise because they know, or know of, someone it has happened to: a couple adopt a child after years of infertility and follow this event by conceiving themselves. My belief is that in such cases there has been some fear of inadequacy in the woman which unconsciously controlled her fertility. The unconscious resistance to having a child is heavily concealed by the conscious eagerness to have one. Left to nature, this unconscious resistance is more powerful than the conscious wish. Until it is released it will dominate the situation. However, by overriding the natural subconscious power by adopting a baby, the woman proves to her unconscious mind that she can cope and love a child which frees her to have her own baby.

The intensity of pain and the cycle of hope and disappointment caused by infertility is strong enough to disrupt hitherto contented partnerships. Not only the partnership but relationships with friends, colleagues and family are put under pressure. This can last for years as hope in developing technology prevents people from widening their focus of interest. This may affect one or other partner more, but a problem for one is a problem for both in a committed relationship. Understanding hidden fears and insecurities can sometimes resolve the infertility, and at other times it can help people to see that life can be worth living again if they can learn to accept their disappointment.

Key Points

♦ Reproduction and sex are so inextricably linked that a problem in one often means a problem in the other

♦ Many people, even their partners, fail to realise how much infertile people suffer

♦ Psychological factors may be involved in the failure of a couple to conceive

♦ A strong unconscious resistance can be totally powerful in thwarting the conscious wish to have a child.

PART VI

Enduring Love

13

The Power to Change

Sexual Phobias

A phobia is where a fear has developed so that intercourse is avoided, or if it cannot be avoided, a feeling of panic is produced. Some people's fear is conscious and they can acknowledge it, but in others it is unconscious and not recognised by the person.

As we have seen, the gaining of insight about personal attitudes and prejudices allows greater understanding of our own behaviour and increased sensitivity to a partner's feelings, and provides the impetus for a change in behaviour where necessary. This change alters the partner's experience and encourages reciprocal change on their part with mutually increased well-being. When it comes to actual sexual activity, however, there is a complication in this strategy which tends to block a change in behaviour and stops increased insight being put to good use. The problem is that where a phobia has been formed such that sexual intercourse is avoided, this remains as a separate physiological issue which can dominate the situation. The phobic element means that, while a person may mentally want sexual intercourse and with insight now feel quite differently about it, the automatic response of resistance to anticipated anxiety dominates and they continue with avoidance.

When I first started sexual counselling as an analytical psychotherapist, I believed that understanding alone would provide the solutions to sexual problems. I found, however, that as long as we just discussed emotional issues, people enjoyed coming to the sessions but at the same time they usually stopped the attempts they had been making to have sexual intercourse. They sat back and waited to experience the feelings they felt they should be having. In some cases this was waiting for the feelings they had when they were first in love; in other cases, where good feelings had never been achieved, they were waiting for the feelings they had heard about.

I came to recognise that there was a phobic element which was actually amplified by our shared belief that talking was enough and they did not need to struggle with sexual intercourse itself. It became clear that any suggestions to do with change of behaviour, whether simply to suggest more frequent love-making or, in the case of non-consummation, to suggest self-examination or use of tampons, resulted in anxiety and an unwillingness to attend. The counselling sessions therefore came to represent the sexual intercourse they were avoiding. Joan's story illustrates this:

> Joan was very demanding that something must be done about her problem immediately. She complained that she did not like to be touched by her boyfriend and was afraid of losing him. She was upset that I was not able to see her for a month so I suggested some reading for her to do in the meantime. A month later I asked her about the reading and she replied that she had been on holiday and had not been able to do it. The incongruity of the initial urgency with the avoidance of even reading, revealed to us that we were going to have a problem with her fear and resistance.

When I realised that this tendency to stop having sexual intercourse was widespread it became obvious that something had to be done to counteract it. Over the following years I developed and tested a programme which, in its final form, I have found to work for all who use it conscientiously. Where it has failed, one or other partner has resisted certain parts of the programme usually because they have resented having to follow rules. The rules have evolved as experience revealed the need for them. Like the rules of a diet, if they are broken, not only will it not work but any progress that has been made is lost and a sense of failure added to the problem. The other reason for failure is where the partner for whom the programme has been particularly necessary has not achieved enough insight into the reasons behind their problem, or understood the importance of the programme sufficiently, to give them the impetus to make it work.

Without the development of understanding, the programme will be useless. Many people will, I hope, achieve that understanding through reading this book and then feel able to implement the programme themselves. Others may feel that the book opens out possibilities for them but that they need professional help to go further.

The basis of my combination therapy is that it combines the analysis of feelings with a behavioural approach. This encourages the individual to understand and thereby discount their negative feelings towards sex, and to seek the positive feelings within sexual activity. Combination therapy is effective because it integrates the emotional and physical sides of sex. However, the key to making the programme work is that the couple face the fact that they have no alternative: that, if sex is what they want to be able to enjoy, sex is what they must do to find the enjoyment.

The Programme

Essentially, the programme is an agreed timetable of sexual activity, with both partners sharing responsibility for its fulfilment. The natural resistance felt by both partners to such a regime is harnessed in a positive way to demonstrate that effort can also be creative. The timing is regular and frequent and three times a week, and is decided in advance. There are a number of rules, which seem petty and unimportant at first glance, but which have proved over the years to affect the outcome significantly if they are understood and adhered to. These will be described later.

The purpose of the programme is to instil a regularity and frequency into sexual activity that has either been lost or was never achieved in the first place. Avoidance of a disliked activity causes automatic resistance which leads to further avoidance and finally panic if the activity must be confronted. Since the avoidance causes a phobia, which worsens in proportion to that avoidance, there is only one way out of it. Sexual intercourse must be reintroduced, and frequently enough to arrest and reverse this growth of the phobia. That is the primary purpose. A secondary purpose is to acquire the taste for sexual intercourse within a committed relationship in a way that does not rely on being romantically in love. A third purpose is to learn that effort can arouse desire even when age or fatigue diminishes the strength of the Pro-Sex team.

Learning to Make Love

The programme is about many things, but literally learning to 'make' love when desire is not present is the most important. In our society we are used to the idea that we make love because we feel like it. This idea makes us very vulnerable once the excitement of conquest and the recognition of commitment begins to take its toll. Those who want a long-term relationship, and to safeguard their children's security, have to come to terms with this issue because excitement goes out of every relationship which feels assured.

There is an answer to this problem but it requires a change in attitude. It means being prepared to have a different set of expectations and to discover the means of achieving success within these expectations. The following, therefore, is for people who value their relationship and who can understand the importance of sexual intercourse as the healing foundation of that relationship. It is dependent on both partners being prepared to make efforts, and to do so more than once! It involves being prepared to separate romance from love-making and to recognise that sexual arousal is as much achieved by touch and tenderness as by sexual attraction as long as there is goodwill and the willingness to make love.

The first thing the programme achieves is to even out the discrepancy of desire. Sexual activity usually begins because one partner feels sexually aroused. Except at the beginning of the relationship or on special exciting occasions, the chance of both partners being aroused at the same time becomes increasingly unlikely and, where one of you has a phobia, never happens. Under the terms of the programme, because sexual intercourse is not at a time of personal choosing for either, neither partner has been motivated by primary sexual desire. This means that both have to make an effort, which seems much fairer and removes one of the biggest bones of contention: the power struggle which results from unbalanced sexual desire in the partnership. Whether it is the woman who wants a relationship but no sexual intercourse, or the man who withholds his sexual interest, both individuals must agree to suspend hostilities and run with the programme.

A wide variety of people can be helped in this way, from those who are only very mildly phobic to those who have not had sexual intercourse for several years. The programme can deal with both of these extremes as long as those involved face the fact that there is only one way back from the precipice of phobic avoidance – and that is to have regular sexual intercourse.

The Rules

For the programme to be successful, you have to accept the rules and, more importantly, understand the reasons behind them. The rules were created and changed as problems revealed themselves over the early years of the programme. They have therefore been through a process of evolution, and although they may seem arbitrary, each has its purpose.

You have to understand that you must totally invest in the programme, because there is no magic to get you back into having regular sexual intercourse other than by actually doing it. You must understand the important fact that if you do not regularly make love, the sexual side of your relationship is doomed, and that may also signal the eventual doom of the relationship as a whole. You have to proceed with hope, and trust the idea that, with the phobia removed, you will be free to develop a new sexuality which will emerge from the insight you have achieved from reading and understanding the other chapters of this book and practising the exercises therein. Your sexual relationship will not necessarily be as it was when your relationship began, but it has the potential to be better in certain respects. It will not depend so much on the vagaries of your mood. Affectionate feelings rather than inspired passion will be enough to initiate sexual activity, which then climaxes in just as powerful a way as it used to when being 'in love' was the drive.

Because of the physiological difference between men and women, there is a difference in the programme depending on who has the phobia. This is because while the woman does not have to be aroused to be penetrated, the man does have to be aroused to penetrate. As we shall see, one of the rules is that sexual intercourse shall take place three times a week. The woman may not like this idea and, indeed, may feel that it is the last thing she can do. The fact is that if she has had sexual intercourse in the past she <u>can</u> do it and the real question is <u>will</u> she do it? Women do not have to be aroused to have sexual intercourse, they just have to be prepared to allow it to happen. This means that women must face the fact that when they say they 'cannot' accept penetration they are really saying they 'will not' which has quite a different meaning. A woman who has not had sexual intercourse for years will often have a big resistance to accepting this, but it is fundamental to overcoming the problem.

On the other hand, where a man is phobic it is no use just telling him that he must regularly penetrate a woman because without an erection he cannot. It can be argued, of course, that like the woman he 'will not', but the fact is that it is different. The woman has conscious control over penetration and can consciously make herself accept it, particularly with aids such as lubricating jelly, just as she would accept a speculum to have a cervical smear test.

A man, however, cannot consciously produce an erection if his unconscious does not want him to be aroused. For him the programme means that he can only consent to make love, he cannot consent to penetrate. Nevertheless the programme is helpful by stopping him from avoiding the issue and forcing him to face his feelings.

For a man, the only answer is to come to understand the basis of his resistance and to build up his confidence gradually, but confidence only comes with satisfactory experience. There is often a vicious circle of unsatisfactory experience undermining confidence which leads to more unsatisfactory experience and so on. There is sometimes, therefore, a case to be made for a healthy man, who has previously been used to satisfactory sexual intercourse and who has gained insight into his anxieties, to add weight to his Pro-Sex team with a boost to the strength of the testosterone competitor through hormone treatment. The temporary extra pull this lends to the team can overcome the 'fear of failure' component of his Anti-Sex Basic Insecurity anchor. Fear of further failure is always a powerful extra anxiety for a man, over and above the anxiety behind the original failure. Normally testosterone treatment is reserved for those who are depleted in the hormone, and it is not useful as a long-term medical treatment of impotence, but I have found it useful in the very limited sense described above. And now, of course, we have Viagra. It is still too early to evaluate fully its place in the treatment of psychosexual problems. We do know, however, that where unconscious anxiety is very great it cannot be overwhelmed by Viagra. Viagra is clearly useful in helping moderate anxiety and where there is mild loss of vigour but it does not take the place of insight.

Many women have stopped having intercourse because they find it painful. Some have always found it so, while others have developed pain. Some find it painful with one partner but not with another. Some have operations to enlarge their vaginas. The interesting thing is that where a woman makes a commitment to do the programme despite the pain she expects to feel, she finds that the pain disappears. This is because the pain is an unconscious attempt to make the partner stop, and when the woman decides to go through with it anyway the unconscious recognises that it is beaten, the muscles relax at the entrance to the vagina and painfree sexual intercourse follows. The only time I have found that this doesn't work is where the woman is not fully committed to the whole programme, and intends to wait and see whether the pain will go before making a full commitment. Since the conditions are not then met, the pain will not go and so the programme will not work.

A most important aspect of the programme is that it shall be followed exactly. This is because there will be a considerable internal struggle necessary to follow the programme since your unconscious mind will try to get out of doing it and will use all means available. It will welcome illness, tiredness, extra work and periods as reasons to avoid sexual intercourse. It may engender conflict to provide an excuse to avoid the anxiety that having sex induces. You have to be prepared to fight these understandable but destructive feelings because my experience was that minor and even major illness increased with the programme.

We now come to the specific rules of the programme which must be agreed and the reasons for them understood. The rules are:

1. **Commitment:** love-making should be three times a week
2. **Planning:** the day and time are to be decided in advance, either at the beginning of each week or a fixed timetable for longer periods, and must be well spaced through the week
3. **Timing:** daytime or early evening is best
4. **Catching up:** any occasion missed for minor illness must be made up the next day

First Rule: Commitment

This rule is to remove any confrontation about love-making. The frequency has been agreed and is now controlled by the programme, so any opportunity for game-playing around requesting and refusal has been taken away. The usual criteria that we all use about a decision to make love – do we feel like it? would it be better tomorrow? will our partner be irritable if we don't? are we too tired? – no longer apply.

One has, for the time being, to use love-making in a more experimental way. The programme is purposely very different to the ideal version that love-making should be a mutually desired activity, spontaneous and free. This is because those components are rarely met in a real-life committed relationship. We have to learn a different sort of love-making from romantic love-making.

Second Rule: Planning

Deciding the schedule in advance removes a great deal of worry about when to make love or whether it can be avoided. Paradoxically, it makes the partner with the problem feel more free, because for four days out of seven they don't have to guiltily wonder about it. They know when they must make an effort and when they can relax.

The three sessions must be spread out through the week in order to eliminate long gaps which allow anxiety to grow again. There should be absolutely no more than three days without a session of love-making for the duration of the programme. As we have seen, avoidance creates phobias, and this regularity prevents the build up of anxiety. It also implants a sense of routine into sexual activity, so each particular incidence of love-making is less important than when it is a rare event. A disappointing episode is less of a disaster when both of you know that there will soon be another chance.

Third Rule: Timing

Because the programme needs effort and there will be some anxiety in both of you, it is important to relieve the tension and conserve energy by making love as soon as possible in the day. It is natural that we should procrastinate about something we dread, which means that we end up watching the late-night film and then feel tired and flat. Putting it off also means that there will be some tension for the whole evening. A daytime or early evening session leaves you feeling good because you have made the effort to fulfil your agreement and can relax without worrying for the rest of the day. You will feel closer and are more likely to have a good evening together instead of one overhung by a feeling of reluctance towards a pending duty.

Fourth Rule: Catching Up

Illness is a tricky issue because it is so difficult for us to judge how ill we really are and how much we are using this intangible issue to avoid sex. The first people to test my programme tended to return with stories of how well it had all gone until one or other had 'flu, after which they had never been able to get back on track. This still happens, but not as much since I introduced the rule that any missed episodes must be made up the next day.

One of the most interesting examples, because it demonstrates the power of unconscious wishes to alter physical processes, was when Josephine agreed to use the programme. She reported that all had gone well until she had her period but that instead of this lasting the usual four days, it lasted twelve. She could not accept my advice that if the bleeding was not too great, sexual intercourse could still take place. Thinking this was a 'one-off' occurrence she started the programme again but eventually she found that while on the programme she always had a long period, but as soon as she stopped the programme, all returned to normal. The only way this could be overcome was for her to agree to have intercourse despite the bleeding, at which point it stopped.

Another interesting case was where a man, who seemed enthusiastic that at last he would be having intercourse after several months of rejection, went home and dug the garden so vigorously that his back 'went' and he spent six weeks lying flat, unable to engage in the programme. This demonstrated how important it was to warn men who appeared to have no problems (because it was their partner who had the phobia) that they, too, might avoid the programme because of finding the need to make love to order rather threatening, as many men are used to only making love if they feel like it.

If the unconscious mind finds that having a headache succeeds in aborting the programme, headaches will come thick and fast. In reality, people are going to have gaps for illness or because one partner has to go away, but it is important to be ready to counter the attack from the unconscious which will come after a gap when resistance to starting again will be very great. Childbirth is notorious for producing this type of phobic reaction. By the time intercourse has not taken place for two months and new responsibilities cause fatigue and anxiety, there is often great resistance to starting again.

The Third Week Warning

The usual report from participants is that the first week, when both are determined to succeed, goes surprisingly well. The second week is a little more of a struggle as willpower wanes, and in the third week participants often succumb to small set-backs. Perhaps one thinks the other doesn't seem very keen, or the schedule is interrupted and the next day rule forgotten, or some other apparently trivial thing can lead to the downfall of the programme. I have found that warning participants of the need for extra determination in the third week often succeeds in getting them through to the calmer water of the fourth week. Those who reach week four have fully accepted the programme which usually means that it will work for as long as necessary.

Making the Effort

In order to make an effort, we have to see it as worth our while. We then have to try to influence our feelings so that they will allow us to act as we wish. It is, perhaps, obvious that it is easy to have sexual intercourse when you want to but very difficult when you have no desire or feel phobic about it. We must, therefore, search for ideas that can help us put into practice what we know to be right for us but feel to be wrong.

First, it is important to put yourself in your partner's shoes and remember how humiliating it is to be unwanted. If you love your partner, you do not want to humiliate them, but it is only too easy to forget this when your tug-of-war teams are reaching a crucial point in their struggle. Unfortunately, in my experience, it is often people who have suffered such humiliation themselves who are most reluctant to recognise that they may be avenging their own remembered pain by affecting indifference.

Secondly, love – as we have seen – is a complicated idea containing a host of different varieties and qualities. Most would agree that the uniting attribute is a willingness to put the loved one first. While we are usually willing and even eager to do this when we are 'in love', most of us find it increasingly difficult as the magic of that state diminishes. It can be argued that love is more true when some effort for the partner is made than when it is effortless. However, this contains the frightening idea that we should forever put ourselves second, which will produce a rebellion in us. Nevertheless there are three important points to consider. First, making an effort for our partner helps our own resistance and opens up the possibility that we can have a satisfactory sex life. Secondly, it often takes us a long time to recognise that there is personal satisfaction to be had in making the partner content. Thirdly, we are very vulnerable if we rely on magical, transient feelings for our love life, but we are very powerful if we discover that a certain type of effort can induce just as good an erection or orgasm as when the sex was driven by strong attraction alone. Making effort is, then, about trying to create love – literally, to make love – and, with it, desire.

Thirdly, it is important to remember the skills you have used in other situations to bring about a successful outcome, whether a job interview or an attempt to interest a member of the opposite sex. Everybody does this when they want to but are unused to bothering with their partner unless they want something. We have to try putting this ability to use in creating loving sexual encounters with our partners. It can be done by becoming very involved in the task and making a positive input of interest, as people do with their children or their jobs in the natural course of events. For example, after a break from responsibility over holidays or even a weekend, I frequently do not feel like spending the morning counselling or doing anything else for that matter. However, I would be a complete failure and would humiliate the people I was seeing if I allowed that feeling to dominate. To compensate I take an extra-strong interest in the first person and their problem and, hey presto, I become involved and interested in my work for the rest of the week. This is what has to be done. By taking an interest and behaving in the way you wished you felt, you find out that you actually can feel that way.

Since this is easily forgotten as our anxieties control us, and since our body responds so much, through hormones, to our thoughts, it is important that we think positive things when we are about to make love. It is helpful, therefore, to have an aide-memoire to produce on the designated day. This should be a list of all the things about your partner that you really value and appreciate. It will serve to remind you how much better life feels after love-making because the intimacy this provides gives a sense of well-being that nothing else can match.

Reactions

The reaction to the programme varies because of a number of factors, some obvious, some not so obvious. The most obvious is the conscientiousness with which it is tackled, so that dutiful people usually make it work best while rebels are difficult to help. To them, change seems like surrender, and they have to understand their resistance before they can make it work. Sometimes one partner fails to share the responsibility, and sometimes each looks to the other to take an initiative which should not have to be taken.

Disappointment

One of the problems with the programme is that it is merely a means to an end. It will disappoint if more is asked of it than it can give. Just as couples have difficulty with sexual intercourse if they have an infertility problem and must get aroused at specific times, so the same complaints come back with the programme. It is cold, they say; it is premeditated; it spoils sex because it is not spontaneous. True, it is all those things. It is a tool and therefore all the possibilities for satisfaction lie in the users of the tool and never the tool itself. Why should having to make love on a Tuesday be so terrible if it provides an opportunity to share enjoyment with the one you love? If love-making can only be done at the bidding of some chemical call, this diminishes the human attribute of harnessing sex to love.

One of the common disappointments is experienced by those women who complain of pain on intercourse and find that while the pain disappears when they accept the programme, they find that arousal and excitement do not immediately replace it. They have spent so long justifying their avoidance because of pain that they have come to believe their own publicity, and really think that their resistance has only been about physical pain. As in all sorts of disappointment due to disillusion, this can provide a reason not to bother. It is often necessary to acquire or reacquire the taste for sexual intercourse, and this takes time. How much time clearly depends on so many factors that it is impossible to generalise. Sometimes a month will completely relieve the phobia, sometimes it is largely relieved but leaves a small amount of resistance which is less recognisable than it was before but which may still be enough to prevent complete enjoyment. Sometimes six months is necessary to bring about the necessary changes.

Along the way of the relationship, a number of habits will have been acquired which must be either lost or replaced with new attitudes. Perhaps the most important of these habits to be lost is that of using sexual intercourse as a gift to give or withhold as punishment for the daily frustrations of living together. New attitudes include learning to give greater attention to the partner's feelings and facing the need for effort which means never lying back and hoping for a quick release. It is necessary to learn to confront each other in a different way. If this can happen, love-making can be used to heal differences rather than to create more wounds because of differences.

Long-Term Contentment

It is an important corollary that the programme teaches a skill for life which means that when the hormonal drive begins to diminish, which it is less likely to do anyway when there has been regular sexual intercourse early on, couples know that with a little effort love-making can be maintained into late life.

As the years have gone by, I have been surprised by the number of couples who have reported that they have wanted to continue the programme in some form or other once they have re-established a satisfactory sex life, and have decided to include it in their lifestyle. They have found that unless they do this, even though avoidance has stopped, the fact of busy lives means that sexual activity tends to get pushed to the bottom of the list of priorities. In theory the idea is that once the phobic aspect has been dealt with there is no need for a programme and couples can rely on spontaneity. In an unstressful world this would probably be the usual outcome but, particularly in committed relationships where there are children to deal with and both partners work, love-making can always be put off until tomorrow. This makes it easy for large gaps to appear and tension to creep back in. In these circumstances three times a week is often too much for most couples, and once a week can be enough to keep sex alive once the phobic element has been resolved.

The exploration of a sexual problem gives people an opportunity to learn a great deal about themselves. Through the uncovering of pain and distress can come greater understanding, and a greater ability both to enjoy life ourselves and to use our insight to free children from negative attitudes passed down from previous generations. With sexual activity, however, understanding is not enough to solve problems without the willingness to make an effort to supplement the insight.

INDEX